Decoding the Cosmos

Decoding the Cosmos

God, Physics, and the Search for Deeper Explanation

EMILY QURESHI-HURST

CASCADE *Books* · Eugene, Oregon

DECODING THE COSMOS
God, Physics, and the Search for Deeper Explanation

Copyright © 2025 Emily Qureshi-Hurst. All rights reserved. Except for brief quotations in critical publications or reviews, no part of this book may be reproduced in any manner without prior written permission from the publisher. Write: Permissions, Wipf and Stock Publishers, 199 W. 8th Ave., Suite 3, Eugene, OR 97401.

Cascade Books
An Imprint of Wipf and Stock Publishers
199 W. 8th Ave., Suite 3
Eugene, OR 97401

www.wipfandstock.com

PAPERBACK ISBN: 978-1-6667-8565-4
HARDCOVER ISBN: 978-1-6667-8566-1
EBOOK ISBN: 978-1-6667-8567-8

Cataloguing-in-Publication data:

Names: Qureshi-Hurst, Emily [author].

Title: Decoding the cosmos : God, physics, and the search for deeper explanation / by Emily Qureshi-Hurst.

Description: Eugene, OR: Cascade Books, 2025 | Includes bibliographical references.

Identifiers: ISBN 978-1-6667-8565-4 (paperback) | ISBN 978-1-6667-8566-1 (hardcover) | ISBN 978-1-6667-8567-8 (ebook)

Subjects: LCSH: Physics—Religious aspects—Christianity. | Physics—Religious aspects. | Religion and science. | Religion—Philosophy.

Classification: BL240.2 Qu47 2025 (print) | BL240.2 (ebook)

For Jack
(it's all for you)

Contents

Acknowledgments ix

Prologue xii

Introduction 1

1. Creation 19

2. Design 50

3. Providence 77

4. Incarnation 114

5. Salvation 145

Conclusion 181

Bibliography 183

Acknowledgments

THIS BOOK IS THE culmination of around a decade of research, which means I am indebted to a great many people who have informed my thinking on the relationship between Christian doctrine and modern physics. I cannot hope to mention everyone by name, so I will just say up top that I am endlessly grateful to my wonderful family (especially my lovely mum), my friends, and my academic community for all the ways you have supported, steered, and shaped me. I would not be who I am without you.

My first explicit thanks must go to my editor at Cascade, Robin Parry, who invited me to write this book and gave it its jazzy (if ambitious!) title. Thank you for putting your faith in me and allowing me to take on this mammoth project. I have so enjoyed bringing all the disparate strands of my academic research together into a single book, and without you that would not have happened.

I am also extremely grateful to my Grandad Jeremy, my partner Jack, and my brother Ben, each of whom read an earlier draft of the manuscript and offered their feedback. You helped keep the writing accessible, and I appreciate your wisdom and your encouragement immensely.

Now for the long list of Oxford colleagues, each of whom played an important role in my decade spent at the university. First, I must thank Professor Alister McGrath, who supervised me during my master's and doctoral degrees, during which much of the research that forms the basis of this book was carried out. His endless wisdom, patience, and support have been invaluable to me over the years. It was a true privilege to work with one of the greatest living theologians, and I do not take that for granted.

Huge thanks are owed to Chris Bennett, who has generously sacrificed many hours to reading (and robustly criticizing!) this and other writings. Thank you also to George Klaeren, who has patiently discussed these ideas with me many times over the years. I couldn't have asked for better companions on this weird and wonderful academic journey than the two of you. I also owe immense gratitude to Mark Schunemann. Our theological travels began side by side as bright-eyed undergraduates, and we have argued about God more times than I could count in the decade that has followed. Thank you for sharing with me your boundless enthusiasm for ideas, and for offering your thoughts on this manuscript as it was being prepared. Thank you also to my dear friend Rebekah Wallace, whose companionship on this academic journey I simply could not be without.

I am also very grateful to Andrew Moore, who first introduced me to science and religion during my undergraduate days, and has remained a friend ever since. I found our many disagreements stimulating and inspiring in equal measure. Thank you to Shaun Henson, whose insightful comments on the manuscript and steadfast mentorship are greatly appreciated. Without the support of Justin Jones, who gave me my first academic job, neither this nor any of my other books would exist. I can never thank you enough. I must also thank my colleagues at the Religion and the Frontier Challenges programme at Pembroke College, University of Oxford: Barney Asprey, Imen Neffati, Tobias Cremer, Christopher Wadibia, Gehan Gunatillake, Tim Middleton, Raffaella Taylor-Seymour, Austin Stevenson, and Muhammad Faisal Khalil. Not many humanities scholars get to work in a research group with such diverse interests as this. Those three years with all of you were the happiest years of my career.

I would also like to thank my colleagues from my time at Oriel College at the University of Oxford, particularly Mark Wynn and Richard Swinburne. Two years of regular Joseph Butler society meetings have sharpened my philosophical acumen and stimulated my thinking immensely. It has been an honor to be among you. Thank you also to David Fergusson at Cambridge and Mark Harris at Oxford, both of whom have supported me as I wade through the murky waters of early career academia.

I also want to thank my students, particularly those in my recent Theology and Natural Science classes at the University of Cambridge. Much of the material of this book has formed the basis of my lectures, and the book in turn has been informed by your excellent comments, challenging questions, and passion for the subject. Thank you for bringing your enthusiasm to class every single time, even when we had to meet at 9 A.M.

A final thanks goes to each and every reader. If no one read my articles or bought my books, I would not get to do what I do. Thank you from the bottom of my heart for your support and your interest, and for allowing me to continue pursuing my lifelong dream of being a writer. It means the world to me that I get to spend my days writing about these fascinating issues. Thank you, thank you, thank you.

Prologue

DECODING THE COSMOS FALLS into the interdisciplinary field known as science and religion. A very natural question stems from this: are science and religion compatible? In a sense, this question is the beating heart of the project, out of which all other questions flow. You may find it odd, then, that I will not be able to give you a clear answer. In fact, in its refusal to give a simple answer to the question of how religion and science ought to relate to each other, *Decoding the Cosmos* will be unlike any kind of book you may have come to expect from the field of science and religion. Many of its most popular books for non-specialist audiences tend to fall into two camps: first, a book explaining how mighty science disproves meek religion. Second, a book of apologetics that tries to defend a specific religion against critiques from science. These books are typically written by scientifically minded atheists or religious academic theologians, and this book is a little different because I am neither a scientist nor a theist. As such, I have comparatively little skin in the game.

Let me be clear at the outset, though, that I am an atheist.

In theology and religious studies, "atheist" can sometimes feel like a dirty word. Perhaps this is because some rather loud atheists spent much of the beginning of the twenty-first century extolling the virtues of atheism and disparaging religion as backward at best and harmful at worst. I do not wish to be tarred with this brush. The fact that I am not religious does not mean that I want to write a book disproving religion from a scientific perspective. I am not interested in such a project, and I do not think that "science" can refute "religion" anyway. What I mean by that statement, and why I have used scare quotes around what you might think are ordinary and commonsense terms, will become clear as we proceed through the arguments of this book. It is worth stating now, though, that my atheism does not blind me to what I believe to be obvious truths:

many aspects of religious life fall outside the reach of science, and much of religion is highly valuable to both individuals and societies whether or not it can be scientifically "proved." Art, history, and culture would be far poorer without religion, and it is clear that religion can give community and a profound sense of meaning to people's lives. I happen to believe that theological claims about the existence of a higher power (God, gods, or spirits) are false, but my aim is not to convince readers of the same. What I am interested in is exploring the extent to which science and religion can enter into dialogue with one another, and what new insights such a dialogue might bring.

A particularly well-known example of a group of atheists who believed that science and religion must exist in a state of perennial conflict is the New Atheist movement that enjoyed cultural prominence at the beginning of the twenty-first century. This movement was led by the so-called Four Horsemen of atheism, Richard Dawkins, Sam Harris, Daniel Dennett, and Christopher Hitchens. According to them, science easily disproves religion. As a result, religion should now either vanish into obscurity, or, if it doesn't have the good grace to disappear on its own, it should be abolished. Its continued existence is harmful. The New Atheists defended what is known as the "conflict thesis" or "warfare model" of the science–religion relationship. The conflict thesis frames science and religion as forces locked in perpetual warfare that must rage on until one side claims ultimate victory. Other voices, including my doctoral supervisor Professor Alister McGrath, have argued that science and religion can coexist harmoniously and that claims of conflict misrepresent what is in fact a complex and often mutually beneficial dialogue between two different—but compatible—ways of explaining the world.

My own position falls somewhere between these. I agree with the New Atheists that the evidence for God's existence is not ultimately compelling, but I wholeheartedly reject the idea that science can answer every question we might have. Nor can science give ultimate meaning to our lives. Most of the things I care most about cannot be reduced to the realm of scientific explanation without something essential becoming lost. The loving embrace of my spouse, the peace I feel when sitting in my garden, the joy that comes from listening to a particularly good piece of heavy metal music, and the obligation I feel to keep a promise lose their magic and their unique subjectivity when we try to cram them into the box of empirical science. We should not look to science for a totalizing explanation of the world. Professor McGrath is right that science and religion can be strengthened by being in dialogue with each other and so they should not be siloed off and left to "get on with it," so to speak. There are many areas of compatibility between the two disciplines. One can acknowledge this while also recognizing that areas of conflict, tension, and downright incompatibility exist also. Essentially, neither the Christian apologist nor the New Atheist gets everything right. Across history and today, when religion and science meet the results are messy, dynamic, and deeply fruitful. Each interaction has its own unique story to tell.

In the decades since "science and religion" entered the academic scene, excellent scholarship has been produced exploring their historical relationship. These histories reveal that nuance and complexity permeate each and every interaction between scientist and theologian, between religious doctrine and scientific theory. I am taking some of this history for granted here, although we will explore a few key historical moments. Instead of a broad and general exploration of religion and science, I want to focus on one particularly rich set of debates: the interface between modern physics and Christian theology.

The book you are about to read is formed out of the lectures, articles, and books that I have written on physics and Christianity over the previous decade. It surveys the field, but it will also contain much of my own original research carried out while working at the University of Oxford and the University of Cambridge. As it is for a wider audience than some of my other academic writings, I have opted to go for a more readable style that is less bogged down by copious referencing and dense footnotes. At the end of each chapter a "further reading" section has been included, for those who wish to delve deeper into the chapter's intersecting themes. My hope is that this book will be valuable to Christians wanting to learn more about science and to anyone else who might be interested in exploring the rich interface between God, physics, and philosophy.

Together, let us dive into the sweeping narratives that tell the story of our universe, from the laws that govern it to the human beings who call it home. Let us explore how these narratives have been constructed and reconstructed by religion, science, and philosophy in humanity's endless search for deeper meaning. Perhaps, by the end, we may be a step closer to decoding our beautiful and majestic cosmos.

Introduction

MODERN PHYSICS IS AN extraordinarily rich resource for theological and philosophical reflection. More accurate in its predictions than any other science, its domain stretches from the very smallest objects in existence to the structure of the cosmos itself. The field of physics is a powerful example of human ingenuity, and the technological advances that have been seen over the past century are as sublime as they are successful. It is a privilege to be alive at the same time as tools as specialized as the James Webb Space Telescope that allow us to peer back into the distant past, capturing some of the earliest moments in the universe's evolution. Just as astounding is the discovery of the Higgs boson by the Large Hadron Collider at CERN. The technical achievements that both of these experimental set-ups represent is a testament to the intellectual capability of our species. Another admirable demonstration of human ingenuity is the sheer amount of physics data we have amassed—more than any one person could read in their lifetime, in fact. There is quite literally an abundance of knowledge to be devoured, and for every piece of information you sink your teeth into there will be tens of new findings waiting to be discovered. What a delightful and overwhelming thought.

Delight aside for a moment, the abundance of data available makes writing a book like this one a challenge. The purpose of *Decoding the Cosmos* is to introduce readers to the fascinating world of physics and theology. While I would love to detail each discovery in the history of physics and explore all the philosophical and theological implications that follow, I would need several lifetimes to do so. And you, dear reader, would probably rather not spend your entire life reading a single (very, *very* long) book. For this reason, decisions have been made about what to include and what to leave out. Each expert in the field would likely pick a slightly different set of materials to discuss, based on their own research interests and which themes seem most important to them.

I have decided, in this book, to structure the physics material around the theological material. My focus will be on five big ideas from Christian theology, beginning with creation and ending with salvation, exploring providence, design, and incarnation along the way. I will be asking whether these ideas can thrive in the world of modern science. Because of this, the physics that will be discussed is the physics that directly influences, impacts, or instantiates these central theological ideas. Inevitably, some areas of physics will not be mentioned, and others will be only explored in passing. Many of the books written on God and physics have the physics as the center of gravity and the theological issues in orbit, offering a slightly more comprehensive treatment of physics than I am able to offer here. For the interested non-believer such a structure may work, but for the Christian it may be alienating. In my view, regardless of one's position on the existence of God, the clearest way of seeing how a particular religion and science fit together (if, and to the extent that, they do) is to take a systematic approach to the theology and bring science into dialogue with it as and where appropriate. Christian theology, the specific religious focus of the book, is a self-contained system. Therefore, we ought to begin with that system as theologians and religious believers understand it.

How well a theological system conforms to modern physics depends partly on one's interpretation of the doctrines and partly where physics is at currently. In order to chart the implications of current physics for theology effectively, I will present the theological doctrines in a simplified form. Academic theologians may be dismayed in those moments where simplicity has been chosen over nuance, but I hope the choice will be a helpful one for those for whom this book is intended. We are not here to get bogged down in doctrinal disputes. We are here to investigate how Christian theology and modern science interact, with a focus on key themes and not the minutia of academic disagreements. Going back to basics offers conceptual clarity. It allows us to explore those places where the sweeping currents of science and theology have swirled together, forming vortices of creativity and innovation. Before immersing ourselves in these depths, it will be worth briefly wading into the waters of the discipline into which this work falls: science and religion.

DEFINING "SCIENCE" AND "RELIGION"

Both "science" and "religion" are tantalizingly tricky terms. Everyone understands what they mean when using the terms "religion" and "science" in day-to-day conversation. Statements like "I am religious" and "according to the science . . ." are not hard to comprehend, and often appear in day-to-day conversation. Nevertheless, philosophers, theologians, and scholars of religion have long argued over which definition(s) of religion and science best capture the essence of each discipline, both historically and today. These are foundational questions. Our understanding of the meaning of these concepts invariably shapes how we perceive their scope and interaction. Because of this, we must begin our foray into the "science and religion" domain by trying to ascertain what each half of the pair actually is. Once we have a firm grasp of the foundations of the field itself, we will be able to delve deeper into physics and Christianity more specifically. Let's begin with science.

Science

The very existence of the term "science" implies that there is a single discipline with neat boundaries and a set of essential properties shared by every branch of scientific enquiry. This not the case. Rather than *science*, there are *sciences*, ranging from quantum mechanics' study of atomic and sub-atomic particles to geology's study of the Earth's deep history. Although this is a fairly widely accepted point in the study of science and religion and in the philosophy of science, there are a couple of different definitions of science that have been cited as plausible options. First is the idea that science is a body of knowledge. On this definition, science is a set of objective facts that we add to cumulatively throughout the course of scientific history. Each discovery, and each new theory those discoveries become, builds upon what has gone before, creating a layered epistemic structure that we call "scientific knowledge" or "scientific fact." This definition, which is probably what most people think of when they think of science, contains two assumptions: first, that there is objective truth out there to discover, and second, that science progresses toward that truth. The issue is, neither of these assumptions can be straightforwardly shown to be correct. It may well be the case that science is only able to give us data, and the theories we generate are laden with conceptual categories, metaphysical baggage, and human biases.

Despite these reservations, the "body of knowledge" approach is generally how science is taught in schools. For example, we are taught the periodic table of chemical elements, the structure of the atom, and the internal workings of the cell. This approach—namely teaching individual scientific theories and models—implies that science is comprised only of facts, and that there is little to no disagreement over how to interpret scientific findings or whether science aims at objective truth or not. It is a good approach insofar as it enlightens children to the inner workings of the physical world. However, it risks overemphasizing the fixity of these facts and overlooking the extent to which disagreement and human biases seep into scientific study.

If science were a body of knowledge, or a set of objective facts, then we should assume that most important matters are settled. That is, that the most important matters are agreed upon by the majority of experts and are unlikely to change. Yet a mere glance at the scientific landscape, both today and across history, reveals that there is not a scientific consensus on many important questions. This does not mean that we should be skeptical of everything scientists tell us. When it is gathered in a robust and reliable way, the data can be trusted. It is when *interpreting* the data that disagreement comes in, and this makes it difficult to call science a body of knowledge. This is best explored through a concrete example from a lively and hotly contested branch of science: quantum mechanics.

Disagreement between experts on how to interpret the data is never clearer than in the ongoing debate over the various interpretations of quantum mechanics. Quantum mechanics is by far the most successful scientific theory we have ever had. Physicists are able to use the theory to make predictions that have been confirmed to a truly staggering degree of accuracy. One example is a phenomenon known as the magnetic moment of the electron. Here, the theory matches the data to an accuracy of about one part in a trillion, a phenomenal feat that far outstrips anything else in the history of science.

Quantum mechanics is primarily comprised of mathematical formalism—i.e., equations—that describes the behavior of particles like electrons, protons, and photons. Despite it being our most successful scientific theory, meaning the equations are exceptionally effective in telling us what to expect when we look at specific features of the world, there are several different interpretations of what wider worldview the mathematics discloses. Each interpretation is, in effect, its own theory about the nature of the universe. What's more, they are empirically equivalent, meaning that they make the same predictions about what happens in the actual world. Because of this, *no experiment could decide between them.* This alone shows that science is more than just a set of facts about the natural world that we discover through empirical investigation. Interpretation of the data must occur. We need to build an understanding of what the data teaches us about the nature and structure of reality.

Although the various interpretations are empirically equivalent, they paint utterly different metaphysical pictures of how our world is structured at the most basic level. The Copenhagen interpretation of quantum mechanics is indeterministic, meaning it claims that chance and uncertainty are baked into the very foundations of reality. On this interpretation there is a single universe, and that universe is indeterministic at the quantum level. Physical causes underdetermine the outcomes of quantum events, meaning that some level of genuine randomness has always been hiding in the smallest corners of the cosmos. We cannot perfectly predict the future because there is no fixed future; until a quantum event takes place a range of possibilities can occur, and we have no way to know exactly which one will happen until we perform a measurement.

Another interpretation, equally viable, claims that the universe is continually splitting into multiple worlds, each of which goes on to evolve slightly differently. According to this view, at a quantum measurement event, instead of only one outcome occurring, all outcomes occur. The catch is that each outcome occurs in a separate branch of the universe which splits off from this one at the moment of measurement. As science-fictiony as this sounds, the Everett, or Many-Worlds, interpretation is a legitimate scientific theory that claims we live in a quantum multiverse. This quantum multiverse is deterministic, as everything that can happen (i.e., is compatible with the initial conditions and the Schrödinger equation) does happen. For that reason, we can predict with certainty which outcome will occur, because *every* possible outcome will occur. There is no genuine randomness in the world itself, only perspectival uncertainty about which world—and thus which outcome—you will observe.

Very reasonable questions to ask are: According to quantum mechanics, are we living in a multiverse or a universe? Is it deterministic or indeterministic? These are fundamental questions, and scientists do not agree on the answers. The situation is not unique either. There are similar disagreements across all sciences, both historically and today, some of which will be explored in later chapters. Given this disagreement, some questions follow. How is the world structured, according to quantum mechanics? What are the "objective facts" that quantum mechanics tells us? There are no straightforward answers. Thus I, and many other philosophers of science, argue that science is not best understood as a body of knowledge. It is not clear enough which pieces of knowledge would make the cut.

Another common answer to the question "what is science?" is that science is defined by its empirical methodology. The so-called scientific method involves generating theories out of observational data and empirical evidence. In effect, it involves examining the world on its own terms and generating theories about how it works from what we discover. If, for example, we see that apples fall from trees and moons orbit planets, perhaps we might infer, as Isaac Newton did, that there is a single underlying force that causes both of these phenomena. Without empirical observation and scientific experiments, we would not be able to get past simple armchair philosophy. It is true that science is fundamentally empirical, meaning it is, at its most basic level, about observing and experiencing the natural world to generate theories about its functioning. Nevertheless, there is a significant problem in using the scientific method to draw boundaries around science.

The problem is, there is no single scientific method. Other than highly vague claims about science being about observation, repeatable experiments, and evidence, very little unites the way we study the Earth's geological history, the way we study sub-atomic particles, and the way we study the behavior of Siberian tigers. For this reason, there is a growing consensus among philosophers of science that there is no single scientific method. Instead, there are scientific method*s* (plural), each of which arises to suit its particular object of study. In addition to this, there are also fringe cases that raise questions about where the boundaries of "science" should be drawn. Where do we place social sciences like economics and sociology? These are cases where there is disagreement regarding whether the discipline is a "proper science" (whatever that means).

Historians of science, including John Hedley Brooke and Peter Harrison, both of whom have held Oxford's prestigious Andreas Idreos Professorship in Science and Religion, remind us that the term "science" has been used in a variety of ways to mean a variety of different things over the last few centuries. Although proto-scientific investigations can be understood to have begun with Aristotle, science-proper emerged with the work of the early modern natural philosophers, including Galileo Galilei, Isaac Newton, Robert Boyle, and René Descartes. Natural philosophers studied nature holistically and included philosophy, mathematics, experimentation, and even theology in their intellectual arsenal. In fact, in its infancy, science was infused with a distinctly theistic flavor. The 1771 *Encyclopaedia Britannica* defined science as "denoting doctrine from self-evident principles," showing that science was viewed as a way of arriving at theological conclusions from principles apparent to reason and evidence gained via the senses. As is becoming obvious, landing on a clear and stable definition of science is far harder than one might initially imagine. Matters are even worse for religion.

Religion

When we hear the term "religion" in the West, we typically imagine a set of beliefs about a supernatural being (or beings) and the desire to enter into a relationship with that being (or beings) that often includes some form of ritualized worship. We might also assume that we can uncontroversially talk about ancient religion, or religions in cultures separate from our own. Scholars of religion urge caution, and with good reason. In fact, one of the first things we teach theology and religion undergraduates is that there is no universally agreed upon definition of religion. I want to use this section to offer a few reasons why religion is extremely difficult to define in a way that captures everything we want to include, such as Christianity, Sikhism, Jainism, and Islam, while excluding all the things we want to exclude, like cults, superstition, and football fanaticism.

Let's begin with the idea that religion is a set of beliefs. The first question to ask is: Which beliefs are distinctively religious? By this I mean which belief functions as a smoking gun that allows us to say, "Ah yes, that's religion!" We need an answer if we are to distinguish religious beliefs from beliefs that characterize cults, ideology, or spirituality, none of which are synonymous with "religion." Some group-identities we want to call religions believe in a single all-powerful God, but many others subscribe to the existence of many finite or flawed gods. Some believe in spirits, both good and bad, some in forces beyond our control. Some believe in no God at all but instead in repeating cycles of birth, death, and rebirth. Saying "religion is belief in x" becomes very difficult to maintain, whatever x ends up being.

Perhaps we might keep it rather general and say, as I did at the opening of this section, that religion is about belief in the supernatural. Well, as it turns out, we make a grave error if we suppose that religion in the main is primarily about belief at all. Many things that anthropologists want to call Eastern and Indigenous religions are primarily comprised of ritual, behavioral practice, and community. In other words, they are ways of life. As we develop an appreciation of all this, it becomes ever clearer that extracting "religion" out of the deeply interwoven strands of political, cultural, and social life that the "religious" is inextricably tied up with is a fool's errand.

Moreover, "religion" is not a universal concept. As the historian Peter Harrison has persuasively argued, the category of "religion" did not exist until it emerged in the West after the Reformation and following European exploration, and colonization, of other cultures. It is a distinctly modern and Western notion without proper counterparts across cultures and throughout history. Before the Reformation, what Westerners now think of as an individual's religiosity was intimately bound up with their social and cultural existence. The idea that one's "religion" was a distinct entity that could be distilled out of the milieu of one's life and that might vary cross-culturally was not well understood. The closest term in the Middle Ages was the Latin word *religio*, which meant something much closer to personal piety or devotion than a system of belief and practice.[1] Historians are now aware that they risk misrepresenting the past if they impose this contemporary category on historical actors who did not have such a concept. Modern anthropologists, too, encounter problems when attempting to study "religion" in other cultures when using the term in the Western way.

Why might employing the modern usage of the term "religion" cause so many problems? Well, one important reason is that the modern Western understanding of religion is heavily based on the framework provided by Christianity. Although Christianity is more than *just* a system of belief, assent to a set of agreed upon doctrinal claims is generally understood to be foundational to the faith. The Nicene Creed, for example, contains twelve doctrinal articles that begin with "we believe . . . ." This doctrinal approach could be understood as drawing borders around what counts as orthodox belief, with anything on the wrong side of the line deemed as heretical. Those who assent to the orthodox credal statements are Christians, and those who do not sit outside of the faith. Indeed, the history of Christianity is marked by many controversies about how one

---

1. Harrison, *Territories of Science and Religion*, 34–44.

ought to understand its doctrinal claims. The Nicene Creed itself was born out of a series of controversies, and many so-called heretics have been kicked out of the church for disagreeing with it. This history serves to reinforce the idea that Christianity is, at its core, about intellectual assent to a set of propositional claims.

In his latest book *Some New World*, however, Peter Harrison questions this, suggesting that the understanding of the Nicene Creed *at the time* was more about trust in God and the church than belief in the modern sense. It was *belief in* as opposed to *belief that*. Despite this, later thinkers have used this history to conceptualize Christianity as being primarily about belief in the modern propositional sense. Religion is about *belief that* God exists and intellectual assent to the truth claims made in religious texts like the Bible. As a consequence, for those raised in societies constructed within the intellectual framework provided by Christianity, religion does tend to be framed first and foremost as a system of supernatural beliefs in a higher power, i.e., in God or gods, and moral beliefs concerning how to live one's life in light of teaching provided by that God or gods. This is, however, a distinctly modern Western notion.

We now know that religion as a system of belief is not—and never has been—representative of religiosity on a global scale. In fact, Harrison argues that not all groups even have a concept of "belief" that maps onto this modern Western notion. He cites much anthropological research on various tribal groups whose theories of mind differ significantly from the understanding of human thought and human cognition that we take for granted—and indeed assume is universal—in the West.[2] Harrison writes, "the cumulative weight of reports such as these has prompted speculation among some anthropologists about whether absence of a notion of belief is less the exception than the rule. Perhaps the Western notion of 'belief,' in the big scheme of things, is the odd one out."[3]

In fact, this is even the case for early forms of Western religions. An analysis of the Latin *fides* and Greek *pistis*, the words that most closely resemble "faith" and "belief" respectively, shows that these terms had meanings that were far more wide-ranging than their modern Western counterparts. We ought not to assume that early Christianity or Judaism were operating with the same epistemic framework as our own. It was only after the Protestant Reformation fractured the medieval church,

---

2. Harrison, *Some New World*, 26–30.
3. Harrison, *Some New World*, 29.

dethroning the ecclesiastical authorities and with them the idea that faith was primarily about trust in the church, that faith as personal belief began to emerge. If there are many churches and many religious authorities to turn to, your personal beliefs and rational capacities play an ever greater role in the development of theological knowledge. As Harrison writes, "the burden of understanding and assenting to sets of beliefs" became an individual's own responsibility.[4] If Harrison is right about this, then it is deeply misguided to frame religion as a system of supernatural beliefs. Applied on a global scale, this definition of religion misrepresents the religiosity of many (probably most) non-Western peoples in a fundamental sense. Not only this, but it likely also misrepresents the Western religions of the past. If we even oversimplify (to the point of distortion) Christianity when we reduce it to a belief system, then that is all the worse for the idea that religion as a whole can be defined in terms of belief in the supernatural.

The lesson here is that what we place within the umbrella of the category "religion" is so multifaceted and uncompromisingly rich that it is impossible to distill from it a single essential property that could work as a definition. Religion is clearly more than a set of beliefs. Perhaps most religions are not even systems of belief at all. But, importantly, only a system of beliefs could be in a relationship with science. It is not possible for the ritual of taking the Eucharist, for example, to be in anything that even remotely resembles a relationship with the experimental set up of CERN's Large Hadron Collider. It is not even clear what that would mean.

Moreover, determining what counts as a legitimate religion and what counts as a cult, spiritual movement, or ideology is not an objective or value-neutral enterprise. Whatever definition we try to give, there remain fringe cases—such as scientology—the religious legitimacy of which is a hotly contested and politicized issue. In societies where religions gain various benefits (e.g., reduced rates of taxation, social status, or political influence), whether your organization counts as a religion is not a purely theological or anthropological question. Social and political issues are never far from the surface, and they frequently bubble up when a group's religious status is brought into question. All of this goes to show that we cannot define religion without acknowledging its historical, social, political, and cultural context. We will return to this idea shortly,

---

4. Harrison, *Some New World*, 66.

when considering the mode of science–religion interaction named by John Hedley Brooke as "complexity."

Despite the difficulty with defining the terms, and thus the conjunction "science and religion," several attempts to characterize the relationship have been made that are worth reflecting on. Some are more helpful than others. I want to consider four broad approaches: conflict, contrast, complementarity, and complexity.[5]

MODELS OF THE SCIENCE–RELIGION RELATIONSHIP

Conflict

The term "conflict" has been used to describe the relationship between science and religion since the work of Victorian scholars J. W. Draper and A. D. White. Although it never faded out of popular discourse as such, it saw a significant resurgence in the early 2000s thanks to the work of the so-called Four Horsemen of New Atheism: Richard Dawkins, Christopher Hitchens, Sam Harris, and Daniel Dennett. It has also been bolstered in recent years by opposition to public health initiatives on the basis of religiously rooted distrust of medical science. A recent example of this was the rise of vaccine hesitancy during the Covid-19 pandemic, an issue to which theologians are giving increasing attention.[6] Similarly, elements of the conflict narrative can be seen in theological opposition to Darwinian evolution by particular religious groups.[7]

What assumptions must be made when characterizing the relationship between science and religion as one of perpetual, irresolvable, conflict? The conflict thesis is committed to the existence of an insurmountable hostility between two separate and easily distinguished disciplines that compete for dominance over the same domain: the natural world. To put it bluntly, and perhaps a little simplistically, the "conflict" thesis has been defended by scientists who are threatened by religion and religious people who are threatened by science. The views of those

---

5. This nomenclature is my own. Other taxonomies for the religion–science relationship are available. The most famous of these, conflict, independence, dialogue, integration, was first presented by Ian Barbour in *Religion and Science*.

6. Stevenson, "Christian Vaccine Hesitancy."

7. Perhaps the most famous example of this was the Intelligent Design movement in the United States. For a summary of the position, see: Dembski, "In Defence of Intelligent Design."

who occupy the former camp can be summed up by Thomas H. Huxley's claim that "extinguished theologians lie about the cradle of every science like the strangled snakes of Hercules; and history records that whenever science and orthodoxy have been fairly opposed, the latter has been forced to retire from the lists, bleeding and crushed if not annihilated; scotched, if not slain."[8] Huxley, also known as "Darwin's bulldog" because of his passionate defense of Darwinian evolution, believed that even in its infancy science is able to destroy religion. This kind of rhetoric has not helped certain religious groups feel less threatened by science, especially if science challenges claims made in scripture.

Why might people think science and religion are—and indeed must be—in conflict? The idea goes something like this: science and religion offer *complete* and *competing* explanations of the natural world. Only one of these disciplines, either science or religion, is true. Proponents of the conflict thesis from the atheism side see science as perfectly rational, objective, and the only reliable means of acquiring knowledge. They see religion as parochial, subjective, and based on the whims of corrupt and corruptible religious authorities. They might point to the great harms done by religious leaders, or the wars waged in the name of religion. No wars have been fought in the name of science (although, of course, without developments in science wars would not be nearly as catastrophic). It is in the best interests of society, they might argue, that religion should be abolished, and science should take its place. Richard Dawkins is an archetypal defender of this position.

Alongside his bestselling book *The God Delusion*, Dawkins made a two-part documentary called *The Root of All Evil?* In his opening monologue, Dawkins makes the following claims which neatly sum up the contemporary conflict position: "I am a scientist, and I believe there is a profound contradiction between science and religious belief. There is no well demonstrated reason to believe in God, and I think the idea of a divine creator belittles the elegant reality of the universe. The twenty-first century should be an age of reason, yet irrational, militant, faith is back on the march."[9] He also makes repeated references to religion resembling a virus that infects the minds of children, spreads throughout populations, and causes untold damage. The only antidote to this way of thinking, for Dawkins, is science. And so, religion and science are at war.

---

8. Huxley, *Lay Sermons, Addresses, and Reviews*, 305.
9. Dawkins, *Root of All Evil?*, episode 1.

Such antagonism is mirrored by religious fundamentalists and many scriptural literalists. Why? At least in part because they believe that human beings are intellectually damaged, prone to sin, and hubristic. Science, insofar as it is the product of human beings, cannot be completely trusted. For this reason, they may also be distrustful of scientific authorities, or the establishment more broadly, which they view as antithetical to their religious identity. Advocates of this view might also look back over the history of science and point out that cutting-edge science two hundred years ago is outdated (and sometimes plainly false) today. Scripture, on the other hand, is the fixed and unchanging word of God and so ought to be held far above anything produced by flawed and fallible humanity. If there is a perceived conflict with science, then all the worse for science.

The problem with this view is that if Christians never listened to scientists, they would still believe the Earth was at the center of the cosmos and the sun revolved around it. Science, when brought into partnership with theology, can help clarify any misconceptions contained in scripture that are an artifact of the historical context of its authors. For the majority of Christian history, the Bible was not read literally as a historical or scientific textbook might be today, and it is unlikely its authors intended it to be read as such. When this is taken on board, scientific challenges to some elements of scripture are no longer an existential threat.

When a theist identifies an apparent conflict between scripture and science that they cannot or will not resolve, this is typically because an overly rigid approach to scripture has been taken. This is a choice that does not have to be made. We will return to this point often in the chapters to come. Similarly, when a scientist tars all religion with the brush of dangerous fundamentalism, as Dawkins does, they are placing all religious people in the same bracket as a small, and lethal, minority. Doing so misrepresents the majority of religious believers, most of whom abhor terrorism and religious violence. If science and religion are doomed to be defined by their worst members, then conflict will persist. But framing these disciplines in terms of intrinsic incompatibility is a result of the belief that either religion or science is the only route to truth and so must eradicate the other. To borrow a phrase from Harry Potter, neither can live while the other survives. Almost everyone working in the academic sub-field of science and religion today agrees that this is the wrong way to look at things. I hope, if you are sympathetic to the conflict position, you may view things differently by the end of the book.

Contrast

The second approach can be neatly summarized by a phrase introduced by the scientist Stephen Jay Gould: science and religion are *non-overlapping magisteria*. Essentially, science and religion are utterly different and contrast completely with each other. Science is about fact, religion is about value, and never the two shall meet. According to this position, sometimes shortened to NOMA, scientists should concern themselves with empirical matters and seek only to understand the inner workings of the natural world. Theologians should be concerned with either theological matters, like understanding the nature of God, or ethical matters, such as how to live a good life. Religion and science need not conflict because they do not overlap in any way. Like oil and water, they can coexist but never mix.

NOMA moves us into more productive territory than the conflict thesis insofar as it recognizes that science and religion are not—nor should they be—totalizing worldviews, each of which is designed to answer every question we might have. Instead, this perspective recognizes that science and religion are, to an extent, domain-specific. They are carried out by radically different methodologies, and they function completely differently in people's lives. You wouldn't go to a scientist for guidance through a difficult period in your marriage, nor would you approach a priest to analyze the results of a medical test. The problem is, NOMA overestimates the extent to which science and religion can be separated. As we have already seen, the histories of science and religion are profoundly entangled. In the words of the writer Nick Spencer, they must be at least *partially* overlapping magisteria.[10]

Complementary

Alister McGrath offers a more constructive third perspective. He argues that science and religion can, and indeed should, be understood as distinct but complementary endeavors that are strongest and most successful when they work together. The history of the relationship between these two intellectual giants is one reason to endorse a more complementary framing. Science has been funded, practiced, and disseminated by religious people for centuries—a far cry from what many proponents

---

10. Spencer, *Magisteria*.

of the conflict thesis would have you believe. A particularly illuminating account of the history of the science–religion relationship is Nick Spencer's *Magisteria: The Entangled Histories of Science and Religion*. It is well worth a read for anyone interested in learning more about how deeply interrelated religion and science have often been.

In addition to historical justifications for viewing science and religion as more intertwined than either "conflict" or "contrast" implies, there are theological reasons. An oft reached-for metaphor is the "two books metaphor." The two books refer to the book of scripture (the Bible) and the book of nature (the physical world). The metaphor positively encourages people to see both scripture and nature as revealing truths about the same God, the author of both. Deepest insights are gained when the books are read together. There is also scriptural justification for such a view, particularly Psalm 19:1, "The heavens declare the glory of God; the skies proclaim the work of his hands." Here we see encouragement to examine the natural world because by doing so we learn more about its creator.

McGrath has written prolifically on many topics surrounding science and religion. He frequently employs an illuminating metaphor provided by the late philosopher Mary Midgley. According to Midgley, we should approach understanding reality as we might approach understanding a particular geographical location, say, the United Kingdom. To understand the United Kingdom properly we need many different kinds of maps, because no single map can capture everything important about a country. We need a geographical map to chart the contours of the landscape; we need a population map to see which areas of the country are densely inhabited and which are not; we need an electoral map to gain an understanding of the political dispositions of the various regions of the country. You get the idea. One map alone cannot convey all the information about a place. Nor can one intellectual enterprise tell you everything about the highly complex reality in which we live. We should avoid reductionistic explanations that distill everything to either religion or science and instead understand these as forming complex and compound knowledge structures.

Applying this idea to science and religion leads to the following position, which McGrath develops in *The Territories of Human Reason: Science and Theology in an Age of Multiple Rationalities*. As opposed to a theory of a single, universal rationality, McGrath moves the debate toward a more pluralistic approach that recognizes multiple, situated rationalities, each of which emerges in a specific context for a specific purpose. He describes his position as one of "epistemological pluralism," which means that there are many routes to knowledge and multiple types of knowledge. None of these should reign supreme. Although each discipline is independent and retains methodological integrity, the rational structures therein are domain-specific, and for this reason they do not come into conflict. Religion has its own rationality, which is suited to explaining and contextualizing the religious dimensions of life. It may be better suited to questions like "how can I live a good life?" or "what rituals ought I to engage in for devotional worship?" Science, on the other hand, is better suited to answering questions like "what is the structure of the atom?" or "how do chemical elements combine with each other?"

Although they ask many different questions, McGrath maintains that there are important areas of overlap where conversations between the two can be highly enriching. Origin questions about the universe and about life on Earth fall into this camp. In fact, Christians should expect to see deep resonances between what religion tells us and what science tells us, because they believe that the Bible and the natural world emanate from the same source. We will explore some of these resonances in the coming chapters. The point is, according to McGrath and many others working in science and religion today, constructive dialogue between science and religion is the best way forward.

Complementarity better acknowledges the many areas in which science and religion can engage in mutually enriching dialogue. Nevertheless, critics have accused all three of the aforementioned categories for being overly simplistic. They each, to varying degrees, assume that we can give clear and well-boundaried definitions of the terms "religion" and "science" that possess historical continuity, which we have already seen is extremely difficult. The final category challenges this assumption.

Complexity

John Hedley Brooke offers a final approach, which I find the most persuasive. As Brooke writes:

> Serious scholarship in the history of science has revealed so extraordinarily rich and complex a relationship between science and religion in the past that general theses are difficult to sustain. The real lesson turns out to be the complexity. Members

of the Christian churches have not all been obscurantists; many scientists of stature have professed a religious faith, even if their theology was sometimes suspect. Conflicts allegedly between science and religion may turn out to be between rival scientific interests, or conversely between rival theological factions. Issues of political power, social prestige, and intellectual authority have repeatedly been at stake. And the histories written by protagonists have reflected their own preoccupations.[11]

Brooke emphasizes that both science and religion are so profoundly rooted in human concerns and human endeavor that it is a mistake to treat them as wholly separate. Not only is it impossible to fully separate them, it is also, as we saw earlier, impossible to neatly define them. For this reason, it is not possible to extract either the religious or the scientific from the social contexts in which they take form. There is typically no single "religious" perspective on a given issue. Often, there is not a single "scientific" perspective on a key issue either.

We cannot escape the fact that "religion" and "science" are broad conceptual categories containing multitudes of ideas bubbling up and vying for dominance. Disputes—and, of course, there have been many disputes—are between *people* not reified disciplines. Indeed, several of the most famous disputes purported to be between "science" and "religion" ended up actually being either conflicts between personalities or disagreements within religion or science themselves. As you progress through this book, exactly how complex the relationship between science and religion is will become ever clearer. That is also why, when peering into the murky waters of science and religion, it is often helpful to focus on a specific branch of science and a specific religion. That is precisely what *Decoding the Cosmos* is here to do.

Perhaps you were hoping we would be beginning this book with some certainty. Alas, in science and religion certainty is rather rare. It is difficult—and often actively unhelpful—to try to give sound-bite answers to these invariably complicated questions. Moreover, the issues under consideration by science and religion are simply too important to consider carelessly.

11. Brooke, *Science and Religion*, 6.

If I meet someone for the first time and they find out I work in science and religion, I am usually asked, "Isn't that a bit of a contradiction?" Even as an atheist, I answer with a resounding "no." Science and religion are not locked in a state of perennial warfare, each aiming to obliterate the other. Not only does this misrepresent their histories, it misunderstands what science and religion are really about. As for a positive answer about the nature and scope of their relationship, clarity is more elusive. Luckily for me, I am not trying to put forth an authoritative account of the religion–science relationship, even if the question of their compatibility runs through the veins of the entire project.

My aim is more modest, and hopefully more achievable. In the following chapters I will take you through some of the significant ways a specific science, modern physics, interacts with the doctrines of a specific religion, Christianity. Even here, no single picture emerges. Some areas are wonderfully harmonious, as though religion and science are singing from the same proverbial hymn sheet. Other areas are far harder to reconcile. I will leave much of the "deciding" to you. Let's dive into the murky waters of physics and theology, pushing ever deeper in pursuit of greater understanding.

FURTHER READING

Barbour, Ian G. *Religion and Science: Historical and Contemporary Issues*. London: SCM, 1998.

Dawkins, Richard. *The God Delusion*. London: Black Swan, 2007.

Harrison, Peter. *Some New World: Myths of Supernatural Belief in a Secular Age*. Cambridge: Cambridge University Press, 2024.

———. *The Territories of Science and Religion*. Chicago: The University of Chicago Press, 2017.

McGrath, Alister. *Science and Religion: A New Introduction*. Maldon, MA: Wiley-Blackwell, 2010.

———. *The Territories of Human Reason: Science and Theology in an Age of Multiple Rationalities*. Oxford: Oxford University Press, 2019.

Spencer, Nick. *Magisteria: The Entangled Histories of Science and Religion*. London: Oneworld, 2023.

1

Creation

IN THE BEGINNING, GOD created the Heavens and the Earth. At least, so says the opening verse of the Hebrew Bible. The claim that YHWH, the Father, the ground of being, or simply *God*, created the physical world is a cornerstone of Christian theology. It is utterly integral to understanding how Christians conceptualize God and the relationship that he has with created persons.[1] There are two accounts of the creation of the world in Genesis, namely Genesis 1:1—2:4a and Genesis 2:4b—3:24. They differ on certain key features, including their scope and the moment at which human beings enter the scene, so some exegetical and theological work is required to ascertain precisely what the doctrine of creation ought to contain. The former narrative has a cosmic focus, while the latter is more concerned with the Earth and humanity. One way of framing these accounts is that the first focuses on the *cosmos* while the second focuses on *creatureliness*. What is shared by these narratives, and is repeated throughout the entire biblical text, is that the world—both physical and spiritual—is dependent upon God for its existence.

The precise mechanics of the creationary process are to an extent ambiguous, and this matters for how the doctrine of creation relates to modern physics. How did God create? What materials, if any, did God use to make the world? What exactly are the opening chapters of the Bible

1. In this book I will be referring to God as "he." Although it makes more sense to me to think of God, if such a being exists, as not being constrained by human-centric notions of masculinity and femininity, I am following historical convention. As this is not relevant to the issues at hand, I won't dwell any further on this point.

really about? Debates rage on over all these questions. What is at stake is no less than the origin of the universe and the reason we exist. Rather important stuff. The point is, the Genesis narratives paint a somewhat mixed picture about whether the creative act took place *ex nihilo*, i.e., out of nothing, or *ex vetere*, i.e., out of old or pre-existent materials.

How one interprets the opening verses of Genesis will depend, to an extent, on how one translates the Hebrew. The two options, each of which are valid and both of which appear in well-known translations, are "In the beginning, God created the Heavens and the Earth . . . ," and "In the beginning, *when* God created the Heavens and the Earth . . ." (emphasis added). The first translation implies creation *ex nihilo*, with God first creating a formless void and then going on to create everything else. This interpretation is supported when God speaks things into existence. God says: "let there be . . ." and then it appears, as if out of nothing. When God creates using materials that already exist, i.e., when he forms Adam from the dust of the ground (Gen 2:7), the biblical author is explicit. There is a clear difference between forming Adam from the dust of the ground and commanding "let there be . . ." which is immediately followed by ". . . and it was so." God is shown to act freely, without constraint or conflict. A creative decision is made, and immediately it comes to pass.

The second translation, "In the beginning, *when* God created the Heavens and the Earth . . ." is more suggestive of creation *ex vetere*, namely out of old or pre-existent materials. It seems as though a formless void is already present when God's creative process begins. God is depicted as hovering over bodies of water while darkness obscures the depths that lie below. The picture here is one of shapeless substance, observed and traversed by God. As the narrative develops, we see this benign primordial material formed into recognizable phenomena as God draws coherent forms out of the fog. There are depths, darkness, and waters over which God's Spirit can travel. These, one might argue, form the building blocks for the creation of our physical universe.

On the creation *ex vetere* interpretation, God's creative work resembles construction. We can conceptualize this kind of creativity by drawing analogies with the type of creating in which we humans engage. As children we build castles out of sand, and as adults we cook dishes for our loved ones out of grains, vegetables, and spices pulled from the Earth. We recognize the creativity involved when an artist designs something extraordinary and builds it out of what is ordinary. We are skilled—some of us more than others, of course—at making meaning out of matter. The second translation of Genesis 1's earliest verses describes creation in this way. God separates out new substances from old materials. He divides light and darkness, day and night, the waters above and the waters below.

Despite the text's suggestions that God formed order from chaos, the standard theological teaching is that God created everything in existence *ex nihilo*, out of nothing. The rest of scripture fits more with the *ex nihilo* reading, e.g., John 1:3, "All things came into being through him, and without him not one thing came into being." This is a denial of the claim that God created out of pre-existent materials. Instead, he created everything that ever has and ever will exist. Similarly, 2 Maccabees 7:28 says, "I beg you, my child, to look at the Heaven and the Earth and see everything that is in them, and recognize that God did not make them out of things that existed."

Moreover, there were powerful theological reasons to endorse creation *ex nihilo*. In order for God to remain all powerful, and for creation to perfectly realize God's plan, God's creative freedom cannot have been constrained by the properties of any materials out of which he created. Similarly, if God is sovereign over all things, then there can be nothing in existence that is not dependent on him. If matter existed without God, then it does not need God to exist nor does it need God to rule over it. The creation-from-chaos picture, then, did not fit with other important Christian commitments: divine freedom, divine omnipotence, and divine sovereignty. By the end of the second century CE, any ambiguities in Genesis 1 had been overshadowed by the reasons to support creation *ex nihilo*. This quickly became the standard understanding of the doctrine of creation, and it has been the orthodox view ever since.

Another important feature of the Genesis narratives is the phrase *God saw that it was good*. There are several overlapping meanings tied up with this refrain, which is repeated six times throughout Genesis 1. Each shines a slightly different light on the value of creation. First, it is good insofar as it is well made. It is ordered, purposeful, and harmonious. Second, it is beautiful—full, verdant, and pleasing to the eye. Third, it is plentiful, in as far as it can sustain a vast range of life, from the vibrant flora to the diverse fauna. Fourth, it is good because it shares in the characteristics of its maker. Creation is imbued with its own creative power; the land and the waters themselves bring forth life. This continuous creative process that is carried throughout the evolution of the Earth is, in effect, creation creating itself. What is required for these goods to transpire is an underlying coherence, a basic structure to reality, perhaps even laws of nature. It is this order that separates creation from what came before, be that abject nothingness or formless void. Genesis 1, then, also teaches us that creation is imbued with a rationality that allows it to evolve in accordance with various laws and principles. Eventually, intelligent beings use this underlying rational structure to develop another mode of understanding the world: modern science.

The narrative arc of Genesis 1 is that God speaks the world into existence through ten utterances, each building on the work of the last, over the course of six days marked by morning and evening. There is a poetic rhythm to the text. God creates, he sees that it is good, and then morning and evening mark the passage of another day. Biblical scholars such as William P. Brown have noted a pleasing symmetry between the two halves of the Genesis 1 narrative.[2] In the first three days, creation is given *form*. First, light is created. Second, the sky is created to separate the waters above from the waters below. Third, we see the creation of land and vegetation. Then, there is a creative shift from *forming* the world to *filling* it. The fourth day sees lights in the dome of the sky which separate day and night and give rise to the changing seasons. Fifth, the skies and the seas are filled with avian and aquatic life. And sixth, the land is filled with animals, humans, and food. Day One mirrors Day Four, Day Two mirrors Day Five, and Day Three mirrors Day Six. This patternicity poetically echoes the above claims about reason, structure, and purpose being part of creation from the beginning. Just as the narratives are thoughtfully structured, with the "forming" days corresponding to the "filling" days, so too is the world thoughtfully structured in such a way that the Earth's various forms perfectly function as habitats for those who will come to fill them.

Clearly, much thought and care has gone into structuring the creation story, and much can be gleaned from analyzing its structure, form, and content. But what overarching points are we to take from Genesis 1? In the broadest terms, the text speaks of God as creator bringing the world into existence and praising the world for its goodness. In rather more technical theological language, God, a *necessary* being (i.e., a being whose existence is guaranteed; there is no possible state of affairs in which God does not exist), created the physical universe, which is *contingent* (i.e., it is perfectly possible for it to have not existed, or for it to have had different characteristics). Christian theology and the philosophy of

---

2. Brown, "Creation in the Old Testament."

religion understand God as the only being whose existence is certain, unchanging, and irrevocable. Everything else could plausibly have not existed and was deliberately and freely brought into being by the necessary creator God. For this reason, everything that exists depends utterly upon God for its continued existence. The doctrine of creation *ex nihilo* is fundamentally one of creaturely dependence upon a creator who created the world freely, lovingly, and as a gift.

Despite general agreement on the above points, many have argued that there is more to the doctrine of creation *ex nihilo* than claims about dependence upon a creator God. Several versions of the doctrine have emerged. Some are perfectly compatible with modern physics, while others cannot be reconciled with modern physics at all. We haven't the scope to go into the minutia of every interpretation here. Instead, I will cover three points of contact between creation and science: Young Earth Creationism, Old Earth Creationism, and the cosmological argument. To set the scene, we begin with physics and Big Bang cosmology.

COSMOLOGY

The discipline known as "cosmology" emerged after the publication of Einstein's general theory of relativity, which allowed, for the first time, a physical theory to model the entire universe. The goal of cosmology is grand: to understand the nature and structure of the universe. This includes, but is by no means limited to, the study of how the universe began. Like the rest of physics, cosmology requires careful experimentation and the formulation of precise mathematical formulas to develop theories that can be tested against what we observe. It also contains a few underlying assumptions, including that the universe proceeds with regularity and that the same substances behave in the same ways across even the vastest reaches of both space and time.

One of the reasons we think we can know anything about the early universe at all is that we assume the physical world is governed by so-called "laws of nature."[3] These laws cause things belonging to certain kinds to behave the same everywhere and at all times. Carbon behaves the same today in a lab in Cambridge as it did in the earliest days of the universe. Gravity behaves the same in our galaxy as it does in a galaxy

---

3. Or, for some philosophers who are wary about committing to something that seems to imply a lawmaker, "physical regularities."

billions of lightyears away. So, we assume (with good reason, given what our observations show us about far-flung galaxies) that we can use our current knowledge to say with reasonable confidence what happened at the beginning of the universe, and what might be happening very far away from us. This is essential if cosmology is going to work. We cannot conduct physical experiments on the primordial cosmos. Instead, we can only look at what we have in front of us now and work backward with knowledge of how matter, energy, forces, and spacetime currently behave. Via careful construction of various models and theories, we can come to know about things we cannot directly observe.

In this endeavor, we are fortunate in many ways. The speed of light is finite, meaning the light from the furthest galaxies we can observe left those galaxies during the early stages of the universe's development. Bigger and better telescopes are being built all the time, with creative names like "the very large telescope" and "the extremely large telescope." These expand our horizons to greater distances than could ever have been imagined by Galileo Galilei, the first person to turn a telescope to the sky four centuries ago. We have gone, in a reasonably short time frame, from being barely able to see craters on our own moon to being able to observe galaxies billions of lightyears away. The richness of the data sets we are now gathering is exceptional. Some images we have now go back as far as 100 million to 250 million years after the Big Bang, allowing us to look into the far reaches of deep time.

Wonderful as this is, a lot happened in the hundred million years between our earliest observations and the origin of the universe. Despite the frankly mind-blowing insights cosmology has been able to offer us in the century since Einstein first wrote down the equations of general relativity, there are problems that persist within the discipline. Not least of which is that science generally relies upon repeatability and replication of results. If I want to learn about the behavior of tigers then I should go to India and observe many different tigers, drawing comparisons between them and looking for behavioral patterns. Similarly, if I want to learn about the efficacy of a particular medication, I ought to test it out on a large number of people from diverse backgrounds to make sure it works effectively and consistently across the populations to whom it might be administered. Of course, when it comes to cosmology, we only have one physical universe (or, at least, we only have access to one universe that we can ever measure). This makes cosmology unique as a science by virtue of having only one object of study.

Despite this potential limitation, cosmology has proved extremely fruitful throughout the century that has passed since its inception. We have gone from believing that ours was the only galaxy in existence to knowing that ours is one of many trillions of galaxies. It has led us to learn that each of these galaxies contains billions of stars, many of which are encircled by planetary systems like our own. It has allowed us to peer back into the infancy of our cosmos, as an ultrasound machine allows us to see into the womb and observe a developing fetus. We have been able to witness the birth of far-flung stars and their violent and explosive deaths. So much has been learned, and the brilliant and terrifying fact is that there is so much more left to discover. Since switching on NASA's James Webb Space Telescope, the most powerful telescope ever built, we have been able to see further back into the universe's past than ever before. For a space nerd like me, this is exceptionally exciting.

Theists of all kinds have marveled at the majesty of the cosmos and the myriad insights about its workings that cosmology has provided. In a broad and general sense, the cosmos's size and its rational and coherent structure have led many to believe that some kind of intelligence is behind it all. Indeed, we will explore such arguments in the next chapter. But there is more for the theist to marvel at than the broad and the general. There are also specific features of the physical cosmos that some have argued are highly supportive of particular theological claims. For now, I want to draw our attention to a discovery of the twentieth century that is of particular relevance for the doctrine of creation: the Big Bang.

The Big Bang

I expect the key idea contained within Big Bang cosmology will not be new to any reader interested in physics and theology. This is, of course, that the universe came into being at some point in the past in something resembling a cosmic explosion bringing space, time, matter, and energy into existence.[4] The four fundamental forces took on their values, as did the physical constants, even the laws of nature themselves came into being. According to Big Bang cosmology, the universe had a violent but definite beginning. Most of us know this. Nevertheless, it is worth going

---

4. Although it differs from any explosion that we might set off here on Earth, it shares certain similarities that make the comparison fair. The Big Bang involved the rapid expansion of space from infinitesimally small to much larger in a very short amount of time, and in this sense resembles an explosion.

over in some detail because it is a fascinating theory with an interesting and rather convoluted origin story.

Cosmology as a sub-discipline of physics is founded upon Einstein's general theory of relativity, a theory about the nature of gravity first published in 1916. General relativity superseded the previous explanation of gravity provided by Isaac Newton centuries before, which described gravity as a force holding between objects. The strength of this force is directly proportional to the product of the masses of the two objects and inversely proportional to the square of the distance between their centers. There was no deeper explanation for why it was this particular formula that gave the strength of gravity, nor of how gravity could act between bodies at great celestial distances from one another. Einstein once called this kind of thing "spooky action at a distance," a quip that captures how odd it is that two bodies millions of miles apart should exert forces on each other.[5] The Einsteinian understanding of gravity was utterly different, although its strength was, of course, the same. Indeed, Einstein's general theory of relativity ushered in an entirely new way of understanding space, time, and interactions between celestial objects. General relativity does not describe gravity as a force. Instead, gravity is a consequence of the warping effect massive bodies have on the fabric of four-dimensional spacetime. As John Wheeler pithily put it, spacetime tells matter how to move, and matter tells spacetime how to curve.

When Einstein first formulated the equations of general relativity, he discovered that they predicted an expanding universe. This stood in direct contrast to the received wisdom of the time, which held that the universe had likely always existed in something resembling its current form. In other words, the cosmos was believed to be homogeneous (the same everywhere) and isotropic (the same in all directions), meaning it held a "steady state" and did not undergo significant changes on the macro-scale. In order to stabilize his equations, Einstein inserted Λ, the cosmological constant, which served as a counterbalance to gravity and prevented general relativity from predicting an expanding universe.

For reasons we shall see below, Einstein would later remove Λ, calling it the greatest blunder of his life. Instead of using the mathematical formalism to discover some radical and unknown fact about the physical universe, he adapted his equations to fit with his pre-existing expectations about what he believed the universe ought to be like. Funnily enough,

---

5. Although "spooky action at a distance" was a remark directed at quantum phenomena, it applies here as well.

Einstein's "biggest blunder" ended up being an accidental early discovery of what we now call *dark energy*, or the energy density of space. We now know there is some force or energy that acts as a counterbalance to gravity, although Einstein's own use of it to stabilize his equations was misguided. Einstein was, and remains, one of the greatest scientists ever to have lived. Even his biggest blunders turn out to be profound discoveries.

Despite his stumbling upon the cosmological constant as something that would later prove significant for quantum mechanics and the study of the energy density of space, Einstein was wrong to try to contort his equations into giving a static universe. Before long, in 1929 to be exact, the astronomer Edwin Hubble observed that the light from distant galaxies was shifted toward the red end of the electromagnetic spectrum, a phenomenon known as red-shift. Red-shift is an instance of the Doppler effect, namely the effect that you notice when a vehicle with a siren drives past you and the pitch changes depending on whether it is moving toward you or away from you. The sound waves are being compressed as the vehicle approaches, causing a higher pitched sound as a result of the shorter wavelength. When the vehicle is moving away from you, the siren's sound waves are being elongated, causing a lower pitched sound. The electromagnetic spectrum, light, varies in color as it varies in wavelength. The end with the longest wavelengths is on the red side of the visible light spectrum, and the shortest wavelengths are on the blue end. Hubble observed that the farther away a particular galaxy was from Earth, the greater the red-shift. He realized that this galactic red-shift indicated that the universe was expanding, elongating the light from those galaxies farthest away from us and shifting it toward the red end of the electromagnetic spectrum.

It took a bright young physicist and Catholic priest, Georges Lemaître, to articulate this cosmic expansion and its consequences for a universal beginning using the mathematics of general relativity. In 1931, Lemaître published a paper pithily titled "A Homogeneous Universe of Constant Mass and Increasing Radius Accounting for the Radial Velocity of Extragalactic Nebulae." It used general relativity's equations to argue that the universe was expanding, and that the rate at which galaxies were shooting away from each other was proportional to the distance between them. In other words, the farther away galaxies are from each other the faster they are moving away from us. This is known as Hubble's law. If you rewind time, reversing the expanding universe, you end up with a cosmic picture in which galaxies were much closer together. Eventually, you end up at a point of almost infinite heat and density at which point everything in the universe occupied the tiniest spatiotemporal point.

What happened before this point, or even whether that was a sensible question to ask, no one was certain. Unease rippled through the scientific community. Perhaps it was the resonance these ideas had with the doctrine of creation. Perhaps physicists were made uncomfortable by the potential discovery of a boundary point; a moment in the universe's history beyond which we may never be able to go. Is this where science ends? What discipline might we turn to if we hope to hop up on the boundary and glimpse whatever (if anything) lies beyond?

The consensus that grew around the expanding universe model was gradual, piecemeal, and fascinating. Neither Lemaître's paper nor Hubble's observations were sufficient to secure the position of scientific orthodoxy, although they certainly helped. Einstein and Lemaître discussed the paper, and although Einstein could not fault Lemaître's impeccable mathematics, it was the physical consequence of that mathematics—an expanding cosmos—that Einstein could not accept. Was it the theological shadow cast by Lemaître's equations that caused Einstein's unease? Whether or not Einstein was put off by the implications of an expanding universe, others later certainly would be. If the universe was expanding, that means it could have exploded into existence from a point of nothingness. And that seemed too much like another familiar creation account that many believed had no place in science.

Lemaître himself did not have theological reasons for providing physical proof of an expanding universe nor a universal beginning. He seemed to see science and religion as occupying distinct spheres, believing that the biblical writers were informed on theological matters but on matters scientific they were as wise or as ignorant as their generation. Although he called the beginning of the universe a "primeval atom," he became uncomfortable with the adoption of this idea by Pope Pius XII who, in 1951, called the scientific discovery of an expanding universe evidence of a moment of creation and thus proof of the existence of God. Lemaître was deeply wary of tying science so tightly to theology and urged the pope to hold back on drawing theological conclusions from scientific data. Although the pope acquiesced, this connection between Big Bang cosmology and "let there be light" has persisted, and for obvious reasons. It is a pleasing quirk of the history of science and religion that the fact that the universe had a beginning was demonstrated by a Catholic priest, who nonetheless advised the pope against drawing any theological conclusions from the discovery. It is easy to see why the pope may have been tempted to ignore his advice.[6]

Lemaître's insistence on keeping theology and science apart was noble and methodologically prudent. Science has a clearly defined methodology which ought to proceed without external influence. That being said, when it comes to universal beginnings, it is simply impossible to disentangle philosophy, physics, and theology. How the universe began is a boundary question. It sits at the very limits of what we can know, and certainly what we can demonstrate empirically. Science alone may not be able to answer it, and even if science can provide us an extremely compelling account, philosophers and theologians will always want to offer their own contributions. For this reason, the debates between rival cosmologies in the middle of the twentieth century strayed far beyond the realm of science into metaphysics, and even theology. For better or worse, cosmology rarely stands alone when looking back to the birth of the universe. The question is simply too important.

It was not merely metaphysics that divided opinion on the universe's beginning. There were profound disagreements over the science too. A particularly vociferous opponent of the expanding universe model was astronomer Fred Hoyle. Hoyle defended the alternative theory, known as "steady state" theory, in which the universe remained static and largely unchanging, having existed always. Hoyle explained galactic red-shift by the suggestion that matter was being continuously created and destroyed, a violation of the conservation law. It was already known that energy—and thus matter, as Einstein had proved their equivalence via his equation $E=mc^2$—can neither be created nor destroyed, but is instead only ever converted to other forms. Nevertheless, Hoyle clearly believed this was a price worth paying to rid science of the distinctly theological claim that the universe came into existence at a finite moment in the past.

A spirited debate raged on between Hoyle and his steady state companions and those who preferred the alternative Big Bang model. Interestingly, it was Hoyle himself who coined the term Big Bang in 1949 in an attempt to disparage the position, inadvertently giving it a jazzy and enduring title. Lemaître and Hubble had given us good reason to suppose the universe had a beginning, but the data failed to be conclusive. More evidence was needed to decide: Had the universe always existed, or had it burst into existence in a Big Bang?

---

6. Spencer, *Magisteria*, chapter 15.

It would take decades for the debate to be decided in favor of the Big Bang theory. In 1964, radio-astronomers Arno Penzias and Robert Wilson discovered that some form of background noise was interfering with their radio that was built to detect extremely faint radio waves. To make the delicate measurements, they needed to eliminate all background interference, and yet there was a particular consistent noise coming from all directions. They could not get rid of it. Initially they assumed fault with their machinery, and indeed they did discover an unfortunate family of pigeons nesting in the antenna, which had to be removed. But the noise persisted. What they had, in fact, discovered was what we now call the Cosmic Microwave Background radiation: the afterglow of the Big Bang. Far from a family of pigeons, indeed! It is truly remarkable that we humans have managed to build machines capable of detecting radiation that was first emitted billions of years ago at the very moment our entire cosmos burst into existence. One can only imagine how Penzias and Wilson felt when they realized that what they were hearing was in fact the echoing birth cries of the cosmos itself. They ultimately won the Nobel Prize in 1978 for their discovery.

A further discovery that contributed to the now robust reputation of Big Bang cosmology was offered by Stephen Hawking and Roger Penrose. They developed a mathematical proof of the existence of the so-called singularity, a point in spacetime at which gravity is so strong that light itself cannot escape. At a singularity, spacetime collapses in on itself creating a point of no return. Singularities are typically surrounded by event horizons, namely boundary points that, once crossed, cannot be turned back on. Once something crosses an event horizon, it will never return. Because of this, singularities are often surrounded by black holes.

Black holes, fascinating in their own right due to their alluringly dangerous nature, also serve as confirmations of the very strangest consequences of general relativity. A black hole is formed during the death of a star. At the end of a star's life, when its fuel runs out, it is no longer able to withstand the immense pressure exerted by gravity upon it due to its mass. At this point, the star will collapse back in on itself to such an extent that light, matter, energy, and even time cannot escape. At the center, a singularity, a point of almost infinite spacetime curvature, draws everything inexorably toward itself. Penrose developed the mathematics explaining singularities, for which he won the Nobel Prize for physics in 2020. With the help of Stephen Hawking, he applied the singularity theorem to the universe itself, showing that at the Big Bang, the universe was a singularity. Out of this, everything in the physical universe emerged in an explosive moment of rapid expansion. This was yet another confirmation of Big Bang cosmology, which now enjoys widespread support throughout physics.

In summation, Big Bang cosmology states that at some finite point in the universe's past—now believed to be around 13.75 billion years ago—there existed a singularity. At this point of almost infinite heat, density, and spacetime curvature, the entire universe was smaller than a single subatomic particle. Everything you have ever seen, smelled, touched, or read about in a physics textbook was compressed into a single point with more extreme physical conditions than we can imagine. Then, and we are still a bit shaky about what happened next (for reasons that will become clear in the next chapter as we discuss inflationary theory and cosmic fine-tuning), something caused this singularity to burst forth in an explosion of energy. For the next 380,000 years or so the universe was an entirely opaque soup of protons, neutrons, and electrons. Eventually, these subatomic particles formed into the first atoms of hydrogen and helium, allowing light to travel through spacetime instead of being scattered by a dark ocean of prehistoric particles.

After several million years, small pockets of slightly denser material began to coalesce under the force of gravity, forming clouds of dust and particles that would ultimately form into stars, illuminating our universe for the first time in its history. These stars were drawn together in clusters, forming the first galaxies. Around these young stars swirled protoplanetary discs of dense gas that themselves would coalesce into gaseous planets like Jupiter and, in the end, rocky planets like our own planet Earth. Ever since the Big Bang the universe has been expanding and cooling, meaning that space itself is growing and pulling galaxies away from each other. Plausibly, at some point in the future, all other galaxies will be so far away from Earth that we will no longer be able to see them. If human descendants survive here, they will have to take the existence of other galaxies as an article of faith. There will be no way to detect them anymore, as the light they emit will have disappeared over the horizon. To whatever beings remain, the universe will appear cold and lifeless.

The history of the cosmos is one about which we know a lot and yet very little. We can sketch out ideas about how celestial bodies formed using the mathematics provided by Einstein and general relativity, and we can use telescopes like Hubble or James Webb to peer back into the universe's distant past and see those ideas empirically confirmed.

Nevertheless, there is so much we still do not know. We struggle to model what happened in the first microseconds of the universe's existence, as physics is incomplete. It is also almost impossible to say what happened before the Big Bang, if we can even ask that question. The Big Bang may well be the event during which time itself came into existence. If so, it is meaningless to ask what happened "before." There can be no "before" if there is no time.

Moreover, there is now some dispute about whether cosmology supports any reading of the doctrine of creation that requires a beginning of the universe. If we live in some kind of multiverse which contains either cycling phases of Big Bangs followed by Big Crunches (a universe collapsing back on itself when the contracting force of gravity overcomes the expansive force of the Big Bang) or an infinite number of universe "bubbles" living side-by-side, then perhaps our Big Bang was not in fact the beginning of everything. This thrilling but uncertain prospect will pop up from time to time throughout this book. For now, we can say this much: the universe we live in came into existence at a finite point in the distant past. It is with this fact in hand that we shall proceed to the next section, where we will be exploring what this means for different theological accounts of creation. The first is an account of creation that is in conflict with the account of the origin and evolution of the universe provided by modern science. The second is an account of creation that is a complementary companion to contemporary physics.

CONFLICT: YOUNG EARTH CREATIONISM

As discussed in the introduction, the conflict thesis or warfare model understands religion and science to be fundamentally incompatible. In the case of Young Earth Creationism, the position is typically associated with a literal reading of Genesis, reorienting the purpose of the text toward that of a literal history of nature or a scientific textbook. Young Earth Creationist Dr. Terry Mortenson summarizes the position as follows:

> Young-earth creationists believe that the creation days of *Genesis 1* were six literal (24-hour) days, which occurred 6,000–12,000 years ago. They believe that about 2,300–3,300 years before Christ, the surface of the earth was radically rearranged by Noah's Flood. All land animals and birds not in Noah's Ark (along with many sea creatures) perished, many of which were subsequently buried in the Flood sediments. Therefore,

creationists believe that the global, catastrophic Flood was responsible for *most* (but not all) of the rock layers and fossils (i.e., some rock layers and possibly some fossils were deposited before the Flood, while other layers and fossils were produced in postdiluvian localized catastrophic sedimentation events or processes).[7]

Mortenson, and others who endorse the view, give a variety of scriptural justifications. First, they proclaim that Genesis 1 is intended as a historical text detailing exactly how the physical cosmos came to be. The primary reason for endorsing this view is that, in their view, Genesis 1 follows the same literary techniques as other passages of the Bible that are intended to be historically accurate. Mortenson gives Genesis 12–50, most of Exodus, and Joshua 1 as examples. He argues that Genesis 1 is distinct in tone and style of prose from other Hebrew texts that are poetic or parabolic. He also argues that the Hebrew word *yôm* means a literal day, a meaning that is solidified by repeated references to morning and evening. Moreover, he notes that God speaks animals and humans into existence immediately, without any hint in the text that this came about gradually over a process of millions of years. In addition, he points to several other places in the Bible that indicate the other biblical authors believed the creation accounts to be literal and historical. E.g., Mark 10:6, "But from the beginning of creation, God made them male and female." According to Young Earth Creationists like Mortenson, this is not compatible with a gradual process of evolution out of which humans emerged.

As is clear, Young Earth Creationism stands in sharp contrast to the Big Bang cosmology detailed above. It also rejects evidence from geology that the Earth is approximately four billion years old, evidenced by the fossil record and carbon-dating, and that biological life emerged via the evolutionary process and not through a single decisive creative act. Exact points of contention with scientific consensus are below. Again, I will use Mortenson's own words here:

> The order of creation in Genesis 1 contradicts the order of events in the evolution story in at least 30 points. For example, the Bible says the earth was created before the sun and stars, just the opposite of the big bang theory. The Bible says that fruit trees were created before any sea creatures and that birds were created before dinosaurs (which were made on Day 6, since they are land animals), exactly the opposite of the evolution story.

7. Mortenson, "Systematic Theology Texts and the Age of the Earth," np.

> The Bible says the earth was covered completely with water before dry land appeared, and then it was covered again at the Flood. Evolution theory says the earth has never been covered with a global ocean, and dry land existed before the first seas.[8]

Mortenson is right that, read as a literal account of the history of the cosmos, Genesis 1 cannot be squared with cosmology, geology, and evolutionary biology. But if Genesis 1 is taken as literally true, then it also cannot be squared with Genesis 2 and 3! In Genesis 1 humanity is created on the sixth day, after the creation of land and sea animals. In fact, creating humans is the final act in the Genesis 1 creation saga. In the alternative creation account given in Genesis 2, man is formed of the dust of the ground (Gen 2:7) before the land is populated with other animals who are created later to keep him company (Gen 2:19). Indeed, God allows Adam to name these other animals (Gen 2:20), implying that he has an encyclopedic knowledge of the natural world and watched it come into being at God's side. Biblical literalism generates a contradiction. Humans must simultaneously be held as coming into being before other animals *and* after them. It is hard to imagine that the biblical authors were unaware of this, a fact that suggests a level of symbolic interpretation was intended for these narratives. To resolve the contradiction, some form of non-literalism must be introduced into biblical interpretation. Once those doors are opened, why close them in the face of overwhelming scientific evidence about the age of the universe?

We have already considered the evidence in favor of Big Bang cosmology, and the vast expanses of time over which the universe evolved. This evidence from physics about a very old cosmos is corroborated by geology's evidence of a very old Earth. In the eighteenth century, Scottish geologist James Hutton was the first to postulate that the Earth was far older than had previously been imagined. He examined rock formations in the Scottish Lowlands, noticing that they exhibited features that indicated gradual change over extremely long temporal scales. For example, the presence of volcanic rock running through sedimentary rock in Edinburgh's Salisbury Crags, or angular unconformities with vertical layers of sedimentary rock beneath and above horizontal layers of sedimentary rock. All these geological phenomena indicated that the rocks had undergone significant changes over vast stretches of time. Millions of years,

---

8. Mortenson, "Systematic Theology Texts and the Age of the Earth," np.

in fact. Hutton famously saw in these rocks "no vestige of a beginning, no prospect of an end."[9] Later geologists would call this "deep time."

Modern geological techniques confirm this old Earth hypothesis. First, geologists provide evidence about the age of the Earth from radiometric dating, a technique relying on the predictable decay of radioactive isotopes of carbon, uranium, potassium, and other elements, which allows scientists to extrapolate back and determine the age of particular geological objects. This technique, specifically U/Pb dating, which measures the amount of lead present in uranium, was first performed in the 1950s by C. Patterson, G. Tilton, and M. Inghram, and yielded the now commonly accepted age of 4.5 billion years. Combined with other dating techniques—including examining annual rock layering and rates of geological change—geologists can confidently claim that they see scales of "deep time" in the Earth's history. Similarly, the fossil record shows millennia-old creatures whose ancient skeletons have become part of the rock and whose presence indicates Earth's lengthy biological and geological history. These are powerful pieces of evidence for the old Earth hypothesis.

Mortenson, along with other Young Earth Creationists, explain the fossil record as the result of the great flood. The flood, they claim, covered the entire Earth and killed all animals that were not in Noah's ark. It also radically restructured the Earth's surface. They deny that the fossil and rock records are evidence of deep time, instead arguing that they are evidence of the great flood. The problem is, we know that the rock structures that we observe take much longer to form than a few thousand years. Moreover, radiometric dating places the age of these rocks far, far, beyond the age of the Earth endorsed by the Young Earth Creationists. As this book focuses on physics, and not geology or biology, I cannot go into much more detail here. Others have written excellent work giving reasons to reject the young Earth account. The papers by Dalrymple and Patterson *et al.* in the "Further Reading" section at the end of this chapter provide solid evidence as to why geology demonstrates that the Earth is billions, not thousands, of years old. Ultimately, the Young Earth Creationist account fails to stand up to scientific scrutiny.

Before moving on, it is worth noting that the Young Earth Creationist has recourse to an alternative tactic, which is to shift the nature of the debate from a purely scientific one about rival theories to a philosophical

---

9. American Museum of Natural History, "James Hutton."

debate about the scientific paradigms within which data is interpreted. A scientific paradigm, a term first introduced by philosopher of science Thomas Kuhn in *The Structure of Scientific Revolutions* (1962), is an intellectual framework that contains all the commonly accepted views about a subject, conventions about what direction research should take, and methodologies dictating how research ought to be carried out. Scientific paradigms also contain standards for evaluating research findings. The idea that science was comprised of paradigms was radical when Kuhn proposed it, and a healthy amount of debate still surrounds the idea. What we *can* say, though, is that Kuhn's invaluable contribution to the philosophy of science was his conviction that science does not proceed via a steady accumulation of knowledge that gets closer and closer to objective truth.

Many assume that empirical science, at its best, ought to be wholly objective. This means that it should collect data and let the data speak for itself about what it reveals about the natural world, remaining impervious to the biases of researchers or their assumptions about what the data should tell us. Kuhn argued that this does not ever really work in the real world. Instead, prevailing scientific paradigms become intellectual contexts for interpreting the data that is gathered. Kuhn argued that so-called normal science is carried out for a period of time, until it hits up against more and more anomalies that are incompatible with the theories that comprise the dominant scientific paradigm. The cumulative effect of these anomalies brings about a crisis—the old framework has too many weaknesses that mean it is no longer coherent. At this point, a scientific revolution must take place. Following that, a paradigm-shift. During this phase of scientific development, we see the emergence of an entirely new scientific paradigm that is incommensurate with the previous one. A good example of this is the revolution that saw general relativity replace Newtonian mechanics. The question is, can these insights from the philosophy of science help the Young Earth Creationist?

Earlier we discussed an instance of the expectations of a particular paradigm causing incorrect conclusions to be drawn, namely Einstein's cosmological constant. The prevailing paradigm contained a static universe, so Einstein moulded his equations to fit with these expectations. In so doing, he made what he considered to be the greatest blunder of his life. Science is full of errors like this, and sometimes these errors have significant consequences. It is important to be aware of the limitations of both science and those who practice it. We cannot allow any single discipline to take a position of intellectual supremacy. Instead, careful consideration of each piece of evidence is necessary when weighing up alternative explanations of something as important as the cosmos itself. That being said, we also see throughout the history of scientific practice that science eventually course-corrects. Again, we saw this happen with the cosmological constant. Without this course correction, science would never move forward. We would still believe in a flat Earth and a geocentric cosmos. Are we in a moment of paradigm-shift at the moment? Are we about to see creation science overturn the old Earth hypothesis?

The short answer is no. Philosophy of science has also taught us that there is no such thing as science; rather we have sciences, a set of distinct scientific disciplines each of which has its own research methodology, norms of practice, grounding assumptions, and theories. We have good reason to trust that the Earth is billions of years old because many disparate sciences converge on the same answer. Geology, chemistry, biology, and cosmology all agree that the Earth has been around for somewhere in the region of 4.5 billion years, and the cosmos even longer than that. If this was a quirk of a single scientific paradigm, we should not expect to see such widespread agreement from various different sciences. In my view, this is powerful evidence in favor of the old Earth hypothesis.

The Young Earth Creationist disagrees by virtue of taking a different starting point, namely that the Bible is the only objective source of truth that can be trusted without question. Because the biblical authors are believed to be divinely inspired, the Bible becomes the intellectual context, or paradigm, through which all data is interpreted. While this is not so dissimilar to the practice of empirical science detailed above, it leads to different conclusions because competing evidence pools are being drawn upon. On the one hand, Young Earth Creationists accept that scientific data can lead us toward knowledge. This is clear when they refer, as they often do, to scientific techniques when refuting claims about an old Earth. On the other hand, they reject scientific data that contradicts their literal reading of scripture, making both their use and their rejection of science inconsistent. This leads to what I take to be ad-hoc reinterpretations of selective fossil data into evidence for the great flood (despite the rock record being clearly older than six thousand years, as we know from radiometric dating). It also leads to the significance of certain data points being overemphasized and others being underemphasized. If it is understood as a scientific paradigm, confirmation bias reverberates throughout the Young Earth Creationist project.

Over and above the scientific reasons for rejecting Young Earth Creationism, there are also some conceptual problems with any view that is grounded upon the conflict model of the science–religion relationship. Mortenson exemplifies the conflict view, writing "if the Bible's teaching on death, the Curse and the final redemptive work of Christ is true, then the millions-of-years idea must be a grand myth, really a lie. Conversely, if the millions of years really happened, then the Bible's teaching on these subjects must be utterly false, which is devastating for the gospel."[10] Religion and science are, in his opinion, fundamentally incompatible. In Kuhnian terms, they are incommensurate paradigms that cannot be held together without slipping irrevocably into the thorns of contradiction. Essentially, science and the Bible cannot both be true.

As I have already argued, advocates of the conflict thesis argue that religion and science are in constant and enduring opposition to each other. There are many reasons for rejecting this. First, the idea that science and religion exist in perennial warfare systematically misrepresents the rich and diverse historical interactions between religious figures and scientists, and more abstractly, between theological doctrines and scientific theories. For one, religious institutions have often been significant funders of scientific research, particularly in the early days of science. In fact, some historians have argued that the Catholic Church is the greatest funder of scientific research throughout history. In his book *The Sun in the Church: Cathedrals as Solar Observatories*, J. L. Heilbron argues that "the Roman Catholic Church gave more financial aid and support to the study of astronomy for over six centuries, from the recovery of ancient learning during the late Middle Ages into the Enlightenment, than any other, and, probably, all other, institutions."[11]

The "two books metaphor" illustrates why religious institutions might be motivated to fund scientific research. This metaphor uses the imagery of two books to illustrate God's two creative projects that are available to humanity for interpretation. First, is the book of scripture. Christians believe that the Bible was divinely inspired and contains ethical, historical, theological, anthropological, and spiritual truth. Yet, according to the two books metaphor, God also wrote a second book: the book of *nature*. The book of nature—i.e., the natural world, including both planet Earth and the entire physical cosmos—was also "written"

---

10. Mortenson, "Systematic Theology Texts and the Age of the Earth."
11. Heilbron, *Sun in the Church: Cathedrals as Solar Observatories*, 3.

(created) by God and was intended to be intelligible. Thus, by examining nature, Christians can come to know their God on a deeper level. Creation reveals the hand of the creator, as the Psalms author emphasizes in Psalm 19:1, "the heavens declare the glory of God, the skies proclaim the work of his hands."

Science allows us to read the book of nature, and so pursuing science need not be in tension with religion. In fact, Christians can trust the insights provided by science because, like scripture, the natural world was authored by God, albeit in a different mode. Scientific insights can inform how to interpret scripture correctly—although science and religion are not equivalent, they can exist in harmony. Together, they sing the song of creation. Although I am not myself religious, it seems clear to me that the pursuit of science is in no way antithetical to faith. What science does rule out is the kind of faith that is hostile to all other intellectual enterprises. The kind of faith that rejects science on the basis of literal interpretations of scripture is a victim of the closed-off conflict mindset. Not all faith needs to be this way.

Second, the conflict model assumes a very flat, one-dimensional understanding of reality—it denies that there can be different levels of explanation of the same phenomena, or that there are a variety of ways one can interpret religious teachings. This means that it fails to recognize that someone could believe both that human beings came about as a result of biological evolution *and* that human beings were created by God. Indeed, many intelligent and reasonable people do claim this. On the biological level, evolution is a sufficient explanation for the emergence of the human species. However, one can also very reasonably believe that God is the architect of the evolutionary process, the driving force behind it, or the creator who set it all into motion and allowed it to unfold on its own terms. Implicit in the idea of "conflict," then, is that two opposing forces, each with stable boundaries and a single perspective regarding core issues, are in a state of war over the same territory. It is perfectly acceptable, however, to view science and religion as distinct categories whose interests overlap but which are ultimately different intellectual projects that can complement each other. We can now move on to an account that does not reject the insights of modern science: Old Earth Creationism.

COMPLEMENTARITY: OLD EARTH CREATIONISM

The position sometimes referred to as Old Earth Creationism is actually a rather diverse umbrella term for all those who reject the Young Earth Creationism account but still endorse some form of the Christian doctrine of creation. Here it will mean, broadly, a denial of a six-day creation period and an acceptance of the cosmologist's account of the age of the universe, the geologist's account of the age of the Earth, and the biologist's account of the evolution of species over extended periods of time. These positions are not in complete opposition, however. Old Earth Creationists share the Young Earth Creationist's aforementioned commitment to the total dependence of the physical cosmos upon God. They agree that at some point in the finite past God created the world out of nothing and has continued to sustain its existence at each moment since. Old Earth Creationism also echoes the claims about creation being a supreme act of divine love; a radically free act by a benevolent creator upon which all our existences depend. Had God not acted to create the cosmos, nothing at all would exist. Creationists of all stripes subscribe to these claims and find evidence for them in the books of the Bible. For this reason, it is totally appropriate to retain the word "creationism" as a defining characteristic of the old Earth position, despite the unfortunate fact that the term is now generally considered (in popular discourse, at least) to be synonymous with the young Earth account discussed above. In fact, it is rather difficult to be a Christian and reject all forms of creationism, given the place the doctrine of creation holds both in scripture and in the theological corpus.

Where the Old Earth Creationists depart from their young Earth counterparts is, unsurprisingly, in the age of the universe that they endorse. Old Earth Creationists are perfectly happy, by and large, to accept the data from cosmology, geology, and biology that indicate that the Earth (and thus also the cosmos) is billions of years old. What scriptural justification might be sought for such a position? After all, the Bible does *seem* to say that the Earth was created in six days, not over billions of years. The answer to this is actually rather simple and has deep roots in the theological tradition. The idea that scripture ought to be interpreted literally is a rather new phenomenon. Saint Thomas Aquinas, for example, argued that the doctrine of creation is wholly compatible with the idea that the world has always existed. Even a beginningless world would be utterly dependent upon its creator for its continued existence, which is the core claim of the doctrine of creation. Although Aquinas did ultimately endorse a moment of creation, and thus a finite universe, he believed the everlasting alternative was theologically consistent. Scripture, in Aquinas's day, was not typically read as a factual account of world history. It was understood as a sophisticated text layered with a multiplicity of meanings that had to be carefully unpacked and thoughtfully contemplated.

As will already be clear, the question of textual interpretation is of the utmost importance in these debates. How should Christians read the Bible? What meaning is mapped onto the scriptural passages that concern themselves with creation? There are many ways of approaching these foundational questions. For the purposes of this particular book, which is most concerned with the interface between theology and modern physics, and the nature of explanation offered by each, I say the following: Old Earth Creationists interpret the scriptural texts that focus on creation, particularly the six-day creation account of Genesis 1, as rich in symbolic, theological, ethical, and anthropological meaning. In the broadest terms, it is to be read as an exploration of the world's dependence on a creator. The texts are concerned with ethical issues surrounding our relationship to our planet, with mythical explanations about the order in which things came to be, and theological proclamations of God's radical creative freedom when bringing the physical cosmos into being. Genesis 1, on this view, is not a scientific or historical textbook. Indeed, one makes a category error in assuming that this mythical text should be interpreted literally.[12]

At this point, if you are sympathetic to a literal reading of the text, you might be feeling suspicious. You may be worried that I am advising Christians to put science above religion and only reinterpret theology through a scientific lens. This approach has caused problems in the past because the science keeps changing. If we adapt theology too much, tying it too closely to the science of the day, theology risks becoming either stale and irrelevant if science moves on or fickle if it tries to move along with it. This type of God-of-the-gaps reasoning is not one that I encourage.

---

12. A category error is a mistake that occurs when one ascribes certain properties to something that belong to another category. An example would be the statement "that fish smells blue"—blueness is not a property of smells, so a category error has been made. In the case at hand, it is a category error to suppose that an ancient text could be offering something like a modern scientific explanation. We misplace the meaning of the text if we assume it was meant to be interpreted as a literal scientific treatise and not a metaphorical, symbolic, and spiritual reflection on creation.

However, this symbolic and layered approach to textual analysis actually stretches back to a time long before modern science (and certainly before cosmology!). If we look to the writings of the early church fathers, particularly Saint Augustine of Hippo, we see a consistent willingness to interpret scripture in non-literal ways. As my colleague at Cambridge David Fergusson argues, this suggests that symbolic readings are not the invention of modern thinkers, intent merely on accommodating scripture to contemporary secular thought. Instead, non-literal readings of Genesis have deep roots in Christian tradition.[13]

Non-literal approaches to the creation texts hold that Genesis should be read as being steeped in layers upon layers of meaning that can only be unearthed through careful attentive reading, perhaps with the help of a book like this one. What Old Earth Creationists take from scripture is not that it is a blow-by-blow account of a six-day-long creative period. Instead, they interpret the text as a proclamation that creation was nurtured into being by a creator God who has a plan for how it ought to unfold. Moreover, creation is good—it makes manifest this divine plan and allows God's creative energies to emerge as an enduring and spectacular universe. Old Earth Creationists also see evidence of *creatio continua* in the creation narratives—God encourages the land and seas to bring forth animals, an indication that the creative act is ongoing and that the world itself has creative power. This can be interpreted as compatible with evolutionary accounts of the emergence of species.

There are some Old Earth Creationists who wish to read the text in a slightly more literal way, taking the empirical content to be more than mere affirmation of a universal beginning. Advocates of this approach turn to the claim that God created the Earth in six days and attempt to unpack exactly what the term "day" is supposed to mean in this context. They take a modicum of interpretive latitude, rejecting the idea that "day" here means a fixed period of twenty-four hours (which only has meaning as a "day" because this is how long the Earth takes to spin on its axis, making it an irrelevance in the early universe when planet Earth did not exist). Instead, they affirm that the universe was created in six creative epochs. These epochs, they claim, echo the scientific account of the evolution of the universe.

First, God said, let there be light. This fits closely with Big Bang cosmology's account of the universe bursting into being in a moment of

---

13. Fergusson, "Creation."

magnificent energy. Then, the sky comes into being, bringing with it the separation of sky from land and sea. This could be interpreted as conveying the coalescing of cosmic dust into galaxies, stars, and planets. At this point, our planet Earth is formed, undergoing a period of geological time known as the late great heavy bombardment in which it underwent violent change before taking a form that would be hospitable to life. Because the Earth is spinning on a tilted axis, likely knocked there by a violent collision with a celestial object, we are able to enjoy seasons as well as night and day. This shares resonance with Genesis 1:14–15 in which God says let there be seasons and days and years. Once the Earth settles into a rhythmic seasonal pattern and becomes stable enough to allow life to emerge, it does so remarkably quickly (in geological terms). Genesis 1:24 speaks of the Earth bringing forth living creatures, before, finally in Genesis 1:26, God creates humanity in his own image. Physics, the object of this book, can only speak to the earliest portions of the Genesis narratives. But it is worth mentioning that, interpreted as broadly indicative of creative epochs, geology and biology do fit rather nicely with the Genesis description. Some of the similarities are remarkable, given the biblical authors' inability to access the kind of scientific knowledge we enjoy today. Although things do not line up perfectly, modern science does not refute the Genesis accounts if we rid ourselves of the literal interpretation of a six-day creation.

The most striking similarity between the Genesis accounts and the Big Bang cosmology that receives endorsement from modern science is this commitment to a universal beginning. Indeed, it was on this basis that Pope Pius XII proclaimed that "the science of today, by going back in one leap millions of centuries, has succeeded in being a witness to that primordial *Fiat Lux*, when, out of nothing, there burst forth with matter a sea of light and radiation."[14] Nonetheless, for those whose views align with Georges Lemaître, and who remain wary of the pitfalls of carving up theology with the knife of modern science, the symbolic reading of Genesis remains available. Lemaître warned the pope against this kind of language. Theology then becomes vulnerable if, and when, science moves on. For this reason, holding science and religion as complementary and compatible companions but *not* equivalent disciplines is the most fruitful mode of engagement. It allows the disciplines to have porous boundaries

---

14. Quoted in Spencer, *Magisteria*, 50.

and to learn from each other. This route, in my view, is the most likely to lead to deeper understanding.

We have focused a lot in this chapter on scripture, but there is much more to theology than the contents of a holy book. For centuries, philosophy has been a bedfellow of theology, and for good reason. In the final section of this chapter, we will briefly turn to a philosophical argument that relates to creation, known as the cosmological argument.

THE COSMOLOGICAL ARGUMENT

There are two types of cosmological argument—the Kalam argument and the argument from necessity and contingency—which, roughly, have Islamic and Christian roots respectively. We will consider each in turn.

The Kalam Argument

The Kalam cosmological argument has its roots in the medieval Islamic theology of Al Ghazali. The version discussed in philosophy of religion today is presented by Christian philosopher William Lane Craig, who is responsible both for naming it the Kalam argument and for bringing it back into contemporary discourse.[15] The argument goes something like this:

Premise 1: Whatever begins to exist has a cause of its beginning.

Premise 2: The universe began to exist.

Conclusion: Therefore, the universe has a cause of its beginning.

If Premise 1 (henceforth P1) and Premise 2 (henceforth P2) are true, then the conclusion must be true. This is what is known in philosophy as a *deductive* argument, namely the kind of argument where the truth of the premises guarantees the truth of the conclusion. If you want to refute such an argument, you cannot do so by attacking the reasoning from premises to conclusion. Instead, you must try and show that one of the premises is false. So, can we say that both P1 and P2 are true?

Let's begin with P2, as it is the more straightforward of the two. Big Bang cosmology, our best theory about how the universe came to be, says that P2 is true, the universe in which we live began to exist. So far, so

---

15. Craig, *Kalām Cosmological Argument*.

good for the Kalam argument. Craig also offers some philosophical arguments for P2. Essentially, these rest on claims about actual infinities being impossible. Although mathematicians use infinities all the time, these are not concrete instances of an infinite number of some object or entity but are instead abstract mathematical objects. Craig argues that it is not possible for an actual infinite to exist in the world, and so there cannot be an actual infinite number of past days in the universe. Instead, the universe must have had a beginning. There is much debate about these arguments in the philosophy of religion, with many remaining unconvinced that the quirky properties of infinite sets make their concrete existence physically impossible. Whether these arguments are persuasive or not is somewhat tangential to our present concerns, as Big Bang cosmology allows us to say with some confidence that the universe had a beginning. We can set aside multiverses for now, because the premise is not "our universe came into existence out of nothing," it merely claims that our universe began to exist. Even if it was birthed by the destruction of a previous universe, our particular universe did come into existence at some point in the past. As far as we know, approximately 13.75 billion years ago.

What about P1? It certainly seems a reasonable enough assumption. I began to exist in 1995 (or 1994 if you believe I existed before I was born, e.g., at conception), and the cause of my beginning to exist was my parents' decision to have a baby. The Tower of London began to exist in the 1070s, and the cause of its beginning was William the Conqueror's desire to have a mighty stone tower at the center of his London fortress. Is this the case for all objects? It is not clear that quantum objects like electrons have causes for their existence, as they have been observed popping in and out of existence completely randomly. Craig makes note of this point and argues that we can weaken P1 and rephrase it as "if the universe began to exist then it had a cause for its beginning." Craig says this is intuitively obvious to everybody, but other philosophers have questioned the universality of these intuition claims. Perhaps this is a statement Craig cannot make. We are not able to say what happened before the Big Bang with any confidence, given the limitations of our current scientific understanding. Moreover, for this to work as a religiously relevant argument, a further premise and conclusion need to be added. Here, further problems lie.

Premise 1: Whatever begins to exist has a cause of its beginning.

Premise 2: The universe began to exist.

Conclusion 1: Therefore, the universe has a cause of its beginning.

Premise 4: No scientific explanation (in terms of physical laws and initial conditions of the universe) can provide a causal account of the origin of the universe, because physical laws and initial conditions are part of the universe.

Conclusion 2: Therefore, the cause must be personal (explanation is given in terms of a non-natural, personal agent).

It may be the case that there cannot be a *scientific* explanation of the origin of the universe. We don't know yet, because there is much about physics we are yet to discover. We do not yet have a theory that unites general relativity (the theory about spacetime on which cosmology is based) and quantum mechanics (the theory about subatomic particles). This is quite important in terms of universal origins, as the cosmos was once the size of a quantum object. Until we have a theory that can make sense of this, we are intellectually in the dark about what went on within, or even before, the singularity. Even if no scientific explanation can be given, this does not rule out that some physical explanation exists if only we were smart enough to work it out. It is possible that something existed before the Big Bang, say, a quantum field or a contracting universe, that caused our universe to come into existence. Not out of nothing, instead out of some causally prior physical state.

Craig creates a false dichotomy between scientific explanations and personal explanations. Science is a contingent human enterprise that is constrained by the limitations of those who practice it. We may never be able to discover what went on during or before the Big Bang. This does *not* mean that there is no in-principle physical explanation. What I think Craig is doing here is conflating epistemology (concerned with knowledge) with ontology (concerned with reality or existence). Just because we cannot epistemically access a physical cause of the Big Bang, this does not entail that no physical cause exists. We do not have to choose between a scientific or a personal explanation. We have a third option: a physical explanation. Such an explanation would rely only on physical causes to explain how the universe came to be, even if we may never come to develop or discover it. If we are left in this position, we have no scientific explanation (because we never develop science to the point that it could explain something like the beginning of the universe) but nor must we invoke a personal explanation such as the existence of a creator God.

Another problem that is also raised for the argument is the following. It is by no means clear why the God of Christianity is the personal explanation Craig is looking for. The argument—at its very best—only gets you to a personal explanation, not to the Christian God. I argue it does not even get us to the personal explanation. For these reasons, the Kalam argument cannot take us convincingly to its conclusion that the universe had a beginning, and that this beginning is evidence for the existence of God.

Necessity and Contingency

The version of the cosmological argument that has its roots in the Christian tradition is that which is encapsulated in the third of Aquinas's Five Ways of demonstrating the existence of God. As the philosopher Immanuel Kant noted, the cosmological argument begins with existence itself. Its aim is to show that the existence of the physical universe is good evidence of the existence of God. The argument is grounded on the idea that was later reframed by Gottfried Wilhelm Leibniz as the "principle of sufficient reason." According to this principle, everything that occurs must have a reason for its occurrence. Another way of phrasing the principle is similar to the causal principle we encountered above in the work of Craig: everything that exists must have a cause for its existence. The principle remains controversial; however, it functions in the argument as follows. Everything that exists has a reason for its existence. Because the universe exists, it has a reason for its existence. The universe and everything in it is contingent, meaning that it could have not existed. Philosophers might put this by saying there are logically possible worlds (i.e., worlds that could exist, even if they do not actually exist) that do not contain our universe, or that contain universes very different from our own. According to the argument, contingent entities cannot have purely contingent explanations for their existence. Instead, a necessary being (a being whose existence is guaranteed; i.e., there is no possible world in which this being does not exist) is required to account for the existence of contingent objects. That necessary being is God. Therefore, God exists. It can be expressed as a formal argument:

> P1. A contingent being (a being such that if it exists, it could have not-existed) exists.

P2. All contingent beings have a sufficient cause of or fully adequate explanation for their existence.

P3. The sufficient cause of or fully adequate explanation for the existence of contingent beings is something other than the contingent being itself.

P4. The sufficient cause of or fully adequate explanation for the existence of contingent beings must either be solely other contingent beings or include a non-contingent (necessary) being.

P5. Contingent beings alone cannot provide a sufficient cause of or fully adequate explanation for the existence of contingent beings.

P6. Therefore, what sufficiently causes or fully adequately explains the existence of contingent beings must include a non-contingent (necessary) being.

P7. Therefore, a necessary being (a being such that if it exists, it cannot not-exist) exists.

P8. The universe, which is composed of only contingent beings, is contingent.

C. Therefore, the necessary being is something other than the universe.[16]

The cosmological argument can be fleshed out in several ways, but this version uses the existence of a contingent being (often considered to be the universe itself) to argue that a necessary being (God) must exist and must have brought the universe into existence.

There have been many criticisms of the cosmological argument, which together leave it in a rather vulnerable position. First, David Hume argued that it commits the fallacy of composition. This philosophical fallacy is committed when one assumes that what is true for the members of a set must be true for the set itself. For example: bricks are small, so the Great Wall of China must be small. Clearly, this is faulty reasoning. Hume argues that if all the members of the set "the universe" (i.e., all the physical objects and events within the universe) have a reason for their existence, it is not reasonable to ask for a reason for the existence of the set (the universe) as well.

A second critique was offered by philosopher Bertrand Russell in a radio debate with Jesuit priest Frederick Copleston. Russell remarked

---

16. This version of the argument is found in Reichenbach, "Cosmological Argument."

that the universe was a "brute fact," namely something that defied explanation. It just *is*. This response could be considered a cop out, a refusal to engage with the terms of the debate. Perhaps you will be thinking this, and maybe you are right. But Russell wasn't trying to be facetious. Instead, he was pointing toward a fact that has cropped up a fair bit in this chapter. That is, we must at some point reach a boundary that human knowledge cannot cross. There are questions too big for us to be able to answer, limited as we are by our cognitive apparatus and our technological capabilities. Perhaps determining whether the universe is contingent or necessary, caused or causeless, is one of those questions. We know the universe exists because we live in it. Maybe we just have to accept that as a basic fact, building our other knowledge structures on top of it, rather than trying to dig beneath and see what, if anything, lies below.

As I hope you will agree, the interface between science and religion on the topic of creation is as vast as it is fascinating. On the question of origins, no subject can proceed alone. Science, philosophy, and theology all weigh in, making this one of the richest areas of discourse that science and religion scholars tackle. As luck would have it, we are only at the beginning. There is much left to explore. With that, let us turn from creation to a related but distinct area of Christian thought: design.

FURTHER READING

Brown, William P. "Creation in the Old Testament." In *St Andrews Encyclopaedia of Theology*, edited by Brendan N. Wolfe et al., 2022. Online.

Dalrymple, G. Brent. "The Age of the Earth in the Twentieth Century: A Problem (Mostly) Solved." *Geological Society Special Publication* 190.1 (2001) 205–21.

Fergusson, David. "Creation." In *The Oxford Handbook of Systematic Theology*, edited by Kathryn Tanner, John Webster, and Iain Torrance, 72–90. Oxford: Oxford University Press, 2009.

Hazen, Robert M. "How Old Is Earth, and How Do We Know?" *Evolution Education Outreach* 3 (2010) 198–205.

Kragh, Helge, and Malcolm S. Longair, eds. *The Oxford Handbook of the History of Modern Cosmology*. Oxford: Oxford University Press, 2019.

Patterson, C. C., G. Tilton, and M. Inghram. "Age of the Earth." *Science (American Association for the Advancement of Science)* 121.3134 (1955) 69–75.

Reichenbach, Bruce. "Cosmological Argument." In *The Stanford Encyclopedia of Philosophy*, edited by Edward N. Zalta and Uri Nodelman, 2024. Online.

Spencer, Nick. *Magisteria: The Entangled Histories of Science and Religion*. Chapter 15. London: Oneworld, 2023.

2

Design

THE SCIENTIFICALLY AND THEOLOGICALLY rich doctrine of creation is both foundational to Christian theology and, in the form laid out in the previous chapter, incomplete. God, Christians believe, did not simply bring forth the universe arbitrarily and then leave it to its own devices. Instead, Christians believe that God carefully and deliberately designed its every feature with a divine purpose or set of purposes in mind. As scripture records, "The LORD, your Redeemer, who shaped your life in your mother's womb, says: 'I am the LORD. I made all that is. With no help from you I spread out the skies and laid out the earth'" (Isa 44:24). Similarly, "For his invisible attributes, namely, his eternal power and divine nature, have been clearly perceived, ever since the creation of the world, in the things that have been made" (Rom 1:20). Theologians have meditated on such passages, as well as upon philosophical work concerning the origin and form of the universe, and many have found in these some evidence for their theistic beliefs. These reflections about divine purposiveness and evidence of orderliness or beauty in nature contain the embryonic forms of the design argument that tries to demonstrate God's existence by locating evidence of such design in nature. Another name for such design arguments is "teleological arguments," from the Greek word *telos* meaning "end," "goal," or "purpose." This is because teleological arguments seek to identity divine purposiveness in the natural world. In other words, teleological arguments detect evidence of God's design in nature by noting particular natural phenomena that seem especially well designed for some ultimate aim. Such aims range from something as specific and fine-tuned as the acute functionality of the human eye to something as basic and general as the existence of life itself. Such arguments have waxed and waned in terms of their perceived success and popularity over the centuries, and I will explore some of that history in this chapter.

In a very broad and general sense, teleological or design arguments begin by identifying apparent patterns in nature that indicate purpose, order, and structured or specified complexity. Then, it is claimed that such purpose, order, and complexity could not have arisen by chance, but instead reveal the careful hand of a supremely intelligent creator who brought about the world we inhabit and designed its particular features. These arguments sit within the theologically controversial tradition known as natural theology, and it is here that we will begin.

NATURAL THEOLOGY

As distinguished theologian Alister McGrath notes in his "Natural Theology" entry of the *St Andrews Encyclopaedia of Theology*, the conceptual category of natural theology has several distinct, albeit overlapping, meanings. One way of understanding natural theology is that it is the use of natural human resources, principally reason, to gain a deeper understanding of God without the use of revelation. On this view, it is doing theology using human reason and not the Bible. Another way of understanding natural theology is that its aim is to infer the existence, or discover some attributes, of God by examining the natural world. The idea behind this is that we should expect a creation to hold evidence of its creator. Thus, by studying nature, say, through the empirical sciences, humanity can learn more about God. Just as the undulating curves of a pot will reveal evidence of the fingers that shaped it into existence, so too can we understand natural theology as looking for divine fingerprints impressed into nature. Something about the artist can always be discovered by looking at their art, and the closer you look the more you can learn. A mere glance at a pot can tell the trained eye whether it was crafted on a spinning pottery wheel or whether it was manually constructed. Looking in more detail should show signs of the kind of artist who created it. Did they have small hands? Did they work quickly? What kind of clay did they use, and what does this choice reveal about their nature or preferences? An even closer inspection may even reveal a signature at the base of the pot; something intentionally left behind for later onlookers to discover. A mark placed there for those who may later wonder: Who made this, and why?

The point of this metaphor is to argue that there are both intentional signs of artistry, such as the signature the artist leaves on their work, and unintentional signs of the artist embedded in the shape, the structure, and form of their pieces. Natural theologians ask, if a God created the cosmos, should we not expect to see similar signs of his creative presence? These signs may echo something about the designer's nature—perhaps goodness, power, or intelligence—or they might resemble more intentional signs, like an artist's signature etched into the base of a vase.

Those who are sympathetic to natural theology argue that we should be able to make rational arguments about God from what we independently discover about nature. Through the use of human reason, we can come to know God in ways not revealed by the scriptures. Despite the fact that the scriptures take a backseat in natural theology, theologians engaging in this type of work would balk at the idea that they are going against what scripture teaches about how to come to know God. In fact, they may look to scripture itself to make their case. Justification for natural theology comes from several sources, but one is Psalm 19:1, which states, "The heavens declare the glory of God; the skies proclaim the work of his hands." This psalm suggests that examining the world on its own terms will reveal truths about the God whose "hands" brought it into existence. Recall the two books metaphor discussed in the previous chapter: God wrote both the book of nature and the book of scripture. These can legitimately be read side by side.

Another source is, of course, the creation account in Genesis that we explored in the previous chapter. Here, the Bible is abundantly clear that God created the world *and* imbued it with certain moral properties (i.e., goodness) that reflect the divine nature. A third, and deeply significant, reason natural theology finds justification through scripture is the proclamation in the prologue to the Gospel of John that Jesus is the "Word" or the divine *Logos*. This idea of Jesus Christ as the divine *Logos* has been interpreted as claiming that Christ is the agent of creation, through whom everything came into being. The *Logos* both represents and embodies the divine rationality through which the world was created, and it is precisely this rational structure that makes the world intelligible. This point was made by theologian Thomas F. Torrance when he argued that the incarnation continuously affirms that creation is intelligible, albeit contingently. In fact, some have argued that without the concept of a divine lawmaker, physics, insofar as it seeks to discover natural laws, would not be possible. McGrath echoes these sentiments throughout his many writings on natural theology. Creation is not only dependent upon God for its existence; it was also designed by God in order to express something of the depths of the divine nature.

Despite this, natural theology does not receive resounding support from all theological corners. In fact, one of the leading Protestant theologians of the twentieth century, Karl Barth, vociferously opposed natural theology on the grounds that we have no justification for trusting human reason when it comes to theological matters. Though these ideas have deep theological roots, they were solidified for Barth during the 1930s and 1940s when he observed many of his contemporaries offering theological justification of the horrors perpetuated by the Nazi regime. Instead of allowing their theology to shape their political ideology, Barth saw these theologians using their political ideologies to shape their interpretations of theology, leading them to horrific conclusions. He was profoundly disturbed by this phenomenon and became convinced that human beings could not be trusted when it came to matters of God. Barth's theological explanation of this was that human reason is deeply corrupted by sin and thus is distorted by human fallenness. Sin tempts us to center ourselves and our selfish desires instead of centering God, the only legitimate source of theological truth. Without God's gracious self-revelation through Jesus Christ and the continual working of the Spirit, humanity would not be able to know God at all.

Barth was committed to the idea that there exists what he called an "infinite qualitative distinction" between humanity and God. God is radically and wholly other and thus the divine personhood remains transcendent and unknowable. Because of this, humanity is in a state of profound ignorance about theistic matters that can only be overcome through divine grace. In other words, humanity can never come to independent knowledge about God. All theological knowledge, then, comes as a result of God's saving grace and not through human rational capacities.

As theologian Keith L. Johnson explains in *Barth on Natural Theology*, in whatever creaturely mode human beings encounter the divine self-revelation, they are encountering the eternal God who transcends creation and history. Humans can only receive revelation directly from God, through the proclaimed word of Christ, which breaks into both time and history from above. Such revelation is radically discontinuous with creaturely existence and should summon humanity to faith and obedience, *not* to engage in their own theological reflection on the basis of human reason or the natural world.

Natural theology, for Barth, is cut off at the knees because it is not grounded in Jesus Christ. By constructing theological knowledge out of insights gained from examining the natural world, we risk creating a system of human ideals rather than producing an accurate representation of God. Barth thus gave a resounding "NO" to natural theology, arguing that we must only passively receive revelation perpendicularly from above. Such revelation came originally in the form of the incarnation of Jesus Christ and is indirectly reported through scripture.

Although it is important to note that there is some significant opposition to natural theology, it does have a rich history and is seeing a fascinating revival in the form of design or teleological arguments from cosmic fine-tuning. For this reason it is well worth considering these arguments at length, even if one wishes to keep the Barthian warnings in the back of one's mind.

Design Arguments

The piece of natural theology most relevant to the theory of evolution is the aforementioned teleological argument, or the argument from design. The teleological argument reasons from premises about the natural world, specifically its order, complexity, functionality, and beauty, to conclusions about the existence of a designer God who created the world to exhibit these desirable characteristics. There are a few different ways of fleshing out a teleological argument, but one extremely simple version can be set out formally in the following way:

P1: The world exhibits evidence of design.

P2: If something exhibits evidence of design, then it is reasonable to infer that it has been deliberately designed by an intelligent agent.

C: It is reasonable to infer that world was deliberately designed by an intelligent agent.

There are clearly some missing steps in this basic argument that stop it being watertight, but it still captures something essential about teleological arguments, and so it is useful for our present purposes. This argument uses the term "world"—an ambiguous referent. World can mean our planet, our cosmos, or even in some contexts a particular grouping of countries, regions, or things (e.g., the English-speaking world, or the biological world). I have intentionally used an ambiguous term here because the teleological argument has a history that precedes our ability to observe other galaxies, or even other celestial bodies in our own solar system, with any greater resolution than the human eye can provide. Its rich history has included a multitude of points of focus. The teleological argument has, at times, referred to the Earth and its biological inhabitants, and at other times has had a wide enough scope to encompass the entire observable universe. To a significant extent, its object of study has been determined by the scope of our scientific understanding. A teleological argument could not have focused on our technically defined observable universe before telescopes existed to reveal to us just how extensive that universe is. Nevertheless, some thinkers today still prefer to focus on local features of our own planet than the cosmos as a whole, so this is not a hard and fast rule. Essentially, "evidence of design" in the "world" has been drawn from one or more of the following:

1. The world is highly ordered and complex.
2. Each component part works harmoniously with others for the good of the whole.
3. Creatures seem to function extremely well for their intended purpose.
4. The universe seems perfectly suited to the flourishing of abundant life.
5. Nature is extremely beautiful.

Some forms of the argument draw analogies between natural objects with the properties listed above, and artificial objects that exhibit similar properties, including machines with many interlocking component parts. We would not infer that a machine containing features that appeared carefully constructed and highly specialized had arisen by chance; instead we would infer that it was created by an intelligent mind for a particular purpose or purposes. Similarly, if the world exhibits these features, then the argument suggests that it was designed by an intentional, highly intelligent, creator with a purpose in mind.

The argument from design has a long history. Traces of such arguments are present in ancient Greek philosophy, and a rather short version is found in Saint Thomas Aquinas's Five Ways. Nevertheless, it was popularized in the Early Modern period. One thinker responsible for the argument's prominence during this time was William Paley. In 1802, Paley published *Natural Theology*, an extended argument for the existence of a creator God who expertly designed the natural world and everything within it. *Natural Theology* contains very detailed discussions of various features of the natural world that seem to reveal the hand of a designer. In other words, features so complex or so perfectly able to thrive in their environment that they cannot have come about through chance alone. The eye, for example, is both extremely intricate and highly specialized. It functions exceptionally well for its given purpose. Paley argued that such a perfectly functioning organ could not have accidentally popped into existence. It must have been carefully created by a designer God in order to fulfill its purpose of providing vision to the animal of which it is part.

What Paley offered was a theological explanation for natural phenomena. That explanation was: that God had created all species in their current forms, expertly shaping them into forms that would thrive in the demands of their environment. From the long necks of giraffes perfectly suited to eating high-up leaves, to the whale's ability to go long periods without breathing in search for food, Paley argued that animals have been created to flourish in their habitats. He illustrated this point with the infamous watchmaker analogy. Paley asks readers to imagine they are walking upon a heath and that they discover a watch upon the ground. The watch has many interlocking component parts, each of which appears perfectly crafted to enable its perfect functioning. We would not assume such an object had arisen by accident, blown together by a strong wind. Instead, we would infer on the basis of its properties that this object was designed and created by an intelligent being who crafted it with a specific purpose—namely telling the time—in mind. The designer may be hidden and unknown, but the watch's craftsmanship reveals both their existence and agency. It is a paradigmatic case of a designed object. The analogy is intended to demonstrate what we should be looking for if we want to look for design: specified complexity, purposive functionality, and even elegance and beauty. Even if the designer is not directly visible, they can be inferred from what they designed.

Paley argues that the world is relevantly similar to the watch insofar as its component parts are continuously engaging in complex interactions with each other in ways that show they are perfectly suited to their environment. The continual, rhythmic dance of predator and prey shows how well suited each partner is to their role. The lion is sufficiently stealthy to catch enough wildebeest to be nourished, yet the wildebeest is strong and fast enough to escape most of the time, ensuring both populations remain stable. Moreover, the natural world as a whole seems bursting with beauty and abundance. Paley wrote: "It is a happy world after all. The air, the earth, the water teem with delighted existence. In a spring noon, or a summer evening, on whichever side I turn my eyes, myriads of happy beings crowd upon my view."[1] Paley argued that from all this we ought to infer that the world and all it contains was intentionally designed by a supreme intelligence.

There is also scriptural justification for concluding that God created species in their final forms, designed specifically to thrive in a way suited to their kind. Genesis 1:25 says, "God made the wild animals according to their kinds, the livestock according to their kinds, and all the creatures that move along the ground according to their kinds. And God saw that it was good." It is easy to understand how, for centuries, Christians believed that God created the world and everything in it in the forms they have today.

This theory, in its raw and original form, no longer stands up to scientific scrutiny. Following Charles Darwin's voyage on HMS Beagle and his subsequent development of the theory of evolution by natural selection, we now know that biological life has developed over the course of billions of years from single-celled organisms to the complex life forms we see in abundance today. Of course, an entirely separate book could be written on the relationship between God and modern biology, and so this description may read as rather thin. Nonetheless, what we need to know for our present purposes can be summed up in the claim that Darwinian evolution offered a *naturalistic* explanation for natural phenomena, supplanting Paley's *theological* explanation. We simply no longer needed God to explain certain features of the natural world, for the theory of evolution did this perfectly well.

Many now recognize that Darwin's theory provides an explanation that leaves Paley's redundant. Why? Because the mechanism of natural selection shows how the features of the natural world that appear designed *could*, and in fact *did*, come about as a result of chance, randomness, and accident. The undirected evolutionary process accounts for the emergence of species. It can also explain why species seem so well suited to their environment. In evolutionary theory, nature is not directed

---

1. Paley, *Natural Theology*, 238.

toward any specific end, goal, or purpose. Rather, the evolutionary process is guided blindly by chance and mutation. In fact, the man known as Darwin's bulldog, Thomas Henry Huxley, claimed that teleology received its deathblow at Darwin's hands. In recent years, Richard Dawkins has gone even further, claiming that the blind natural processes behind evolution have ridden us of God altogether, leading to his description of nature as a "blind watchmaker," a description explicitly designed as a rebuttal to Paley.[2]

Despite these strong proclamations, the critics of teleological arguments spoke too soon. Design arguments as a whole have by no means suffered a fatal blow at Darwin's hands. One option has been to push the explanation back a level and claim that rather than God designing the *products* of evolution he designed the *process*. Another option is to look for evidence of design in arenas beyond the biological. As this is a book about modern physics, we will only consider the second option.

Cosmic Fine-Tuning

Teleological arguments from cosmic fine-tuning shift their point of focus away from the biological world and toward the domain of physics. More specifically, they look at data from cosmology concerning the laws of nature, the initial conditions, and the values of the universe's many constants. Proponents of arguments from cosmic fine-tuning claim that these numbers look "fixed" in some way. The basic argument is this: various properties of the universe could (as far as we know) have taken many different values to the values we actually observe. In fact, the range of possible values is staggeringly vast. Yet the values we see are those that are perfectly suited to the flourishing of complex life forms. According to our best physics, most universe-configurations that are compatible with the laws of physics are life-prohibiting; they are cold, lifeless voids in which no living beings could possibly have emerged. Therefore, the fact that we see life-conducive conditions has led some theists to claim that the universe has been "fine-tuned" by a designer God *so that life will emerge.*

By focusing on physics, modern proponents of the teleological argument distance themselves from the unfashionable organismic teleological arguments of Paley, with the hope that they will clothe themselves in renewed credibility. The structure of the argument is the same, but

---

2. Dawkins, *Blind Watchmaker*.

the content—specifically, the evidential basis upon which the argument is founded—is different. If you want to construct a design argument on the basis of so-called fine-tuning, you must begin with data from physics. Specifically, you must examine the fundamental features of the universe that make possible the evolution and existence of complex life. These include (among other things) the laws of nature, the values of the fundamental constants, and the distribution of particular types of matter.

An axiomatic claim of fine-tuning arguments is that our physical universe is perfectly suited to the flourishing of complex life. Let's take a moment to really think about what that means. We live in a vast—perhaps infinitely vast—universe that contains billions of galaxies, each of which is home to billions of stars. Many of these stars have solar systems much like our own, with rocky, gaseous, and icy bodies swirling in orbit around the only nearby grain of light and warmth in the silent and expanding darkness. These suns provide essential heat and light, without which life could not emerge. Just by looking at the data we have about other planets, it becomes clear that we are very lucky on Earth to have "Goldilocks" conditions that are *just right* for life to not only emerge but to flourish. This in itself is pretty staggering, especially given that our extensive search for extraterrestrial life on other planets has thus far led to nothing. Perhaps we are alone in this vast cosmos. Even if we are not, planets that can support life seem to be rather rare.

But we need more than a rocky planet at a suitable distance from its star to support life. Much, *much* more. Yes, our planet could have been knocked far out into the distant reaches of our solar system and become too cold to allow anything living on it to survive. But it would still be the case that other distant planets could in principle support thriving lifeforms, even if our world plunged into the icy depths of the Oort cloud that encircles the farthest reaches of our sun's gravitational field. Our cosmos contains the right ingredients, even if they are rarely combined into a recipe that leads to life.

The point is, fine-tuning arguments go much further than noticing the perfect conditions we have on Earth. They point to the fact that an extremely specific—and by no means guaranteed—set of circumstances must have held in the universe as a whole to allow any matter to exist *at all*. In fact, modern physics seems to indicate that we are stupendously, ridiculously, unimaginably lucky to be living in a universe whose conditions are such that life is able to flourish. Either that, or someone fine-tuned the conditions for us.

It is widely believed to be the case that the conditions we observe in the universe occupy an extremely small range of the possible values that could have obtained. And what's more, most of the possible options would lead to universes being sterile; devoid of anything resembling habitats stable enough to support the fragility of early lifeforms. What do we mean by these conditions? Well, the first set of relevant conditions are the strengths of the four fundamental forces, namely gravity, the strong nuclear force, the weak nuclear force, and the electromagnetic force. Another group of conditions are to the natures of the fundamental particles, including photons, electrons, protons, etc. And, finally, the initial conditions, meaning the velocity, density, and distribution of matter-energy in the earliest epoch of the universe. These conditions have certain values, and those values are well-suited to the flourishing of intelligent life.

We don't know exactly how life began, but we do know that it must have required a highly delicate balancing of conditions to produce a reasonably warm, wet, and stable environment. Before all this, life requires chemical elements. Before that, matter-energy itself. And, of course, we also need forces like gravity that regulate the interactions between the pieces of matter that eventually coalesce into living centers of meaning: human beings.

Physicists are able to use our best theories to work out how many possible universes with various configurations of the above are compatible with those theories. As it turns out, the physical laws and initial conditions could have been vastly different from the ones we observe. Out of the set of all possible universes, only a very small proportion are able to support life. Only a small number of possible universe configurations are compatible with stable matter that can form into stars, solar systems, and galaxies. These must exist, and persist for long enough, that life can both begin (no easy feat) and evolve into intelligent beings who can study the early universe and write books like this one. We know that, on Earth, intelligent life took billions of years to emerge. In effect, fine-tuning arguments look at the order, structured and specified complexity, and apparent purposiveness in the universe, and claim that this requires explanation. Why do we see such abundant life when life seems so unlikely? To get a feel for just how unlikely life really is, we must take a deep dive into the data.

Evidence of cosmic fine-tuning is gathered from just after what is known as the Planck era, approximately 10^{-43} seconds after the Big Bang. At this time, the universe was in an extremely hot, dense state. Physicists are not currently able to model the universe before this time due to an area of incompleteness in the intellectual framework of theoretical physics. As previously mentioned, physics contains two highly successful and beautiful theories: general relativity and quantum mechanics. The former describes the very big (the cosmos, stars, planets, etc.) and the latter describes the very small (sub-atomic particles, photons, etc.). The problem is, they're incompatible. We don't know what happens when the cosmos, i.e., something governed by general relativity, is the size of a quantum object. The Big Bang involved the universe being smaller than the smallest object we can currently measure, even if it was for an incredibly brief point in time. To understand how it behaved, we need what is sometimes rather grandly called a "Theory of Everything." Basically, a theory that unites quantum mechanics and general relativity. Until we can extrapolate back to the Big Bang, we must begin our examination of the empirical evidence after the Plank era.

Our current scientific understanding begins in what is sometimes referred to as the inflationary period, a period in the universe's early history during which it grew by at least a factor of 10^{25} in 10^{-30} seconds or less. This means it went from smaller than a sub-atomic particle to roughly the size of a grapefruit in the smallest fraction of a second. This was an extremely critical period at which point the conditions we observe in the present day were set. The four fundamental forces crystallized: gravitation, electromagnetic forces between charged particles, the weak nuclear force giving rise to nuclear processes such as decay of neutrons into protons, and the strong nuclear force binding the nuclei of atoms together. Sub-atomic particles and anti-particles were formed, creating the building blocks for the chemical elements crucial for the evolution of life.

A critical factor in the formation of stars and galaxies, necessary places for life to evolve, are the physical constants.[3] They are given this name because their value is the same everywhere and at every time. There is a range of possible values these physical constants could have, and as far as we know it seems as though only a very narrow range could give rise to a universe that could support life of any kind. An example of a fine-tuned constant is the cosmological constant represented by the Greek letter Λ. It is the value of the energy density of the vacuum of space, and so it acts as a counterbalance to gravity. Λ is absolutely critical in determining the rate that the universe expands and the extent to which gravity can cause

---

3. Barrow and Tipler, *Anthropic Cosmological Principle*, 372.

matter to condense into vast clouds that eventually collapse to form stars and galaxies.

Because the universe is expanding, scientists now assume that Λ has a value of very close to (but not quite) zero. According to our best theories, the value of Λ could have been anywhere within a truly staggering range of possibilities—its minimum possible value is 120 orders of magnitude smaller than its limit. Why does it have the value it has? We simply do not know. That it is so close to zero is extremely important for the evolution of life. While a change in the value of most constants would have prevented life *as we know it* emerging—but could perhaps be compatible with life of a very different kind—if Λ differed only slightly from its actual value then this would have prevented the emergence of *life itself*. The universe would either have expanded too rapidly for the formation of stars and galaxies or collapsed back in on itself soon after the Big Bang.[4] Most people—atheists, agnostics, and theists alike—agree that some kind of explanation is needed. The odds are so stacked against us that "chance" just won't cut it. Of course, there is impassioned disagreement about which explanation is best.

Evidence of fine-tuning abounds in physics. Another piece worth considering is the amount and distribution of carbon. As far as we know, carbon is required for all forms of complex life. It is particularly suited to the task because of its molecular structure. Its valence number, namely the number of electrons in the outer shell, is four, which means it is able to bond with lots of other chemical elements. Electrons are essential to chemical bonds. The physical chemistry behind all this is reasonably complicated and only tangentially relevant. Without going into too much detail, if there is space in an electron's outer shell then it can take electrons from other elements into its own shell and create a bond. The maximum number of electrons that can occupy this shell is eight. If a carbon atom's outer shell was full, it could not easily bond with other elements. If it was almost empty, then it would be much more unstable. Carbon's valence number means it can bond with up to four other elements at once, allowing a truly vast range of possible molecules that can remain stable for long periods of time. These long-chain carbon compounds are also known as organic compounds—the building blocks for life.

Essentially, carbon is perfectly suited to forming compounds with other elements without being so reactive as to prevent stable structures

---

4. Rubenstein, *Worlds Without End*, 15–16.

being constructed. This is hugely important when trying to build lifeforms that need flexibility, dynamism, and stability to grow and replicate. Moreover, their long-term stability means that carbon-based compounds are excellent at storing information. We don't yet know whether it is theoretically possible for other elements (like silicon) to form the basis of life. What we do know is that carbon is perfect for the job.

So, we need carbon for life, or at least life as we know it. An abundance of carbon requires a delicate balance of the four fundamental forces. For example, an increase or decrease of more than 0.5 percent in the strength of the strong force, or more than 4 percent in the strength of the electromagnetic force, would lead to negligible amounts of carbon and oxygen being formed, thus making life very unlikely. These variations represent an extremely small range within the range of possible values those forces could take. There are many more examples like these, but the above is enough to give you an idea of just how remarkable it is that life exists at all, anywhere in the universe. As philosopher of religion Richard Swinburne writes, the data reveals that "there are several small islands within the space of possible values of constants and variables within which human life could evolve."[5] Why does our universe exist on one of those islands? Some kind of explanation is required.

INTERPRETING THE EVIDENCE

Theism

The first explanation of fine-tuning data we shall consider is the theistic explanation. That is, the teleological argument from cosmic fine-tuning. Swinburne presents one of the most sophisticated versions of the argument, so we can take his work as representing the argument's greatest chance of success. Swinburne suggests that given the teachings of Christianity, and the theistic worldview they paint, we should expect to see a world that is teeming with life. God has good reason to create a world containing intelligent beings who can enter into a relationship with him, and so the fact that we see a world that is so hospitable to intelligent life is good evidence of the existence of God.

Swinburne argues that it is extremely unlikely that life-conducive conditions arose by chance or accident. The way Swinburne himself

---

5. Swinburne, "Universe Makes It Probable That There Is a God," 227.

argues against what we might call the "chance-hypothesis" (namely that the universe is the way it is by chance alone) is by appealing to probabilities. One way to think of it is like this. Imagine you are at a casino, and you want to place a bet on a roulette wheel. This is no ordinary roulette wheel, however, as it has many trillions of numbers on it. What's more, you only win the jackpot if you pick a single number before the wheel is spun and then the ball lands on that exact number. Given that each number on the roulette wheel is equally likely to be the winner each time the roulette wheel is spun, your chance of success is one in trillions. In other words, it is extremely unlikely indeed. In fact, it is so unlikely that you would probably not waste your money on such a bet. If you did, and you happened to win, you would almost certainly wonder whether there was some other explanation at play. Perhaps someone had fixed the wheel.

Theistic supporters of the argument from fine-tuning argue that finding yourself in a fine-tuned universe is like winning on such a roulette wheel. It is so unbelievably unlikely that you win by chance, given how highly the odds were stacked against you, that a deeper explanation is required. Just like each number on our roulette wheel, the probability of any one universe occurring is roughly equal. But if only a tiny minority of possible universes could support life, then any randomly occurring universe is far, far more likely to be sterile than fertile. You're much more likely to lose at roulette than win.

The theistic explanation, then, is that the universe appears perfectly suited to the flourishing of abundant life because it has been designed with life in mind. Gravity is the right strength to allow planets to form, but not so strong that the universe implodes. There is enough carbon to form the basis of DNA. Stars are able to burn for billions of years, giving complex life lots of time to evolve. All of this has allowed rudimentary lifeforms to emerge and evolve into highly intelligent life. Swinburne explains the fine-tuning data in terms of the intentional action of a person. This person, God, directly and deliberately fine-tuned the universe so that intelligent life would emerge. This is sometimes called the Strong Anthropic Principle (SAP). *Anthropic* refers to humankind, and the SAP makes the strong claim that human life *must* emerge in the universe. The theist's version of the SAP is that the universe was designed for the specific purpose of bringing about human life.

In summation, Swinburne argues that cosmology indicates that the Big Bang could have led to many kinds of universe, most of which could not have held any life of any kind. The mere fact we exist is so unlikely on a purely atheistic explanation that it is deeply implausible. In fact, most people (theists or not) agree with this. Some kind of explanation of fine-tuning data is required. Swinburne's explanation is God.

Atheism

God is not the only option, though. A popular naturalistic, namely scientific, interpretation of fine-tuning is sometimes fleshed out via the Weak Anthropic Principle (WAP), which is discussed at length by John Barrow and Frank Tipler in their fantastic book *The Anthropic Cosmological Principle*. WAP maintains that our observations are necessarily constrained by the conditions required for our very existence as observers. It is weaker than SAP because while SAP claims life *had to* emerge, WAP only claims that we should expect to see life-conducive conditions because we are life, meaning it would be impossible for us to observe anything else.

WAP employs the concept of observation selection effects. Observation selection effects are the restrictions or influences that the conditions required for observation have upon that which is observed. These can lead to nontrivial biases in the data or its interpretation. What this means can be clarified by drawing an analogy with fishing. Imagine you are fishing with a net with 5 cm sized holes between the netting. You cast the net many times throughout the day and at sunset you notice that you haven't caught any fish smaller than 5 cm. Does this mean there are no fish smaller than 5 cm in the lake? The evidence from your net seems to point in that direction. Nonetheless, the answer is no. You cannot draw any conclusions about whether the lake has fish smaller than 5 cm in it, for the simple reason that your net's holes were 5 cm wide, meaning the smaller fish would have slipped through the net and evaded capture. What you observed in your net was restricted by the form of the net itself. It could not possibly catch fish smaller than 5 cm, so your catch reveals nothing about whether the lake has fish smaller than 5 cm.

WAP applies this concept to the universe itself, claiming that the values we observe are restricted by the requirements that carbon-based life can evolve, and that enough time has passed for this to occur. Rather than postulating divine intention, WAP insists we must remain conscious of the limits imposed on our observations by the position from which we observe. However improbable life-conducive conditions are, we could not possibly have found ourselves in an uninhabitable region of the universe. We could not observe anything other than conditions suited to the existence of intelligent life, and so we cannot draw any conclusions from these observations. WAP is intended to demonstrate that the force of the argument from fine-tuning is lost when considering the restrictions our location imposes on our observations.

Nonetheless, many have responded that this misses what's truly at stake in this conversation. It is not that we *observe* life-conducive conditions, but rather that they are *there* in the first place. Swinburne offers a useful analogy to illustrate this: imagine you are being held captive by an evil scientist with a machine that shuffles ten packs of cards and draws a card from each at random. If the machine draws an Ace of Hearts from each pack, you will live. Any other result will trigger a fatal explosion. Imagine, then, that the machine is activated and miraculously draws an Ace of Hearts from every pack. You would rightly be extremely shocked and may doubt whether the machine really did pull its cards at random. If the evil scientist responded, "Ah but you shouldn't be surprised to see that you are alive, you could not observe anything else" you would likely feel that this explanation was not good enough. Though you could not observe another outcome, as all other outcomes would involve your death and inability to observe anything, the extremely unlikely event of your survival would drive you to suppose that the machine was rigged in some way. The extremely unlikely event of ten Ace of Hearts being drawn requires a deeper explanation. This analogy draws out the problem with WAP: it cannot adequately account for the improbability of the fine-tuning data. Alone, WAP does not work as an atheistic explanation of fine-tuning.[6]

This doesn't mean the atheist has no options, though. In fact, they have recourse to an additional explanation that makes the point WAP makes much more persuasive: the multiverse hypothesis. The multiverse hypothesis comes in various forms and is generated by several different physical theories, but its most basic claim is that our universe is only one out of many (perhaps an infinite number of) universes. Each of these universes has different properties, some of which are life-conducive and many more of which are hostile to life of any kind. There are at least four kinds of multiverse:

1. A Spatially Configured Multiverse
2. A Temporally Configured Multiverse

6. Swinburne, *Existence of God*, 156.

3. The Everett interpretation of Quantum Mechanics

4. The Modal Multiverse

The multiverse according to (1) resembles a foam with each bubble being a separate universe, all existing co-extensively. By contrast, (2) models the multiverse as a continuous, perhaps infinite, cycle of big bangs and big crunches. Only one universe exists at any given moment, as opposed to the spatially configured multiverse, but over many trillions of years a multiplicity of universes will exist. Approach (3) claims that at every quantum event the wavefunction of the universe branches out into universe-domains each of which contains one outcome out of the range of possible outcomes.[7] Finally, (4) is the most all-encompassing—it claims that everything that can happen does happen somewhere in the universe. The modal multiverse is an infinite expanse of every logical possibility and is by far the least scientifically credible of the options. It is the brain-child of philosopher David Lewis and although fascinating in its own right is less relevant in a book about physics and theology. Multiverses 1, 2, and 3 are seen as ever more credible and are being generated by a greater breadth of theories. That being said, none has been conclusively proved. In fact, whether it would even be possible to prove the existence of other universes that are by definition empirically inaccessible is far from clear.

Physicist Robert B. Mann describes the possibility of a multiverse as a "super-Copernican" revolution because it further displaces the centrality of our cosmic position. The original Copernican revolution brought about the departure from the Ptolemaic geocentric cosmology—i.e., the theory that the Earth was at the center of the cosmos—to Copernicus's heliocentric model of the solar system which placed the Earth among a set of planets orbiting a central star. If we are really living in a multiverse, then this is just another step in the journey of our cosmic insignificance. We once thought we were at the center of everything. We have had to realize we were not only not central in our solar system, but that our solar system itself is just one of many billions of stars in one of many billions of galaxies. Perhaps it should not really come as a shock if it turns out there are billions of universes as well.

---

7. The Everett interpretation of quantum mechanics has been the subject of my research for several years now. Qureshi-Hurst, "Many Worlds and Moral Responsibility"; Qureshi-Hurst, "Many Worries of Many Worlds"; Qureshi-Hurst, "Many Worlds and Narratives of Personal Identity."

As I have already mentioned, several physical theories seem to imply that we may in fact be living in a multiverse. One such theory is string theory, a quantum theory of gravity that holds that at the most fundamental level reality is comprised of strings vibrating at different frequencies to give rise to the various sub-atomic particles. The equations of string theory have up to 10^{500} solutions. Physicists have interpreted this as implying that our universe may be one of 10^{500} universe domains, each governed by different laws, constants, and variables. Let's say for argument's sake that string theory is true, and that we are living in a multiverse. Many of the universes would be uninhabitable. Nevertheless, the greater the number of universes, the higher the chance that some would be suitable places for life to develop.

A multiverse also emerges from the aforementioned cosmic inflationary theory, which posits the existence of a state of matter known as a false vacuum. Its negative pressure energy would have caused the universe to double in size every 10^{-34} seconds. Some unknown mechanism causes this to stop after 10^{-32} seconds, yielding a sliver of true vacuum that contains our observable universe. This false vacuum causes bubbles of true vacuum to bud off generating a multiplicity of universes. If this is the case, then the WAP does end up having persuasive power. If, in an infinitely large multiverse, life-conducive conditions exist somewhere, then it is no surprise that we see them here. Our existence forbids us from observing anything else. To amend the famous words of Martin Luther, "Here I stand; I can be in no place other." According to the opponent of the teleological argument from fine-tuning, this is the superior explanation. But who is right?

DECIDING BETWEEN COMPETING EXPLANATIONS

To decide between a naturalistic and a theistic interpretation of fine-tuning, we need to identify some selection criteria. There are many criteria we could use to decide which explanation should be favored, some of which are as follows. Philosopher of physics David Wallace calls these "extra-empirical virtues" because they exist over and above the scientific (viz. empirical) data itself. First is beauty or elegance. This typically refers to how elegantly the theory can be mathematically expressed. Second is simplicity, which can be understood in a multitude of ways but essentially boils down to what's known as Occam's Razor. That is, all other things being equal, the simplest explanation is the most likely to be true. In effect, if you already have gravity to explain why you are sitting in your chair and not floating up into the ceiling, you do not need additionally to posit the existence of an evil demon pushing you toward the ground.

Third is how well the given theory fits with your other background beliefs. Say you own a naughty dog who loves nothing more than making a mess when you are out of the house. If you come home and see a big mess and a very guilty looking dog, it makes much more sense to believe that your dog decided to wreak havoc on your house than to suppose that a passing delinquent broke into your house just to make a mess before leaving again. Fourth is explanatory power, which refers to how effectively a given explanation can account for the relevant data. Fifth is predictive power, namely whether a theory is able to make testable predictions. There are more, but these are some of the leading extra-empirical virtues that function as selection criteria between theories that cannot be decided between empirically. Several of these could factor into which explanation of fine-tuning you will favor, but the most relevant are (i) how well each explanation fits with your background beliefs and (ii) simplicity.

Fitting with Background Beliefs

One way of understanding cosmic fine-tuning data is that it underdetermines our theory choice. Underdetermination manifests when there are multiple explanations available for a given data set, and the data set itself does not clearly point to which one should be favored. What that means, then, is that the evidence does not lead us conclusively to one theory or the other. A common example of underdetermination is the following: say I know that apples cost £1 and pears cost £2, and I also know that you spent £10 at the apple and pear stall at the market. I can work out that you did not buy six pears, but I do not know how many apples and pears you did buy (it could have been a single pear and eight apples, two pears and six apples, etc.).[8] The evidence is insufficient to draw a single conclusion. This is what it means to say that theories are underdetermined by the data. How might we proceed if our evidence underdetermines our candidate theories?

---

8. Stanford, "Underdetermination of Scientific Theory."

One option is to see how well the theories fit with our other background beliefs. In this case, we might think of background beliefs as either the atheistic worldview or the theistic worldview. If you are a theist, you might follow Richard Swinburne in saying that theism leads us to expect that God will create a beautiful, ordered world full of creatures who are able to live meaningful lives and enter into free and loving relationships with God. Thus, if we find evidence that the universe seems finely tuned to allow the emergence of such life, we should not be surprised. It fits with what theists already believe about the world and its creator. Recall the naughty dog example above, and imagine you already hold the belief that your dog is prone to outbursts of energetic behavior if he is left at home alone all day. Because of this, you are more likely to believe the dog is the culprit behind the mess in your house than to believe that it was an intruder whose only aim was to cause you mild inconvenience. It is the explanation that fits best with what you already believe. Theists, too, may believe that they know their God and that a theistic explanation of fine-tuning data fits better with their beliefs about God's nature than the secular explanations available. We might think of it, in philosophical terms, as requiring a very small epistemic leap or having a low epistemic cost.

Relevant atheistic background beliefs might be a commitment to the *in-principle* (if not currently in-practice) ability of science to explain the universe and its features. This belief might lead atheists to warn against God-of-the-gaps reasoning—we ought not to jump to theological conclusions when our scientific knowledge is incomplete. In other words, it is unwise to add supernatural or spiritual explanatory devices into arguments where a materialist explanation may eventually be found. What one risks doing when inserting God into gaps in our scientific knowledge is rendering God irrelevant when the divine explanation is replaced with a naturalistic, scientific one.

Atheists might point to historical examples of this happening, such as William Paley's own design argument being replaced by Darwinism. The skeptical atheist may prefer the multiverse hypothesis for this reason, as it is not committed to the same faulty reasoning. Indeed, even many theists warn against God-of-the-gaps arguments. Consider these words from twentieth-century German theologian Dietrich Bonhoeffer, written in a letter to Eberhard Bethge, dated 29 May 1944: "how wrong it is to use God as a stop-gap for the incompleteness of our knowledge. If in fact the frontiers of knowledge are being pushed further and further back (and that is bound to be the case), then God is being pushed back with them, and is therefore continually in retreat. We are to find God in what we know, not in what we don't know."[9] Instead of postulating the existence of God, atheists may find the multiverse—as a materialistic explanation—fits better with their prior materialist and non-theistic beliefs. For this reason, the multiverse is a less epistemically costly explanation for an atheist.

Have we actually made any progress here? What this brief discussion has indicated is perhaps we should look for different explanatory criteria. If atheists should favor the secular explanation and theists should favor the theistic explanation, then we haven't really done much to determine which of these explanations is superior on their own merit. Instead, we have split people along pre-existing party lines. If the argument is supposed to be powerful and persuasive, it should be able to show that other explanatory criteria favor it on independent grounds. Theistic proponents of this argument need to show that theism is the better explanation in its own right, not merely to those already committed to theism. By relying only on how well something fits with one's background beliefs, the result may reveal nothing more than biases in our thinking. It can be useful to see how well various explanations fit with our own personal beliefs, but we also want to make sure these beliefs are open to healthy criticism as well. Let's turn to another non-empirical virtue that crops up very frequently in the literature on this topic: simplicity.

Simplicity

Throughout his many writings Swinburne demonstrates a sustained commitment to what he calls the principle of simplicity. He says that it is an *a priori* fact that simplicity is evidence of truth. By this he means it is a self-evident principle, the truth of which is confirmed by logical or rational analysis rather than empirical observation. The principle of simplicity is not merely a philosophical principle; in fact it plays a significant role in scientific practice as well. As Swinburne points out, it is possible to construct an infinite number of theories which yield the same data but whose predictions and descriptions of the world differ. That means that there could be an infinite number of possible explanations of a given data set and, according to Swinburne, without using the principle of simplicity

---

9. Bonhoeffer, *Letters and Papers from Prison*, 310–12.

we can make no step beyond the observable data. Although this claim might be a little strong, as other selection criteria are available, he does have a point about how useful simplicity can be when deciding between competing theories or explanations.

Swinburne's argument, in the context of fine-tuning, is that the principle of simplicity tells us we should favor the theistic over the atheistic hypothesis. In fact, he says it would be the height of irrationality to postulate innumerable universes just to explain the particular features of our own universe when we can explain those features by postulating the existence of God, who is only one entity. Essentially, Swinburne argues that God is simpler than the multiverse, and therefore God is the more likely explanation of the fine-tuning data.

I want to suggest that the principle of simplicity begins to crumble under more in-depth scrutiny. The first criticism of Swinburne's argument is that simplicity does not *entail* truth. It only makes something more likely to be true if all other things are equal. By suggesting that simplicity always provides evidence of truth, Swinburne risks conflating the goal of science with the reality of the world it seeks to explain. This point is made by the philosopher A. N. Whitehead, who writes that "the aim of science is to seek the simplest explanations of complex facts. We are apt to fall into the error of thinking that the facts are simple because simplicity is the goal of our quest. The guiding motto in the life of every natural philosopher should be: seek simplicity and distrust it."[10] We are looking for the simplest *theories*, not a simple world. In other words, we cannot assume the world itself is simple just because we want to find the simplest way to understand it. When assessing Swinburne's use of simplicity, Robert Burns argues that it is a *non-sequitur* to assume that the scientific pursuit of simple theories should be interpreted as a commitment to the cosmos itself being simple.[11] It seems as though opinion is divided about the extent to which simplicity indicates truth.

A good, although not perfect, indication of whether simplicity can be useful in deciding which theory to trust is whether it can be substantiated in the history of science. One should not make the question-begging assumption that the universe is simple *a priori* and then proceed with one's investigation with the simplicity principle firmly in hand. If simplicity is to be preferred, this should bear out in the history of science. But

---

10. Whitehead, *Concept of Nature*, 163.
11. Burns, "Richard Swinburne on Simplicity in Natural Science," 198.

when we look at the history of science, we do not see a journey toward simplicity. If anything, we see a journey toward complexity. A case-in-point example of increasing theoretical complexity is the standard model of particle physics. It is a highly complex model describing the seventeen fundamental particles and their interactions. The standard model developed throughout the twentieth century like a patchwork quilt, with contributions from countless physicists and mathematicians. It is simple neither in its formulation nor its construction. Nonetheless, it is a highly accurate theory. If the criterion of simplicity was the only deciding factor in whether this piecemeal model was to be accepted, it is hard to imagine that it would have made the cut. Less accurate, simpler, theories have often had to give way to more complex ones. Though there are exceptions, simplicity is seldom the single deciding factor.

Swinburne might respond that the principle of simplicity favors the simplest theory that fits with the background evidence, not just which theory happens to be most simple. This is certainly an improvement. Simple theories have given way to more complex ones due to new evidence, so although theories historically have increased in complexity, they have become the new simplest theory that fits with the background evidence. Nevertheless, overuse of the simplicity principle may still lead someone toward the biased assumption of a simple world when choosing between two theories that equally account for the background evidence. This is not vindicated in the history of science. Is this principle, then, strong enough to bear the weight Swinburne puts on its shoulders?

To find our answer, we must interrogate precisely what Swinburne means by simplicity. Simplicity can be understood in a variety of ways. Swinburne claims that "the simplest theory is that which postulates few substances, few kinds of substances, [and] mathematically simple properties of substances determining their mode of interaction with other substances (i.e., mathematically simple laws of nature)."[12] Simplicity is constituted in one sense by the number of things postulated, in another sense the number of kinds of thing postulated. A third sense, often used in science, is the simplicity of the mathematical formalism. This definitional ambiguity leads to a big problem for Swinburne's argument. Each definition of simplicity generates a different answer to whether God or the multiverse is the simpler explanation.

---

12. Swinburne, *Simplicity as Evidence for Truth*, 24.

We must recognize that there is a crucial distinction to be made between quantitative and qualitative simplicity. Quantitative simplicity concerns the *number* of entities to which a theory is committed; qualitative simplicity refers to *kinds* of entities. It works a bit like this. Imagine someone or something has eaten all the raspberries I have been growing in my garden. Struck by a particularly superstitious mood, my theory is that a ghost stole the raspberries as a prank. My partner's theory is that a gang of squirrels came in the night and ate them. My theory is more quantitatively parsimonious than my partner's by positing only one culprit: the playful ghost. My partner's theory is more qualitatively parsimonious because it involves commitment to the existence of something we know exists (squirrels) and we know visits our garden (to dig it up). While one definition of simplicity sees my theory as simpler, because it suggests only one being was involved, another definition of simplicity will see my partner's theory as simpler because it does not require the existence of something it is hard to believe in. In effect, you do not have to make any additional existence claims for the squirrel theory. You already know squirrels are the kind of being that exists, and the background belief that they have a penchant for berries makes the theory even more convincing.

These two kinds of simplicity generate different answers to the question of which explanation of fine-tuning is simpler. The multiverse is less *quantitatively* ontologically parsimonious than theism because it is committed to the existence of many billions of universes, while theism posits just one God. This is Swinburne's point, and it is certainly correct that the multiverse requires committing to the existence of a huge number of universes instead of just one God. That being said, the multiverse is far more *qualitatively* ontologically parsimonious than God. By observing our universe, we have strong empirical evidence to support the claim that universes are a kind of thing we already know exists. Committing to the existence of many more squirrels in my garden is not a very ontologically costly thing to do, because I already know that squirrels exist and at least some of them are in my local area. As for universes, I know they can exist because I am living in one. Whether multiple universes *do* exist is a different question from whether they *can* exist. The latter is settled even if the former remains up for debate. In theological tradition, God, on the other hand, is a being of a radically different kind to any object within our contingent universe. He is transcendent, unique, and non-reducible to the material world. Postulating the existence of such a God requires commitment to a radically higher mode of being, which is far less qualitatively ontologically parsimonious than positing the existence of many more universes.

The third definition of simplicity noted above, namely simple mathematical formalism, cannot be used when deciding between a theistic and a naturalistic interpretation of fine-tuning. A theory is mathematically simple if it uses a small number of variables, mathematical entities, and relations. Multiverse theory is generated by mathematics, so it is liable to mathematical analysis. But it is impossible to translate theism into mathematical terms. It is not a hypothesis of that kind. Theism posits a creator God who is omnipotent, benevolent, and transcendent; a divine subject who is radically transcendent and wholly other. Objectifying God or attempting to translate the rich and diverse tapestry of theism into mathematics would be philosophically reductionist and theologically unjustifiable. God is not a feature of scientific theories, and theism is not a hypothesis with relevant similarity to a claim of science. It is not liable to empirical verification or falsification, as, by his very nature, God transcends the empirical sphere. There is not sufficient theological justification for any attempt to operationalize the variable "God" in a mathematical sense. Thus, the mathematical version of the principle of simplicity is not relevant to the issue at hand.

We are left with two options: qualitative simplicity and quantitative simplicity. Swinburne favors the quantitative notion of simplicity at least in the context of cosmic fine-tuning. But qualitative parsimony remains a live option. If you want to use the principle of simplicity here, my own view is that qualitative simplicity is the way to go. Multiverse theory requires commitment to the existence of entities that belong to a kind of thing we already know exists; it requires a smaller epistemic and ontological leap than theism. This would lead to the conclusion that the multiverse is the better option, at least as far as the principle of simplicity is concerned. Quite the reverse of Swinburne's own argument.

Regardless of which version of the principle of simplicity you prefer, simplicity does not have quite the argumentative power Swinburne claims it does. There are non-trivial ambiguities in how simplicity is defined, and each interpretation yields different results for interpreting the fine-tuning data. The principle of simplicity is difficult to pin down, and as such any argument that invokes it loses some of its persuasive power. Even more damaging is the fact that simplicity as a criterion for scientific theories cannot be substantiated reliably in the history of science. This is not to say that simplicity is never useful. Far from it. It is to say that it cannot be the only way to decide between the two options. The principle of simplicity is not strong enough to establish theism as a significantly preferable hypothesis to the multiverse.

You may wish to return to the question of how well each explanation fits with your background beliefs. If you are already committed to the existence of a transcendent God for other reasons, then the leap from fine-tuning to theism is very small indeed. This raises a question, though. If teleological arguments do not persuade the non-believer, and they are superfluous in persuading a theist who is already committed to the existence of God, then who are they really for?

Perhaps the best answer to this is that they are merely a thread in theism's rich tapestry. Each individual thread's contribution to the tapestry's overall picture is relatively minimal. Similarly for each argument of natural theology. The teleological argument from fine-tuning is unlikely to convince you to be a theist if you are not already one, nor will it keep you believing in a crisis of faith. Alone, it is simply not enough. But for exactly this reason these arguments ought not to be thought of in this way. There are many threads that comprise the tapestry of natural theology, which is itself only a small corner of theism. While they may be valuable, none of these can give us the whole image. Bring each thread together, however, and suddenly you have a complex and valuable picture.

FURTHER READING

Barrow, John D., and Frank J. Tipler. *The Anthropic Cosmological Principle.* Oxford: Oxford University Press, 2009.

McGrath, Alister. "Natural Theology." In *St Andrews Encyclopaedia of Theology*, edited by Brendan N. Wolfe et al., 2022. Online.

Paley, William. *Natural Theology.* New ed. Edinburgh: Oliver and Boyd, 1817.

Qureshi-Hurst, Emily. "Is Simplicity That Simple? An Assessment of Richard Swinburne's Argument from Cosmic Fine-Tuning." *Theology and Science* 19:4 (2021) 379–89.

Rees, Martin. *Just Six Numbers: The Deep Forces That Shape the Universe.* London: Phoenix, 2000.

Swinburne, Richard. "Teleological Arguments." In *The Existence of God*, 53–91. 2nd ed. Oxford: Clarendon, 2004.

3

Providence

As the previous two chapters explored, the Christian story speaks of a God who brought the universe into existence at some time in the remote past. Moreover, this God is believed to have designed the cosmos to be beautiful, ordered, and directed toward a divinely ordained purpose. Each of these doctrines describes an almighty, but perhaps distant, creative force that provides both life and the stage upon which life plays out. In other words, God is understood as the creator and sustainer of the universe, constructing physical laws that allow the emergence of complex life forms like ourselves. These are examples of "general providence," i.e., cases in which God has provided for creation in the most broad and general sense. The Christian has faith in more than a distant creator who brought about the universe and then stepped back and allowed it to unfold on its own, however. Christianity speaks of a personal God who continues to be active within the world he created, overseeing and often shaping worldly affairs.

More specifically, God is believed to act in specific and direct ways in the unfolding events of world history to bring about divinely desired outcomes. These include shaping historical events, revealing God's nature or God's will to human beings, and cultivating relationships with communities of faith (and more things besides these). This type of divine action is known as "special providence," or, sometimes "special divine action." The most obvious example of special providence is the incarnation, the subject of the next chapter, during which Christians believe that God the Son took on human flesh to dwell among humanity. Further examples are the miracles witnessed in scripture, including God speaking to Moses at the burning bush. These biblical passages describe an active God who is present in the lives of human beings, answering prayers, performing miracles, and shaping the course of history.

Despite this, specific references to "providence" in the Bible are rare, as theologian David Fergusson explains in his article "Providence," in the *St Andrews Encyclopaedia of Theology*. Thus, there is no abundance of biblical passages one can look to in which providence is explicitly explored. Nonetheless, broader theologies of providence capture recurring scriptural themes, including God's creation and ordering of the cosmos, God's intervention in the history of Israel and the church, and the many miracle events. Throughout the Christian tradition, theologians have reflected on the various ways in which God provides for creation. As Fergusson writes, "with general and particular aspects, [providence] reflects the divine ordering of creation and subsequent forms of divine action."[1] Understandings of providence thus conceived have ranged in scope, depth, and detail, and we are unable to cover all this extensive ground in the present chapter. Instead of providing a comprehensive account of the Christian theological reflection on providence, I want to focus on the ways in which providence has been brought into dialogue with physics. This means our focus will be on rather recent theologies of providence.

At the very outset it is essential to distinguish the two, interrelated, forms of providence to which Christianity is committed. Together, they must form a coherent and consistent whole that accounts for the myriad ways in which God provides for creation. General providence holds that God creates and sustains everything in existence, including all the objects and events in the universe and the laws that govern their interactions. A multiplicity of names exists for these laws, including the physical laws, the laws of nature, the laws of physics, and, for those who do not wish to commit to the existence of laws, physical regularities. I will use these interchangeably throughout this chapter. Special providence holds that God is active in creation, overseeing its unfolding and interacting with it—performing miracles, shaping the unfolding of events, and answering prayers—as and when he chooses. As both forms of providence are essential aspects of Christian theology that together form the complete picture of divine providence, they ought to be compatible. God's ability to act in the world (special providence) should not be impeded by the

---

1. Fergusson, "Providence," 3.3.

particularities of the laws of physics (general providence). Exactly how the laws of physics and special providence fit together, though, has not always been obvious.

Since the scientific revolution in the Early Modern period, physics has traveled in a direction that seems to problematize special providence. According to many of our most successful scientific theories, the world is governed by fixed physical laws that are never broken and do not require (indeed, cannot accommodate) input from anything external. How can we make sense of ancient miracle accounts and traditional teachings about providence in such a world? Do the laws of physics forbid action from outside the cosmos? Does God have to break the laws of nature he set in place if he wants to perform an action? These puzzling questions have received sustained attention in recent years by those working in science and religion. In this chapter, I want to explore some of this fascinating and creative research. What is at stake in this discussion is whether, and to what extent, God can perform miracles—or any other actions—in the physical cosmos, given our best understanding of the laws of nature. In other words, can physics accommodate the Christian idea that God is a personal agent who acts in our world?

GENERAL PROVIDENCE

General providence is encapsulated by the idea that God is the creator, designer, and sustainer of the universe and everything it contains. As such, little more needs to be said that hasn't been covered in the previous chapters on creation and design. One additional feature worth mentioning is that providential theology understands the natural world as created with an underlying rational structure, or *logos*, echoing the divine personhood of God the Son. Nature is written in a language that the human mind can understand—the rationality through which both were created. Christianity teaches that the world is intelligible to us, making endeavors like science possible, because as creatures of God and bearers of the divine image, humanity, too, shares in this rationality. The world is rational, intelligible, and good. Through this we are able to make sense of it. God is understood as an abundant provider in this broad sense.

Due to its absolute centrality to the Christian worldview, general providence has a rich theological history. For Saint Augustine of Hippo, who lived just before the medieval period and whose influence has reverberated down the generations ever since, general providence must permeate both the natural and the human worlds. In *City of God*, Augustine writes: "it is beyond incredible that [God] should have willed the kingdoms of men, their dominations and their servitudes, to be outside the range of the laws of his providence."[2] Everywhere we turn, according to providential theology, we see the divine purpose unfolding. Nature and history reveal God's hand. In the medieval period, however, modern science did not exist. As such, any dialogue between theologies of providence and physical science had to wait until the scientific revolution in the Early Modern period.

Newtonian Mechanics

Around the seventeenth century, Europe experienced a scientific revolution. There were multiple factors that played into this, including shifting philosophical and theological attitudes toward the natural world on the one hand, and landmark empirical discoveries on the other. This multifaceted and seismic event in European intellectual history starred an English physicist whose revolutionary ideas changed the way we understood the world for centuries to come. This was, of course, Sir Isaac Newton. Newton made a series of discoveries that led to the development of theories, written in the language of mathematics, describing a variety of physical phenomena. One such theory concerned the motion of objects and was comprised of three laws or principles that have come to be known as Newton's laws of motion.

Importantly, Newton realized that physical laws that described the motion of objects on Earth could, and indeed did, hold all across the universe. This led to Newton's discovery of the law universal of gravitation that we discussed in the previous chapter. To reiterate, Newton discovered what he believed to be a universal force that attracts objects toward each other. This same force was responsible for both apples falling to the ground in Cambridge gardens and the cosmic dance of countless planets orbiting billions of stars. Newton was able to describe a multiplicity of seemingly diverse physical phenomena—from celestial motion to the behavior of falling objects—using a simple set of universal principles. These stunning discoveries revealed several things about the natural world. First, there seems to be an underlying rational structure stitched

2. Augustine, *City of God*, 156.

into the seams of the entire cosmos. Second, the processes that drive the behavior of objects in the universe are, in principle, describable using the language of mathematics. Third, and perhaps most importantly, this set of laws known as Newtonian mechanics describe a mechanistic and causally deterministic universe.

The term "mechanistic universe" captures the idea that the Newtonian universe can be thought of as a great machine that operates mechanically in accordance with fixed physical laws. Causal determinism claims that every event is understood to have complete causal explanation in (the set of all past events) + (the laws of nature). In effect, given the state of the world and the physical laws, there is only one possible future. According to causal determinism, whatever you decide to have for breakfast tomorrow was determined at the Big Bang. The initial conditions and the laws of physics make all other breakfast choices impossible.

Many interesting theological reflections followed from this mechanistic, deterministic understanding of the cosmos. The idea that the universe was like a machine has implications for teleological thinking discussed in the previous chapter. Just as a machine must have a maker who created each of its intricate parts and ensured that each one contributed to the machine's purposeful functioning, so too must the universe have had a maker who created each crevice and every corner with a purpose in mind. Newton himself was sympathetic to this view. General providence thus understood is easy to accommodate in a world governed by Newtonian mechanics. God was the first cause, instigator of the initial conditions, and fine tuner of the constants that set the universe in motion. A mechanistic universe, however, does not require interaction from outside of it to keep it running. Like any well-made, well-oiled machine, such a universe could continue in a self-sustaining manner for a considerable length of time.

These ideas led to a particular understanding of the relationship between God and world known as deism. According to deism, although God created the universe and set it into motion, he has not been creatively active in the world since. There is no reason for him to be, as the universe proceeds perfectly well on its own. Alister McGrath characterizes deism as a culturally adapted form of Christianity, popular in the late seventeenth century, that reduced Christianity to just two claims. First, that God created the world, and second, that God formed the basis of human morality. Once God has created the universe, the deist believes that he steps back and never intervenes again.³ Although it enjoyed a brief period of popularity several centuries ago, deism is not enough for the Christian whose theological understanding is shaped by the Bible and by broader Christian tradition. Christians are theists, not deists, and theism claims that God acts in the world in a form of divine action known as special providence. Special providence, however, is much harder to accommodate on the Newtonian picture, leading David Hume to develop a critique of one form of special providence—miracles—that has left a powerful legacy. Because there is little more to say about the relationship between general providence and physics, the remainder of this chapter will explore various ways of understanding the interface between physics and special providence.

SPECIAL PROVIDENCE

Special providence generally refers to specific instances of divine action, such as performing miracles, appearing to individuals in religious experiences, answering prayers, and other deliberate acts that bring about particular outcomes. The mechanistic way of understanding the universe that followed from Newtonian mechanics has raised problems for this type of divine providence.

Miracles and the Humean Challenge

Scottish philosopher David Hume developed a famous critique of miracles, the effects of which have rippled throughout the philosophy of religion ever since its publication.⁴ Hume defined a miracle as a "violation of a law of nature." This means a law of nature must be broken with the specific aim of bringing about an event that otherwise would not, indeed could not, have occurred. The event must also have occurred as a result of the direct agency of a divine or supernatural being. The basic idea is that miracles exceed, or even contradict, what nature can do on its own. The sting of Hume's critique follows from his definition. Nevertheless, the definition has been challenged from a number of angles.⁵ For example, what counts as a "law of nature"? Gravity is a clear candidate for

---

3. McGrath, *Science and Religion*, chapter 4.
4. Hume, *Enquiry Concerning Human Understanding*, section X.
5. For further discussion, see McGrew and Larmer, "Miracles," 1.2.

a law of nature, so a miracle that defies gravity satisfies this definition. But is it a "law of nature" that water cannot turn into wine? At best, we might be able to explain this by appeal to several principles from chemistry, but perhaps not a single "law of nature."

For now, though, let us follow Hume in defining a miracle—or indeed any act of special providence—as a violation of a law of nature. Why might this be a suitable definition of a miracle? Because, by its very miraculous nature, a miracle disrupts the natural order of things. As philosopher J. L. Mackie explains:

> The laws of nature . . . describe the ways in which the world—including, of course, human beings—works when left to itself, when not interfered with. A miracle occurs when the world is not left to itself, when something distinct from the natural order as a whole intrudes into it.[6]

Miracle events would not have happened were it not for the direct action of God at a specific time and place, and they cannot be explained via natural processes. One might see the hand of God in a beautiful sunset, but a sunset is a wholly natural phenomena that can be given a natural explanation. If you see God in the sublime beauty of a fiery orange sky, you might be being moved by an appreciation of general providence—how blessed you feel to be given the gift of living on such a beautiful planet. A miracle is different. A miracle bursts into the world, making something happen that was previously believed to be impossible. Walking on water and parting the sea are examples of events that seem to break physical laws and thus count as miracles. It is these kinds of events that Hume is trying to capture with his definition. In this sense, his definition of miracles aligns with the commonsense understanding.

Another feature of the Humean critique of miracles is the claim that nature is a causally closed system. What this means is simple: the universe is comprised of causes and effects, and this creates a self-contained system that does not require input from outside. According to the hypothesis of causal closure, all physical effects have physical causes. If you couple this with determinism, then it appears that the universe proceeds like clockwork from the Big Bang to the Big Crunch (or Heat Death), not leaving any space for divine action whatsoever. Unless, of course, that divine action breaks or suspends the laws of nature. This type of divine action, or special providence, is also called *interventionism*.

---

6. Mackie, *Miracle of Theism*, 19–20.

Interventionism does not save the day for special providence because it faces both a philosophical and a theological problem. The philosophical problem is known as *Hume's challenge*. Hume argued that we have overwhelming empirical evidence to support the claim that the laws of nature are never broken. Every second of every day I see the laws of nature being upheld. I release an object from a height, and gravity causes it to fall. A chef scrambles an egg; it cannot then be unscrambled. A person dies; they stay dead. These physical regularities are so uniform that we call them laws of nature. According to Hume, each time we see a law of nature being upheld, that is another piece of evidence in favor of the claim that the laws of nature never break. If the laws of nature never break, then miracles (which, as we have already seen, Hume defines as violations of laws of nature) do not occur.

This argument contains an ontological and an epistemological claim, i.e., it contains a claim about the nature of reality (ontology) and a claim about our knowledge or understanding of reality (epistemology). The ontological claim is that the laws of nature do not break, and so miracles cannot occur. The epistemological claim is that we never have justification for believing in miracles because the weight of evidence against them is so powerful as to create an impossibly high standard of verification for each miracle. Thus, according to Hume, miracle claims can never have good enough evidence to be considered credible. This is the philosophical problem with interventionist divine action.

The theological problem with interventionism is set out by physicist, Christian theologian, and pioneer of science and religion John Polkinghorne. In a 2001 book *Quantum Mechanics: Scientific Perspectives on Divine Action*, he writes: "to suppose that God habitually acts against the grain of nature would seem to suggest the theological absurdity of God acting against God, since theologically the laws of nature are to be understood as expressing the faithful will of the Creator who ordains them."[7] If Christians accept that the laws of nature were set in place by God, and that God has absolute creative freedom allowing him to design any logically possible set of natural laws, then we can conclude that the laws of nature that govern the universe are exactly as God intended them to be. It seems theologically incoherent to suppose that God would set up laws that he would have to break to realize his divine will. Thus there is a theological problem with any divine action, or special providence, that is

---

7. Polkinghorne, "Physical Process, Quantum Events, and Divine Agency," 188.

interventionist. Scholars of science and religion have developed a range of solutions that attempt to salvage special providence in the world of modern physics.

QUANTUM MECHANICS AND NON-INTERVENTIONIST OBJECTIVE DIVINE ACTION

The Divine Action Project

Science and religion is a relatively recent scholarly enterprise. One of its most significant multi-disciplinary projects to date is the "The Divine Action Project," co-sponsored by the Center for Theology and the Natural Sciences and the Vatican Observatory. The Divine Action Project was a twenty-year project whose proceedings were published in a series of books entitled *Scientific Perspectives on Divine Action*. During this time, the founder and director of the Center for Theology and the Natural Sciences, Robert John Russell, developed a fascinating proposal that brings God and modern physics into fruitful dialogue. Russell had an esteemed career in both physics and theology, equipping him with the tools to blend scientific and theological insights together when constructing a new model of special divine action. His aim was to give an account of divine action that is *non-interventionist*, meaning that it does not involve God breaking any laws of nature. Instead, God works in and through nature to bring about his will. The arena in which God acts, according to Russell, is the sub-atomic world of quantum mechanics. In a nutshell, Russell argues that God acts in terms of general providence by creating quantum laws and in terms of special providence by working through these laws to act directly in the world.

Russell claims that God is able to perform both objective and non-interventionist actions through quantum processes, bringing about concrete changes in the world that would not have occurred if God had not acted. Crucially, God does this in a way that does not intervene, suspend, or break any existing laws of nature. Recall the theological problem with interventionism raised by John Polkinghorne—God should not be seen to act against himself by setting up laws of nature that he then has to break in order to act in creation. Russell names his proposal Non-Interventionist Objective Divine Action (often shortened to NIODA or

QM-NIODA).[8] If he is successful, then Hume's challenge to miracles is sidestepped.

For Russell, the claim that God acts in the world in concrete ways is absolutely central to the Bible. Therefore, he is committed to making sense of divine action in the context of our best scientific theories. To understand the finer details of Russell's account of how divine action can occur in the quantum realm, we must dive into the weird and wonderful world of quantum mechanics. Quantum mechanics is our most successful scientific theory. Despite its roaring success, it came into being in a manner quite unbefitting of its status today. The "quanta," the first piece of the puzzle, was accidentally and rather reluctantly discovered in 1900 by the physicist Max Planck.

The Quantum Revolution

Around the turn of the twentieth century, Max Planck was preoccupied with something called the blackbody problem. A blackbody is a hypothetical perfect absorber and emitter of radiation that allows physicists to calculate the relationship between the frequency or wavelength of radiation and temperature. In a theoretical setting, a blackbody is typically conceived as a box with a tiny hole in one side through which radiation can be absorbed or emitted. The radiation, once inside, is reflected back and forth between the walls of the box until it is totally absorbed. If a blackbody is heated, then the walls begin emitting radiation. As radiation can only escape from the hole (because the box is perfectly insulated), the blackbody also acts as a perfect emitter. Thus, a blackbody should allow one to calculate the relationship between temperature and the frequency of various wavelengths of electrodynamic radiation.

We have all experienced this relationship between heat and radiation in a more recognizable context. As a metal poker in a fire heats up it will glow a dull red, then a cherry red, moving all the way through various oranges and yellows to a bright white. The rising temperature of the poker causes the light emitted to change color in a predictable sequence. A blackbody perfectly represents this relationship. The blackbody problem, then, involved calculating the spectral energy distribution of blackbody radiation (the amount of energy at each wavelength from infrared

---

8. Russell, "Quantum Physics and the Theology of Non-Interventionist Objective Divine Action."

to ultraviolet) and deriving a formula to reproduce the distribution at any temperature.

Physicists were able to measure the relationship between temperature and the frequency of electromagnetic radiation. What was missing was the mathematical formula, based on the prevailing physics of the time, that could provide a theoretical explanation of why the measurements were the way they were. It turned out that the spectral energy distribution of blackbody radiation was proving almost impossible to derive from first principles. The closest formula available, known as Wein's law, could only reproduce the right energy distribution for certain wavelengths of the electromagnetic spectrum. Wein's law was fatally flawed, as it erroneously predicted that as an object heats up to higher and higher temperatures it should emit shorter wavelengths of light increasing to infinity. This clearly does not happen—we do not observe very hot objects emitting dangerously high amounts of ultraviolet radiation. This problem was dramatically dubbed the "ultraviolet catastrophe." Catastrophe or not, something was wrong with the science.

Planck decided to tackle the problem using a radical working assumption. Rather than assuming that radiation waves were emitted continuously, he dared to suggest that they were instead emitted and absorbed in discrete packets or chunks. To his surprise, this allowed him to derive the right formula. Finally, the mathematics aligned with the measurements. Although he did not believe it at first, what Plank's working assumption revealed was that instead of radiation being emitted in continuous waves that are infinitely indivisible, there comes a frequency below which it cannot be emitted or absorbed. In effect, there is a minimum unit of radiation. These units are functions of h, a new constant of nature that we now call Planck's constant.

It's helpful to think of this like a flowing tap—it might look like the stream of water coming out of the tap is continuous and that we could divide the amount of water in half infinitely, causing smaller and smaller amounts of water to flow out. In actuality, we can't do this, because the stream is made up of billions of individual water molecules. Even if you had the most sensitive valve possible, there is a finitely small unit of water that could come out of the tap: a single molecule. You cannot divide this molecule and make a smaller unit of water, causing even less to flow out of the tap at a time. The same is true of radiation. Importantly, Planck only viewed this assumption as a heuristic that would later either be eliminated or explained away.[9]

As physicists struggled to make sense of this outlandish suggestion, a patent clerk living in Switzerland was working on pushing the idea further. In a flash of genius that would change the course of physics forever, Albert Einstein suggested that instead of radiation only being *emitted* and *absorbed* in certain frequencies, perhaps radiation itself was quantized. In other words, perhaps radiation behaves as though it is particle-like, not wave-like. In 1905, Einstein used this insight to explain a particular phenomenon known as the photoelectric effect. His resultant paper which addressed this issue proposed the existence of light quanta (what we now called photons) and set in motion a slow but certain sea-change in physics. Nonetheless, physicists continued to disagree about whether electromagnetic radiation—light—was particle-like or wave-like. In some contexts, light behaves like a wave, and in others, it behaves like a particle. As it turns out, it is both.

This ushered in a radically new way of understanding the sub-atomic world. Many developments followed, and over the next two decades a more fully formed theory of "quantum mechanics" or "quantum physics" began to emerge. There are many facets of the theory that would take a book of their own to explain. Fortunately, we only need to grasp the essential information here, beginning with the uncertainty principle. The uncertainty principle exposes a fundamental difference between quantum and classical physics by introducing the idea that there are uncertainty relations between pairs of properties that mean that both cannot be known at the same time. An example is position and momentum. Why is this the case? The answer lies in the wave-particle duality of sub-atomic particles.

Sub-atomic entities behave both as particles and as waves, and according to Werner Heisenberg's uncertainty principle, the position and momentum of such a particle has no precise value until measurement takes place. To clarify, while particles are understood to have precise locations, waves are disturbances spread out through space that have a wavelength. Wavelength is related to momentum such that a shorter wavelength corresponds to a higher momentum. Knowing the momentum of an electron, for example, would involve measuring the

---

9. In his book *Quantum*, Manjit Kumar gives an excellent account of this fascinating period of scientific history. I cannot recommend it enough for readers wanting to know more about the emergence of quantum mechanics.

wavelength, whereas knowing the position requires measuring it as a particle. To ascertain the position and momentum of an electron, various waves must be combined into a wave-packet: a quantum object with both position and momentum. Certainty about position is lost as the entity is no longer restricted to a specific point, and certainty about momentum is lost as the wave-packet is comprised of waves with various wavelengths. The more precisely one property is measured, the higher the uncertainty of the other property becomes.

The Schrödinger wave equation explains the behavior of quantum objects in terms of a wave function, which deterministically evolves through time until such an act of measurement takes place (a quantum event). Key to understanding "measurement" in quantum mechanics is the notion of superposition. Superposition follows from the mathematics and holds that a quantum object exists in all possible states until it is measured. The wave packet represents the superposition of the quantum object, and the Schrödinger equation describes its behavior through time. At a measurement event, namely the collapse of the wave function, a range of possible outcomes can occur, and the probability of a particle having a specific position is distributed in accordance with nature of the wave-packet. The act of measurement itself affects the state of the thing being measured, causing it to occupy one state out of a possible range. For the rest of this chapter, I will refer to the collapsing of a wave function as a "quantum event."

The outcome of a quantum event can only be predicted within a probability range which is spread out over the superposition, with various states being more likely than others but none being certain. In other words, the outcome of a quantum event is underdetermined by the physics. The traditional way of understanding quantum mechanics is that it is indeterministic, and this indeterminacy is a feature of the world rather than a gap in our understanding that will be filled with future scientific development. At least, according to the Copenhagen interpretation, an issue to which we shall return shortly.

One of the most popular examples of an experiment that encapsulates quantum mechanics' central features is the double slit experiment. This kind of experiment was first carried out by Thomas Young in 1801. The version of the experiment that we associate with quantum mechanics was initially undertaken in 1927 by Clinton Davisson and Lester Germer and, independently, also by George Paget Thomson and his research student Alexander Reid.[10] The double slit experiment was designed to determine whether quantum objects such as electrons were particles or waves. The experiment involves sending electrons through two slits and onto a screen that will show where the electron lands. Sending particles through just one slit leads to a band-like pattern you might expect if bullets were fired through a slit onto a wall behind. The band would be most concentrated directly in front of the slit, but there may be a few marks that show where a particle ricocheted off the slit and landed somewhere slightly less likely. In other words, the marks will end up mapping the probability distribution of finding a particular electron in a particular location. If you send a wave through, however, you should expect to see signs of interference, a well-known consequence of waves interacting. When two waves meet, one will either see *constructive* interference, where the peaks or troughs combine, or *destructive* interference, where a peak and a trough cancel each other out. If waves are passed through two slits, splitting into two waves, one should expect to see an interference pattern on a screen showing both constructive and destructive interference.

If *particles* are sent through two slits, you might expect to see two bands of dots on the screen, showing where the particles landed, much like you would see after sending them through one slit. Instead, however, we consistently measure interference patterns, as though the electrons are wave-like. This is even the case when we send through a single subatomic particle—it appears to go through both slits and produce patterns that show interference with itself. What is most fascinating, however, is that if we try to set up a device to measure the electron as it passes through the slits, it reverts back to behaving as a particle and only travels through one slit. Something about measuring the position of the electron causes it to behave like a particle, but when it is not observed it behaves like a wave. The double slit experiment neatly demonstrates that quantum particles behave both as particles and as waves, a radical departure from the previous scientific paradigm.

Despite the wild successes of the experiments and equations produced in the early years of the quantum revolution, physicists could not agree on what the theory actually tells us about reality in a metaphysical sense. Physics is more than mathematics and data. It needs to be able to give us an intelligible model of the world, meaning that the various pieces of the conceptual puzzle need to be arranged in such a way that a clear

10. Navarro, "Electron Diffraction chez Thomson."

picture emerges. There now exist several rival interpretations of quantum mechanics, each of which give an account of reality.

The Copenhagen Interpretation

The Copenhagen interpretation was the dominant way of understanding what quantum mechanics says about the world throughout much of the twentieth century. Although many today are moving away from it in favor of other interpretations, it still remains the standard way of teaching quantum mechanics in physics textbooks. Championed by Neils Bohr and Werner Heisenberg, the Copenhagen interpretation holds that at the most fundamental level, nature is indeterministic. There is no fact of the matter about where a particle will appear before it is measured. Instead of there being a single fixed outcome, a range of possible outcomes of a quantum event are possible. Until we measure it, we cannot predict with certainty what the outcome will be. This is a radical departure from the causal determinism of Newtonian mechanics.

According to Bohr, this indeterminacy is ontological, meaning it is a fundamental feature of reality, not some limitation of our knowledge that future generations will correct for us. In the previous physical paradigm provided by Newtonian mechanics, it was in-principle possible to predict with certainty the outcome of a physical event. This is helpfully illustrated through the example of a game of snooker. Right after a player strikes a snooker ball with a cue, it is possible for a physicist to gather all the relevant information to predict exactly what will happen, e.g., the white ball will hit the red ball into the top left pocket. The behavior of the snooker balls is determined by physical processes that hold universally and so always act in the same way. This means that if you could gather all the relevant information—the friction of the table, the mass of the balls, the force of impact, etc.—you can predict exactly what will occur. With quantum mechanics, the outcome of a given event, such as where an electron will end up after passing through two slits, can only be predicted within a certain probability range. There can be no certainty about where it will end up. If the Copenhagen interpretation is right, then at the most basic level of reality, nature is far fuzzier and more unpredictable than most scientists could have dared to believe.

Quantum mechanics is fascinating and challenging in equal measure. Although there is so much more that could be explored, we do not have the space to do so here. The key point for the present discussion is that the quantum revolution overturned the classical, deterministic, conception of nature. Determinism, the idea that the laws of nature + the state of the universe = only one possible future, seemed to leave little room for divine action from outside. Because quantum mechanics has the potential to reintroduce indeterminism back into reality, it has been used by science and religion scholars as the foundation of a new approach to understanding divine action.

NIODA Explained

As I explained above, Russell's NIODA suggests that God acts in and through indeterministic quantum processes to actualize particular outcomes of quantum events, causing material changes to occur in the physical world. Although he does not break any laws of nature, God is able to enact real, tangible, theologically significant change within the physical world. At a measurement event, the outcome is underdetermined by the laws of physics, meaning that a range of outcomes is possible. Russell argues that this is highly fertile ground for divine action. The mechanism is simple: God selects which outcome will occur from the range of outcomes permitted by quantum mechanics and then causes that outcome to occur. This leads Russell to claim that while the scientist may see quantum processes as entirely random, the Christian can infer that God has chosen the outcome from among the quantum mechanically allowed options. The NIODA hypothesis, then, interprets quantum mechanics theologically and claims that God's special divine action is performed in and through quantum processes. The burning question is, does this work?

Scientific Problems

One way to begin answering this is to reflect a little on Russell's use of the science. We must be clear about one very important point. There are several interpretations of the quantum mathematics available, and not all of them contain the collapsing wave function and indeterminism on which NIODA relies. The Copenhagen interpretation has several rivals, one of which is known as the de Broglie-Bohm theory (or "pilot wave" model). This interpretation describes the wave function as a real, physical wave that guides particles. A sub-atomic particle, on this view, has a well-defined trajectory determined by the precise values of position and velocity that it possesses, but is hidden from measurement. As these variables cannot be measured, they are not subject to the constraints of the uncertainty principle. This type of interpretation is known as a "hidden variable theory." Quantum systems are interpreted as ontologically deterministic, with any uncertainty being only epistemic. There are hidden variables beneath the measurements that make indeterminism a feature only of our ability to understand the world and not of the world itself.

In recent years several further interpretations have been offered, all of which are empirically equivalent. This means that they make the same predictions and explain the mathematics equally well, and so no empirical test could decide between them. Each, however, makes radically different claims about the nature of reality. Those working in the field are deeply divided on which interpretation should be favored. Maximillian Schlosshauer, Johannes Kofler, and Anton Zeilinger offer insight into the extent of this disagreement in a 2013 paper in which they present the results of a poll conducted on thirty-three attendees of a quantum mechanics conference. These thirty-three participants, from the fields of mathematics, physics, and philosophy, were asked which interpretation of quantum mechanics they preferred. The findings showed that on these fundamental questions the participants were deeply divided. It showed that 42 percent named the Copenhagen interpretation as their preferred interpretation; 18 percent favored Everett's Many-Worlds interpretation; 24 percent chose the information-based/information-theoretical approach; 9 percent said objective collapse; Quantum Bayesianism and relational quantum mechanics each received 6 percent. "Other" and "I have no preferred interpretation" each scored 12 percent; and the modal, DeBroglie-Bohm, statistical (ensemble), and transactional interpretations each received 0 percent of the vote.[11]

As this snapshot shows, there is no consensus on which interpretation is the right one. Though the Copenhagen interpretation received the highest number of votes, it still received less than half, and these numbers may even be less if a similar poll was conducted today. It is not clear that the Copenhagen approach provides a firm enough basis upon which to build theological proposals like NIODA. Although there was a limited

---

11. Schlosshauer, Kofler, and Zeilinger, "Snapshot of Foundational Attitudes Toward Quantum Mechanics," 1.

sample size of only thirty-three participants, such fundamental disagreement by leaders in the field indicates the extent to which such central problems are unresolved. Quantum mechanics contains many unanswered questions, and future empirical data may vindicate any one of these interpretations. For this reason, NIODA, in so far as it relies on the Copenhagen interpretation, could be seen as resting on shaky ground.

As we have already seen, tying theology too tightly to specific scientific theories contains significant risk. Recall William Paley's 1802 work *Natural Theology*. Paley used the available scientific data to draw theological conclusions. Yet just half a century later Charles Darwin published *On the Origin of Species*, presenting his theory of evolution by natural selection. This work offered a naturalistic account of phenomena Paley had previously explained as evidence of God's creative design. Essentially, new scientific developments displaced Paley's theological explanation. We may view Paley as a cautionary tale here. Constructing one's theology firmly within the framework of the dominant science leaves open the very real possibility that as the science develops and changes (as science so often does), the theology becomes stale or even irrelevant. Is Russell making the same mistake?

Perhaps. But opening oneself up to this kind of critique is inevitable in any science and religion research. As long as theologians and philosophers are engaging with science, they risk their work becoming outdated when the science moves on. Because of this, Russell is not alone in facing this problem. In fact, it is built into the very nature of the science and religion enterprise. We all take these risks by bringing religious and philosophical ideas into dialogue with cutting-edge science. It is the price paid for interdisciplinary creativity, itself such a valuable thing. We should not throw the baby out with the bathwater here. What really matters is how uncertain the science is and, therefore, how at risk the theological conclusions are. I will leave this question open, but I urge readers to give this point some serious consideration. We do not want to penalize Russell for his creativity, but we do not want to risk everything on the success of the Copenhagen interpretation either.

Practical Problems

Another critique worth noting is a practical one, namely whether adjustments in the quantum realm can really have the desired impact. Could any outcome of a quantum event, brought about either by naturalistic processes or by special divine providence, lead to meaningful change of the kind that matters to us ordinary people? Given that the quantum world of sub-atomic particles is very far removed from the realm of our experience, it is hard to imagine how God could use NIODA to respond to a prayer or to bring about a miracle—exactly the kinds of things we think about when we think of special providence. We simply don't see middle-sized objects like cats, cars, and cathedrals behaving in quantum ways. Cats aren't dead and alive at the same time; cars don't tunnel through brick walls; cathedrals never exist in two places at once. Electrons and photons, however, behave in these ways all the time. Quantum tunnelling and quantum superpositions are abundant in the micro-physical world.

The reason we don't see middle sized objects exhibiting this behavior is because of a phenomenon known as decoherence. Decoherence ensures that the weird and wonderful features of the quantum world are for the most part "canceled out" when moving to levels of reality that are described by chemistry, biology, and ordinary experience. Quantum states are highly delicate, and the hot and messy environments of our middle-sized world cause these delicate states to decohere and cease behaving in recognizably quantum ways. If this is the case, we might ask whether divine action in the quantum world really makes any difference at all.

Russell has been critiqued on this point, and he does have a response. NIODA likely *can* make a difference in the world of human experience, but it might take an awfully long time to do so. Minor quantum adjustments can, over long periods of time, generate outcomes that are perceptible in the non-quantum world in which human lives play out. If God were to use NIODA to, say, answer prayers, he would have to determine a vast number of quantum events over a lengthy period of time. The scholar Nicholas Saunders explores this problem by imagining that God wanted to redirect an asteroid to collide with the Earth and exterminate the dinosaurs. Saunders estimates that this would have taken approximately three million years, meaning that God would have had to begin directing the asteroid much earlier in the dinosaurs' evolutionary history.[12] Now this, surely, is a wildly inefficient mode of action. Why would an all-powerful God design such an unwieldy method as his mode of acting in the world? Given the radical creative freedom any omnipotent

---

12. Saunders, "Does God Cheat at Dice?," 540.

being has about which blueprint to draw for creation, it seems doubtful that God would have chosen something so cumbersome. In my view, this raises serious questions for the credibility of the proposal.

Russell responds to this type of claim by stating that meaningful change can be brought about through what's called bottom-up causality, even if it is not the kind of change that we typically associate with special divine action. The sciences supervene on one another: quantum processes affect organic chemistry, organic chemistry in turn affects molecular biology, which then affects life. This view of bottom-up causality begins to explain the way in which quantum processes affect the larger-scale processes that depend upon them. This means that NIODA takes a very long time, but that is why we must locate this type of divine action in the appropriate corner of the cosmos. A particularly important arena for this type of divine action is where the quantum meets the biological: genetic mutations.

Mutations are alterations of an organism's genotype that occur at random, causing variations in physical characteristics. Russell argues that there are both classical and quantum causal explanations for mutations. Mutations, being essential drivers of evolutionary change, are a means by which God could shape the evolutionary process without breaking or suspending the laws of nature. Russell argues that God acts through general providence by designing physical laws that make evolution possible and then by special providence to shape and direct the evolutionary process in real time. One way that this could work is by introducing phenotypic variation (i.e., variation in observable physical characteristics like height or eye color) via mutations in the DNA of an organism.

Mutations can be maladaptive, adaptive, or adaptively irrelevant, depending on which effects they bring about in the organism and how that organism then fares in the environment. Organisms with more adaptive traits have a greater chance of surviving to a stage where they can pass on their DNA. If the mutation does result in adaptive consequences, the mutated DNA will spread throughout the species and become solidified within future generations. Thus, the micro-world of genetic mutations can have significant macro effects, albeit via the rather slow process of generational change. In effect, if quantum mechanics can affect genetic mutations, then God can use NIODA to direct the course of evolution.

Much of the discussion up to now has been rather technical. To sum up, Russell's argument is essentially comprised of three core claims:

1. A theological commitment to extend special divine action to include evolutionary biology.
2. A philosophical decision to interpret quantum physics in terms of metaphysical indeterminism.
3. A scientific claim regarding the role of quantum mechanics in genetic mutation and thus in evolution.

The NIODA hypothesis, then, claims that God participates in quantum process to bring about specific biological outcomes, like the emergence of species. It doesn't matter that this mode of divine action takes a very long time because evolution takes millions of years anyway. God uses quantum processes to affect populations and species, continuously creating via a form of theistic evolution. If quantum processes can directly affect organic processes, and therefore life, Russell's NIODA is no longer restricted to the quantum realm *and* evolution is no longer random and unreflective of divine purpose. NIODA might not be an efficient way of answering prayers or redirecting asteroids, but it may turn out to be an excellent way of shaping the evolutionary process. That solves the practical problem rather nicely. Alas, this response solves one problem while creating another.

Theological Problems

Suppose that God does act in and through quantum processes to shape the course of evolution. An example might be God bringing about a particular characteristic in a species, or even setting into motion a series of mutations that would cause an entirely new species to emerge. In many ways, this would be a beautifully intimate vision of the creator's relationship to creation. God's presence can be found in each apparently random biological event, meaning that Genesis's claims about God creating each species still ring true.

Yet there is a darker side to this view, which ends up being impossible to avoid. Mutations bring about both positive and negative outcomes. Yes, mutations are the means by which a new species emerges, as over millennia multifarious adaptations mold the contours of the animal kingdom. But mutations also cause devastating diseases. If God acts in the realm of quantum biology, bringing about biological events like genetic mutations, then responsibility for diseases that come from such mutations is God's also. Cancer, for example, is caused by mutations in the genes that control cell growth. To put it very bluntly indeed, NIODA might be unable to avoid the conclusion that God is responsible for cancer. Not only the cancer that befalls an elderly person whose full and happy life is ready to come to an end, but the cancer that overtakes the bodies of children and causes tragic and painfully premature deaths. If God can be praised for the mutations that bring about new species, must he be blamed for the mutations that bring about disease and death? This brings us to the crux of this theological concern: the problem of evil.

The problem of evil, or the problem of evil and suffering, is the oldest and most frequently cited argument against the existence of God. While we cannot hope to cover all that has been written on this extremely important issue, we can get to grips with the essentials. In extremely broad brushstrokes, the problem states that evil and suffering presents a significant challenge to the existence of the God of classical theism. Evil and suffering seem to be incompatible with the divine properties of omniscience, omnipotence, and perfect goodness, all of which are essential properties of the Christian God. If God is omniscient (i.e., all knowing) then God is aware of all instances of evil. If God is omnipotent (i.e., all powerful) then God could stop all instances of evil. If God is omnibenevolent (i.e., all loving), then God should want to stop all instances of evil. Yet, evil exists. Atheists and theists alike agree that some further explanation is required to make sense of this.

The argument from evil and suffering comes in various forms, most commonly divided into the logical and evidential problems of evil. The logical problem holds that any instance of suffering is logically incompatible with the existence of God. The argument is a deductive one, meaning if the premises are true then the conclusion must be true. In order to defeat the argument, then, one must show that at least one premise is false. The argument runs as follows:

P1. God is omniscient.

P2. God is omnipotent.

P3. God is perfectly good.

P4. An omniscient, omnipotent, perfectly good being has knowledge of all instances of evil, the power to stop evil, and the desire to stop evil.

C1. If God exists, God will stop evil. (From P1, P2, P3, and P4).

P5. Evil exists.

C2. God does not exist. (From C1 and P5).

According to this deductive argument, a single instance of evil renders the existence of a God with the properties of omniscience, omnipotence, and perfect goodness impossible.

Fortunately for the theist, it is fairly easy to deal with the logical problem. All that needs to be done is to point out that God may have good (but unknown) reasons for allowing particular instances of evil to occur. It is easiest to see how this works, and why it might be persuasive, via the following example. Imagine a very young and seriously ill child who endures great suffering after an invasive operation with a lengthy recovery period. The hospital stay, operation, and recovery all involve much pain, confusion, and fear. That child would likely wonder why their parent, who is usually loving and protective, allowed them to endure this suffering. Such a child would likely only be able to focus on their immediate pain, but their loving parent would know that this suffering was the means to a far greater good: the child's life being saved. The child being unable to understand the parent's reason does not mean that no reason existed.

Opponents of the logical problem of evil make an analogous case with regard to God, which is comprised of one or both of the following claims. First, they claim that some evils are such that their occurrence is logically necessary to allow the occurrence of goods that outweigh them. Second, they claim that some apparent evils serve a far greater purpose to which humans are blind. This position, sometimes called skeptical theism, raises the skeptical possibility that human beings do not (or cannot) understand God's reasons for allowing evil. We are too intellectually and spiritually inferior to ever understand divine motivations, so the argument goes, but the theist should trust that the goodness of God will override even the worst possible evils in the end. All one needs to do to respond to the logical problem of evil is to point this out. Skeptical theism shows that premise 4 (P4) is false, as it shows that there might be reasons an omniscient, omnipotent, perfectly loving God *would* allow evil. By virtue of the argument's deductive form, defeat of a single premise is sufficient to bring the entire argument crashing down. Without P4, the argument collapses. Neither conclusion 1 (C1) nor conclusion 2 (C2) follows. Thus, skeptical theism is sufficient to defeat the logical problem of evil.

This does not mean the entire problem of evil goes away, however, as the evidential problem of evil remains a highly credible alternative. The evidential argument is *inductive* in form, meaning that the premises support but do not entail the truth of the conclusion. Those who endorse the evidential problem of evil cite various different types of evil and suffering as evidence against the existence of God. These pieces of evidence can be placed into several categories:

1. Particular instances of evil and suffering.
2. Particular distributions of evil and suffering.
3. The sheer amount of evil and suffering.

On balance, according to this argument, the evidence supports the atheist, or anti-theist, position. In the present discussion, the suffering caused by disease and death counts as evidence of evil and thus of the non-existence of God. The question we must ask of Russell is whether he can respond to the evidential problem of evil and save NIODA from painting God as callous and perhaps even cruel.

Russell does address the problem of evil, particularly in reference to theistic evolution. He begins by arguing that the problem of evil must be faced by any theological interpretation of evolution and is not restricted to his approach. While this is true, Russell's account does face a particularly pressing version of this problem that is not present in all accounts. Some believe that God designed the evolutionary process but then stood back and let it play out naturally without interference. On this view, God can only be indirectly blamed for the suffering, competition for resources, and harmful mutations. This is still a problem—God can still be accused of designing evolution to be extremely painful, cruel, and wasteful—but God's hands are less dirty on this rather more detached account. Perhaps the theist might say that the evolutionary processes' particular cruelties are consequences of the fall, and not God's imperfect design.

Russell, however, explicitly argues that God acts in, with, under, and through physical and biological processes as immanent creator, bringing about the order, beauty, and complexity of life. This is both *direct* and *objective*. Russell offers an account of divine action that sees God's hand in every natural event, and thus he explicitly rejects attempts to remove God from the detailed history of nature. While he argues that disease and death are natural prerequisites for the evolution of life, that is unable to adequately respond to the problem of evil. God is not simply indirectly responsible for the corollaries of the evolutionary process, such as disease and death, by virtue of his creating and instating the laws by which it unfolds. Rather, God is *directly responsible* for each specific actualization of disease and death by acting in and through the quantum laws that bring these outcomes about. Russell claims that "God is genuinely, if inscrutably, at work, caring for every sparrow that falls."[13] Yet in a very real sense, given NIODA, God is the *cause* of every sparrow that falls. Is this mode of special providence bought at too high a price?

Many solutions to the problem of evil are available, some of which are more effective than others at addressing the suffering caused by NIODA. Solutions typically fall under the heading of either a defense or a theodicy. A theodicy provides a theological explanation of evil. In other words, it is an attempt to give a theologically robust account of God's reasons for allowing evil and suffering to occur in the created order. A defense is either a general attempt to show that the existence of God and evil are not logically incompatible, or an attempt to mitigate the force of observed evil as evidence against God.

The most well-known defense is the free will defense, put forth notably (but, of course, not exclusively) by Alvin Plantinga. This defense states that evil is the result of humanity's free will, itself something of tremendous value. Freedom, for Plantinga, requires that the individual has a genuine choice between all the possible options available to them, including the option to make morally bad decisions and perform evil actions. However, God cannot compel the individual's choice or it would not be free. So while there are possible worlds in which free agents do not sin, whether it is feasible for God to create such worlds depends on the free choices of the agents, not on God. Plantinga says that for all we know every feasible world God could create is one in which creatures choose to sin. He refers to this as the *transworld depravity* thesis. If it is true, then if God is to choose to create a world inhabited by free creatures it *must* be a world containing sin.[14]

Evil, therefore, is a necessary consequence of freedom, meaning God could not create a world in which human beings are free but evil does not exist. At most, God is indirectly responsible by virtue of allowing evil, but this responsibility is outweighed by the good that freedom bestows on the human beings who are able to exercise it. While this solution is very

---

13. Russell, "Special Providence and Genetic Mutation," 222.
14. Plantinga, *God, Freedom, and Evil*, 53.

popular and does hold promise for the kinds of evil things human beings do to each other, it only applies in areas in which free will is relevant. It cannot solve the problem of evil faced by NIODA, as it is the free will of God, not humanity, that is responsible for genetic mutations and the resultant suffering caused.

The next option to consider is the idea that evil is a result of the fall. The idea here is that creation began in a state of perfection, and only degenerated after Adam and Eve made the conscious decision to disobey God, causing both human beings and the natural world to fall into an irreversible state of sin. Accordingly, disease and death are not part of God's design, they are a consequence of the fall. Once again, if God is acting distinctly and directly to bring about various diseases, this does not work. Without wanting to labor the point too heavily, Russell's biggest problem is that his model has God being *directly* responsible for the onset of the disease through bringing about a given genetic mutation. Consider Huntington's disease, for example, a genetic condition that affects brain cells and begins to manifest with radical changes to personality (often resulting in the disintegration of one's relationships) and ends in a painful death ten to twenty-five years after the onset of symptoms. Experiencing the loss of one's parent to Huntington's, and then discovering that one has it oneself, may be an example of the overwhelming anguish that can be caused by genetic conditions of the kind relevant to NIODA.

Another option is the soul-making theodicy first developed by Irenaeus, a second-century Greek bishop, and advanced in the modern day by John Hick. Hick rejects Augustinian-type approaches that rely on a historical fall, as these are much harder to defend in the contemporary scientific context. He argues that humans were never created in an idyllic and perfect state. Instead, we emerged incomplete and immature. Like children, we are in a continuous state of growth and development. The fall narrative is therefore a mythological articulation of the human situation, not a historical text that describes real past events.

According to the Irenaean approach, evil and suffering allow humanity to undergo a process called soul-making. Soul-making is a process by which humans develop into morally and spiritually mature beings. Hick states, "it is an ethically reasonable judgment . . . that human goodness, slowly built up through personal histories of moral effort, has a value in the eyes of the Creator which justifies even the long travail of the soul-making process."[15] He then goes on to say that we should not view humanity's relationship to God like we might view our relationship to our pet, whose life we want to make as pleasant and straightforward as possible. Instead, we should think of ourselves as we would think of human children. Children benefit most when they mature in an environment that is not focused only on satisfying their immediate desires (i.e., to eat nothing but chocolate and chips all day) but in which they can develop into robust adults who experience and benefit from the full range of human experience (even if that means eating broccoli from time to time). To put it rather glibly, it's the theological analogue of "what doesn't kill you makes you stronger."

This holds more promise—we do see people coming out of a period of pain and suffering stronger and more empathetic to the suffering of others. Nevertheless, it still leaves us in the uncomfortable position of claiming that cancer in children is a means by which those individuals undergo soul-making. It feels like an unnecessarily cruel way to bring about personal development, especially if the person's life is brought to an early end by a genetic condition before much soul-making can occur. Ultimately, whether an individual's suffering is worth the potential benefits they may or may not experience can only be decided subjectively by that individual. Some people who suffer immensely do come out of the other side stronger than before. Others do not survive suffering, or survive so damaged that their life is forever overshadowed by past pain. Think of soldiers with PTSD, or those whose childhood trauma so negatively impacts them that they cannot live a stable life as an adult. Not all suffering makes us stronger. In the midst of the fog of pain and suffering, it is often hard to see the kind of meaning some theists wish to find. This has led the theologian Bethany Sollereder to argue that philosophers and theologians should stop trying to solve the problem of evil and should instead focus on finding ways to help people make meaning out of their suffering.[16]

Russell's own response is a holistic one constructed out of many of the ideas we have seen in the previous paragraphs. He begins with the insight that God created the universe with the evolution of moral agents in mind. According to Russell, suffering, disease, and death are intimately connected to the conditions for genuine freedom and moral

---

15. Hick, *Evil and the God of Love*, 256.
16. Sollereder, "Compassionate Theodicy."

development. You cannot have light without darkness. In my view, this kind of response has the potential to leave a sour taste in the mouth. If suffering, disease, and death are instrumental for the provision of genuine freedom and moral development, then that means that God designed a world in which the suffering of innocent individuals is valuable because it provides the possibility of those goods to others. This feels, to me at least, to be rather cold and detached from the harsh reality of those living in abject suffering. A loving God should not want to impose extreme suffering on an innocent child so that other people might benefit. If our moral intuitions tell us anything, they tell us that children ought to be protected and not exploited for anyone else's gain.

Philosopher Marilyn McCord Adams points to an important distinction to bear in mind when considering such theodical questions, namely the distinction between God as a provider of global goods and God as a loving parent of individual creatures.[17] Russell's response appeals to the former divine characteristic by describing suffering as an indirect but necessary consequence of providing particular global goods. It focuses only on general providence and leaves the plight of the individual sufferer wholly unaddressed. An individual suffering greatly due to genetic disease may still justifiably ask why a loving and active God caused, or failed to prevent, the cause of *her* suffering. NIODA cannot answer this question satisfactorily.

Ultimately, Russell's final appeal is to the overarching creation-redemption narrative that sits at the heart of Christianity, arguing that a fully developed theology of redemption is the only adequate response a Christian can give to suffering. Redemption is promised for humanity and creation more widely, a redemption so glorious that suffering will fade away. Creation may, he argues, only be recognized as fully good in the eschatological future. Though this response leaves many questions unanswered (and much to be desired for those who want a concrete answer as to the meaning of their suffering now), it fits within the wider nexus of Christian beliefs. We will explore these themes in later chapters, and I hope the discussion there will provide further tools to assess the success of this response.

For NIODA, perhaps more than other more general accounts of divine providence, the problem of individual suffering looms large. It is precisely the direct action of God—in the evolutionary process or in the

---

17. Adams and Sutherland, "Horrendous Evils and the Goodness of God," 302.

instantiation of specific mutations—that causes suffering. A mutation that causes the onset of terminal cancer in a young mother, for example, comes about as a result of direct divine action. Even if Russell balks at this conclusion and argues instead that God acts only in *some* instances, then God has refrained from acting (in a way that God *does* sometimes act) to *prevent* a mutation that caused the onset of disease. On Russell's proposal as it currently stands, either God causes suffering and disease through bottom-up causality in the quantum biological sphere, or God refrains from preventing the onset of disease and the subsequent suffering which God could do by using the causal mechanism NIODA outlines to stop a genetic mutation occurring in the first place. Either way, the source of suffering is within a domain in which God is causally efficacious and acts regularly.

Ultimately, how damaging one finds these criticisms of Russell's non-interventionist account of special providence will be influenced by one's wider theological commitments. It seems to me, though, that NIODA places God at the heart of the problem of evil. While this is a brave acknowledgment of creatorly responsibility for the sufferings that befall creatures, particularly as a result of genetic mutations, more must be done in order to allay fears that NIODA's God is at best capricious, and at worst cruel.

CHAOS THEORY AND DIVINE ACTION

Russell's proposal for special providence was *bottom-up*. Bottom-up causality affects whole systems by acting on their parts. In NIODA's case, God's action is located at the subatomic level. From there, it reverberates up the causal chain to "higher" levels of reality, bringing about effects that become relevant to biological life forms and ultimately shaping the physical world as a whole. John Polkinghorne offers an alternative proposal for special providence that is *top-down*. What this means is that causes at higher levels, or on the whole of reality, trickle down and affect individual parts. Essentially, God can act in some way upon the entire cosmos, and this filters down to bring about change to specific parts of the universe, including human beings. The scientific framework within which he develops this approach is chaos theory.

Chaos Theory

Chaos theory is founded upon classical physics, meaning that it does not introduce a fundamentally new scientific paradigm in the way that quantum mechanics did. Nonetheless, chaos theory reveals that there are areas of physical reality that are not so easy to predict as Newtonian mechanics initially implied. In the early 1800s, French scholar Pierre-Simon Laplace developed a thought experiment that has since been dubbed "Laplace's demon" in which he suggested that if a superintelligent being possessed knowledge of the state of every single particle in the universe, and every force acting upon them, then that being would have perfect knowledge of the future. We have already explored how the dominant physics of this period, Newtonian mechanics, implied a deterministic and mechanistic world, so it is clear how Laplace came to this conclusion. Chaos theory, however, challenges this view. The extent of this challenge is a matter of scientific and philosophical debate.

You may have come across chaos theory via the famous butterfly effect. The term "butterfly effect" originated from a lecture title in which meteorologist Edward Lorenz asked whether the flutter of a butterfly's wing could set off a chain of causes that would eventually bring about a significant weather event a great distance away. Lorenz argued that this was possible due to a property of weather systems dubbed "chaos." Essentially, because of the highly complex and interrelated nature of physical systems that are "chaotic," even the most microscopic changes can end up bringing about hugely impactful events down the line. Hence the suggestion that a butterfly's wing flapping in Argentina could cause a tornado in Texas a few weeks later.

Lorenz stumbled upon the principles that would become chaos theory when running computer simulations of weather events in the 1960s. This involved inputting numbers that represented measurements of the atmosphere and its various properties and then running a simulation to make predictions about what weather would occur in the near future. On one particular day in 1961, he decided to examine a particular weather system in greater depth. He ran an initial simulation that provided a weather forecast and then checked his findings by running the simulation again. On the second run, however, he took a shortcut. Instead of repeating the simulation from the beginning, he started midway through and typed in the numbers using a printout from the first simulation.

To his great surprise, the second weather forecast was entirely different from the first. Within just a few simulated months, there was no longer any resemblance between the two forecasts. Unsure, at first, whether the computer had malfunctioned, he later realized that the printed sheet had rounded the numbers to three decimal places instead of the six places he had been using in the first simulation. Although the changes in the variables inputted into the simulation were tiny (differing by a maximum of one part in a thousand), over a very short amount of time the resultant predictions diverged completely. Lorenz realized that the type of system he was dealing with was highly sensitive to even the most miniscule of variations. He named such systems "chaotic" and concluded that long-range weather forecasting was doomed.[18] About this, he has largely been correct.

Chaos, generally defined as a mathematical property of a dynamical system, has become a recognizable phenomenon in a variety of contexts over and above the weather. A dynamical system is chaotic if it exhibits a phenomenon known as sensitive dependence on initial conditions. In other words, if even the smallest differences in conditions obtaining in two almost identical systems lead to drastically different outcomes as they evolve. Examples include fluid flows and turbulence, particle accelerators, heart cells, and the erratic motion of a driven pendulum.[19] A chaotic system like the Earth's atmosphere is extremely responsive to the various conditions within it, meaning the smallest variations cause large divergences in how two *almost* (but not quite) identical systems will evolve over time.

What is fascinating about chaos theory is that, insofar as it is based on classical physics, most agree that it is entirely deterministic. Yet it is also impossible to generate certain predictions of how a system will evolve over time. Predictability and determinism are not equivalent. We cannot gather completely accurate information about complex systems like the Earth's atmosphere to the precision of an infinite number of decimal places, meaning that seemingly random and unpredictable outcomes occur. Nonetheless, they follow precise rules and have deterministic causal explanations. Is there room in this picture for divine action?

---

18. Lorenz, "Deterministic Nonperiodic Flow."
19. Saunders, *Divine Action and Modern Science*, 174.

Top-Down Divine Action

John Polkinghorne has argued that chaos theory reveals the potential for a genuinely open future that can be shaped in radical ways by relatively minor interventions. Polkinghorne is theologically committed to the idea that God is a personal agent: a father, not a force. Thus, theists ought to expect God to act in the world in the kinds of ways described in scripture. Polkinghorne is also committed to non-interventionist divine action for reasons discussed above. Thus, he is motivated to find areas of physics that support indeterminism and to explore whether these might be suitable arenas for special providence to occur. Chaos theory's challenge to determinism—and thus its ability to open up a space for divine action in the world of physical causes—is subtler and less obvious than that of the Copenhagen interpretation of quantum mechanics. Insofar as chaos theory is grounded upon classical physics, most agree that even though it might be impossible to predict the consequences of the many variations in the physical world, this is only due to our inability to do such complex calculations. The underlying laws are still deterministic.

The deterministic physics sitting at the foundations of chaos theory is, for Polkinghorne, no more than a helpful approximation that only works perfectly in experimental settings. In the real world, it is impossible to take adequate account of every possible variable, meaning that while Newtonian mechanics can predict the behavior of billiard balls on a table, it cannot fully and completely predict exactly how the entire universe will evolve. The high level of sensitivity to each and every variable in chaotic systems means that they must be considered in the context of their entire environment. Failing to account for the influence of a single electron at a great distance away will, rather rapidly, lead to serious errors in the predictions one might make about how the system will evolve. As Polkinghorne writes, "even so simple a system as air molecules [in a room], in so short a time as 10^{-10} seconds, requires *literally universal knowledge* for a complete description."[20] According to Polkinghorne, then, we only get determinism from the scientific tools we use to understand particular parts of reality, but reality as a whole is not strictly determined in this way. Instead, there is genuine randomness at play in physics. Whether chaos theory really does paint a picture of a deterministic world or an indeterministic one is,

---

20. Polkinghorne, *Science and Theology*, 42 (emphasis added).

according to Polkinghorne, a "metaphysical choice whose answer cannot be settled by present scientific knowledge alone."[21]

Polkinghorne endorses an open future, arguing that chaos theory is compatible with an indeterministic worldview that leaves open the possibility of non-interventionist divine action. He argues that our inability to predict the future is good evidence that the future is open (he calls this the "epistemology models ontology" approach). Polkinghorne's top-down divine action contrasts with Russell's bottom-up approach whereby God acts in the most minute parts of creation, creating effects that echo up to act upon the whole. Instead, Polkinghorne's God acts on the whole of creation in a way that subsequently affects its constituent parts.

In top-down causation, higher level holistic mechanisms affect the parts. An example might be my decision to type this sentence. My mind has the idea for what I want to say, and this thought begins a chain of causes that eventuate in me using my hands to type the sentence. My agency has caused my constituent parts, i.e., my hands, to type. Polkinghorne's proposal for divine action is based on this kind of idea. Divine agency decides to act upon a particular system—either the whole of physical reality or some smaller sub-system within it—and this higher-level causation enters the nexus of physical causes to bring about particular outcomes that would not otherwise have happened but are nonetheless perfectly consistent with the laws of nature that God has ordained in the cosmos. God does not act against God, breaking or suspending the laws of nature. Instead, God uses chaotic systems to bring about his will in the world. Both general and special providence work together in harmony.

The mechanism of such action for Polkinghorne is via information transfers—God inputs active information into the world's open physical processes. The term "information" here means a type of ordering principle that operates without any input of energy into a system. These relatively minute influences amplify rapidly and can allow God to guide the development of the world in accordance with his will. Just like the active information in my mind constituting the idea for the next sentence I will write brings about the physical consequence of the sentence being written, so too can divine agency enter into and shape the physical world. Far from being a rigid, mechanistic cosmos, Polkinghorne argues that the world's supple nature allows for the input of information that will go on to cause macro-level holistic change affecting entire physical systems.

21. Polkinghorne, "Chaos Theory and Divine Action," 247.

This information is broadly understood to be patterns of behavior, which, in chaotic systems, are hugely causally efficacious. He calls his approach strongly antireductionist, which means that we should not prioritize the smallest levels described by particle physics. Instead, we should focus on the whole of reality.

Polkinghorne views Russell's proposal as overly episodic, reducing divine action to the realm of quantum measurements and thus making it piecemeal and sporadic. Russell's God picks and chooses when he acts and then acts in the minutiae of quantum processes. Polkinghorne's alternative allows God to input very small pieces of information that bring about very large and significant affects in the future. Instead of everything being ultimately reducible to quantum mechanics, higher level processes like those described by chaos theory can be equally essential, and, indeed, can bring about effects more quickly than minute quantum adjustments. Polkinghorne admits that there is much still to be worked out in order for his proposal to be watertight, but he is hopeful that he has outlined a fruitful avenue for future development. In a chapter setting out the bare bones of his argument, he lists a few consequences of such a view, some which I shall set out here.[22]

First, this kind of special providence will not lead to testable miracles, or what Polkinghorne describes as naked acts of power. As is characteristic of chaotic systems, the nexus of causes will be so deeply entangled that isolating one and saying, "Ah yes, here is the divine cause" will not be possible. Because of this, Polkinghorne's proposal is difficult to verify. Although no scientific experiment could ever detect it, people of faith may recognize signs of God's handiwork in various places. Empirical verification is not available for many of theism's claims, so this may not be too much of a problem for some readers. The proposal may well be accepted as an article of faith by those who are persuaded by the weight of evidence and are sympathetic to the kind of creator–creation relationship it describes.

Second, Polkinghorne's view contains a world in which human and divine agency can actually make a profound difference. This claim dovetails with including biblical promises that God acts in the world and assurances that our actions matter both morally and soteriologically. Such theological claims make most sense on a worldview within which divine and human actions can shape the future. As opposed to the machine-like

---

22. Polkinghorne, "Chaos Theory and Divine Action," 248–50.

world of Newtonian mechanics that proceeds like clockwork and seems hostile to any intervention from outside, Polkinghorne's open future means that agency of various kinds will be effective in creating the future and shaping the development of worldly affairs.

Christianity, Polkinghorne writes, has always strived to find balance between two extremes—on the one hand a tyrannical puppet master God whose will is the sole determiner of everything that happens, and on the other hand the detached God of deism who sets the world in motion and then disappears, leaving the world to its own devices. The first God does not love creation enough to give it the independence to explore radical self-expression and take a hand in creating itself. The second God does not love creation enough to intervene and save creation in an act of ultimate redemption. Polkinghorne is committed to the substantial effects of agency in both the human world and the natural world. We are, in this picture, freely able to actively participate in the development of our own personalities and build our own lives; similarly, we are free to shape the development of history. Animals and plants, too, participate in the creation of future generations by being constituents of the evolutionary process. The choices of living things have tangible consequences. By a similar mechanism, God is able to act in and through natural processes to provide for creation as he sees fit.

Third, Polkinghorne argues that petitionary prayer is given scientific legitimacy. This is only the case if that petitionary prayer is understood *not* as an attempt to persuade God to do something he had not considered or would not otherwise perform, but as an open acknowledgment of a willingness to work collaboratively with God toward a particular goal. Because, for Polkinghorne, the future is open and can be affected in big ways by small acts of human and divine agency, petitionary prayer can be theologically and scientifically effective.

I would not be surprised if, after reading this section, you are a little confused about what exactly all this means. Although Polkinghorne does provide some detail about how this might work, much of the finer details remains shrouded in mystery.

Critique

My primary concern with this model is Polkinghorne's reliance on the openness of the future, which many physicists say that chaos theory cannot provide. As Nicholas Saunders writes, "detractors of chaotic SDA [special divine action] maintain the underlying physics remains classical and thus fully deterministic. As such, they correctly argue that non-interventionist chaotic SDA is not possible."[23] As I noted earlier, predictability and determinism are not the same thing, and so they should not be conflated. The fact that it is impossible to predict the future states of chaotic systems does not mean that the future is metaphysically open. God, with infinite knowledge of everything in the universe, would know exactly how even the most chaotic of systems will evolve. In slightly more technical language, chaos imposes an epistemic limit, not an ontological openness. Thus, Polkinghorne may have been a little hasty in claiming that chaos theory offers up the possibility of an open, malleable future. Without this open future, many of the theological virtues of his proposal are lost. As such, this is a rather big problem.

The second concern is that chaos may not offer God the large-scale control of entire systems of the kind most typical instances of special divine action require. This point is made by Jeffrey Koperski, who points out that nature might not actually be as chaotic as some thinkers have implied. In fact, in many examples of chaos in nature, the chaos itself is more of a background feature than something that creates large-scale disorder. For God to make effective use of chaos, he argues, the chaos must have a significant impact on the dominant behavior of the relevant system. Often, according to Koperski, this is not the case. As he writes: "to put it crudely, [chaotic quantum determination] describes a causal pathway in which God could alter the arrangement of bubbles in the crest of a tsunami but not redirect its course. Presumably more is wanted from an account of divine agency."[24] Perhaps this is one of the features of chaotic divine action that will be resolved later. After all, Polkinghorne does claim that this is a direction of travel that has not yet been fully worked out. In its current form, however, I think we are justified in concluding that the version of special providence offered by chaos theory cannot give us the kind of action most theists are after.

---

23. Saunders, *Divine Action and Modern Science*, 174.
24. Koperski, "God, Chaos, and Quantum Dice," 557.

CONCLUSION

The picture we gather from the pursuit of finding non-interventionist divine action in physics is a mixed one. Although Hume's challenge has left a powerful legacy, Christians should perhaps not take it as seriously today. A plethora of problems with the argument leave it more than a little unconvincing. If you believe that the Bible is the revealed word of God, you will believe that God does act in the world, not least during the incarnation. This is a fundamentally interventionist act, making one wonder why the search for non-interventionist divine action has occupied such a significant swathe of the discipline of science and religion's brief history. Today, this quest is firmly on the back burner, due in large part to the fact that these proposals were not as convincing as once hoped. Although this area is one that I find most intellectually engaging, and something I have published on several times, it has not been a resounding success. Nonetheless, I hope you have found these arguments as stimulating and creative as I do each time I read them. Perhaps there is promise in them yet. Future developments will decide. Now, we turn to the most significant interventionist act of special providence in the entirety of Christian history: the incarnation.

FURTHER READING

Bishop, Robert. "Chaos." In *The Stanford Encyclopedia of Philosophy*, edited by Edward N. Zalta, spring 2017 ed. Online.

Fergusson, David. "Providence." In *St Andrews Encyclopaedia of Theology*, edited by Brendan N. Wolfe et al., 2022. Online.

Kumar, Manjit. *Quantum: Einstein, Bohr and the Great Debate About the Nature of Reality*. Thriplow, UK: Icon, 2008.

Polkinghorne, John. "Chaos Theory and Divine Action." In *Religion and Science: History, Method, Dialogue*, edited by W. M. Richardson and W. J. Wildman, 253–54. London: Routledge, 1996.

Russell, Robert John. "Quantum Physics and the Theology of Non-Interventionist Objective Divine Action." In *The Oxford Handbook of Science and Religion*, edited by Philip Clayton, 579–95. Oxford: Oxford University Press, 2006.

Qureshi-Hurst, Emily. "Does God Act in the Quantum World? A Critical Engagement with Robert John Russell." *Theology and Science* 21.1 (2023) 106–21.

Saunders, Nicholas. "Chaos Theory and Divine Action." In *Divine Action and Modern Science*, 173–206. Cambridge: Cambridge University Press, 2002.

4

Incarnation

THE INCARNATION IS CHRISTIANITY's defining event, marking a pivotal moment in the narrative arc that structures the Christian telling of our world's history. Although this foundational idea will likely be very familiar to most readers, it is worth briefly setting it out here. That way, the scene will be set for the discussion about how the incarnation intersects with modern physics. According to the doctrine of the incarnation, at a particular historical moment and geographical location, God entered the spatiotemporal world. Born a Palestinian Jew of the Virgin Mary and descended from David, he lived for around three decades fulfilling God's purposes, before being sentenced to death upon a cross. After three days, Christianity teaches that he rose again, in an act that revealed him to be both the Son of God and God the Son. Much theological reflection has been carried out trying to make sense of all this. The incarnation played a highly important revelatory role. Not only did it perform the primary function of revealing to humanity the nature, the love, and the abundant power of the divine, but it also revealed to God what it means to be human from a first-personal perspective. Christian theologians almost universally agree that this is because Jesus Christ has two natures; he is both fully God and fully human.

Christians also believe in the fall, as a result of which humanity and the world plunged into a state of sin and separation from God. Precisely how this occurred (or indeed continues to occur) is very much open for discussion. The fall, as set out in the book of Genesis, was caused by Adam and Eve eating fruit from the tree of the knowledge of good and evil, performing the original act of disobedience against God. The consequence is that sin (and, potentially, death) are brought into the world for the first time. It is a matter of theological debate whether the Christian should believe in a literal historical fall—either occurring exactly as the Bible describes or taking the biblical account as a symbolic presentation of a historical event—or a mythical fall, with the scriptural stories symbolically representing a profound alienation that exists between God and humanity. Whichever interpretation one opts for, Christianity is committed to the idea that both world and humanity are fallen in the sense that they are estranged from God and err toward evil. According to the Bible, human pride caused sin to seep into our veins like a powerful poison, rotting us from within. And, like a poison, an antidote is required to save us from death and destruction. This is where the incarnation comes in. Jesus Christ, Son of God, the second trinitarian person, sits at the centerpoint of history because he brought a soteriological (i.e., concerning salvation) transformation that changed the course of history forever. Before, creation was fallen. After, there was hope for redemption.

Christianity is also committed to the doctrine of the Trinity. This is the idea that although the Christian God is one substance, he is three persons: Father, Son, and Spirit. According to the Christian doctrine of the incarnation, the second trinitarian person, God the Son, took on human form and entered the spatiotemporal world of fallen material existence to die for humanity's sins and save us from an otherwise inevitable fate. We will examine the soteriological dimensions of this claim in the next chapter. Here, we will be concerned with how to understand the idea that a non-physical divine being clothed himself in human flesh. What does it mean to say that Jesus Christ was fully God and fully human? How does the incarnation relate to physics' understanding of space and time? How might we understand the incarnation if life—perhaps even intelligent life—exists elsewhere in the cosmos?

CHRISTOLOGY

Christology refers to the study of the nature and personhood of Jesus Christ. It is one of the most widely written on areas of Christian theology, and for good reason. Christology concerns itself with questions including: Who was Jesus of Nazareth? What does it mean to be fully God and fully human? How much did Jesus know about his own divine identity?

Both scripture and tradition are rich theological resources for answering these questions, so it will be worth spending a moment briefly discussing each before returning to modern physics.

Scripture

Throughout the Bible, Jesus is depicted as both human and divine. The prologue to the Gospel of John, for example, contains a poetic and deeply philosophical articulation of the incarnation:

> In the beginning was the Word, and the Word was with God, and the Word was God. All things came into being through him, and without him not one thing came into being. . . . And the Word became flesh and lived among us. (John 1:1–3, 14)

According to these verses, Christ was with the Father at the moment of creation. He is the Word—the divine *Logos*, i.e., the rationality that imbues the created order—through which everything was created. Although Christ is not identical with the Father, they are one in being (John 10:30). The Word is both *with* God and *is* God (John 1:1). He has come "to do the will of him who sent me and to complete his work" (John 10:34). They are separate persons, yet there is a deep connection between them. If you know Christ, you know the Father (John 14:7).

The Synoptic Gospels—Matthew, Mark, and Luke—also speak to Jesus' divinity, showing Jesus acting as only a God could act. He forgives sins (Matt 9:6), heals the sick (Luke 4:40), and elects those to whom he will reveal the Father (Luke 10:22). Nonetheless, he is also depicted as fallible in ways only a human can be. He appears not to know the timing of his return (Matt 24:36; Mark 13:32), knowledge only the Father possesses. He also seeks solitude, feels fear and anguish about the suffering he has to endure (Luke 22:39–44), and has uniquely creaturely needs like hunger (Matt 21:18). He is born, as all humans are born, lives a human life, and dies a terrible death.

Obvious puzzles emerge when trying to work out how to understand the appropriate theological formulation of Christ's nature. According to the Bible, this historical figure who ate with his friends, preached on a mountain, and died on a cross is one and the same person as the Word of God who existed with the Father before time began. How can someone be God, at the Father's side before the cosmos existed, and human, able to suffer and die on a cross in a specific geographical location at a particular moment in time? Jesus was able to shout, "my God, my God, why have you forsaken me?" (Matt 27:46; Mark 15:34) while also stating "before Abraham was, I am" (John 8:58). The first utterance implies a radical disconnect between God and Jesus, showing that at the moment of his death Jesus felt totally abandoned by God. Yet the second utterance not only indicates that Jesus pre-existed Abraham, it also identifies Christ with God by echoing one of God's Old Testament names, the great "I Am." Over many centuries, careful work has been done to understand the appropriate theological interpretation of these texts.

Tradition

How has Jesus been understood across the two thousand years that have passed since his birth? Entire libraries could be filled by books trying to answer that question, and entire libraries we do not have. I must attempt to give the extremely condensed version here and ask any theologians reading to forgive me for the necessary brevity. The theologically orthodox understanding of Jesus Christ's nature was developed in the patristic period, following a number of disagreements and controversies. This period of time in the church's early history was named after the church fathers who developed many of the Christian doctrines endorsed by Christians today. After a period of intense debate and much theological reflection, a consensus formed around what we now call the Chalcedonian definition, so named because it was developed during the fourth ecumenical council of the Christian church, held in Chalcedon in 451. According to the Chalcedonian definition, Christ is fully God and fully human, sharing one substance with God while also having a completely human nature. Theologian Oliver Crisp identifies five central Christological claims that are contained with the Chalcedonian definition:

1. Christ and the Father are of one substance.
2. Christ is eternally begotten of the Father according to his divinity and temporally begotten of the Virgin Mary according to his humanity.
3. Christ is one theanthropic (divine–human) person who has two natures that are held together in a personal union.
4. Christ's two natures remain intact in the personal union, but are not confused or mixed together to form some sort of hybrid entity.

5. Christ has a fully divine nature and a fully human nature, respectively, his human nature consisting of a human body and "rational" soul. He is not half God half man.[1]

Jesus Christ must be understood as God *and* man; flesh *and* spirit; infinite *and* finite. His nature is a paradox. As Paul Tillich reminds us, however, this paradox should not be confused with irrationality. A paradox neither contradicts logic, nor does it show that something has gone wrong with the reasoning. When we look at the origin of the word, this becomes clear. If something is "paradoxical," then it contradicts *doxa*, namely "opinion," which is "based on the whole of ordinary human experience, including the empirical and the rational."[2] Crucially, this experience-based opinion has been formed in the finite world under the fragmented and fallen conditions of existence. So, for the Christian, Christ's nature is paradoxical in that it contradicts *what we believe to be possible*. It goes above and beyond this world while remaining fully within it at the same time. It is in this sense that his nature is a paradox.

In addition to the metaphysics of the incarnation, we must consider its dual function. The incarnation is about *salvation*, and it is about *revelation*. We will tackle salvation extensively in the next chapter. For now, all that needs to be said is encapsulated by the words of David Moser: "the theology of the incarnation assumes that God has touched our flesh so that he might draw us into his very life. . . . [E]very feature of the human being has to be assumed by the Logos in time, except for sin, in order for this union to bring about our salvation."[3] The theme of revelation is taken on by twentieth-century theologian Karl Barth. Barth argued that the incarnation is God's ultimate act of self-revelation in and through which God discloses himself to the world in a radical act of love. Humanity cannot actively participate in this revelation; we must only passively receive it from above. In order to understand what God was revealing, and the extent to which modern physics ought to shape our interpretation of this revelation, we must examine what it means for God to take on human form in both time and space.

---

1. Paraphrased from Crisp, "Incarnation," 161.
2. Tillich, *Systematic Theology II*, 92.
3. Moser, "Jesus' Preexistence and Incarnation."

TIME[4]

To understand how a theology of the incarnation ought to interact with the nature of time, we must first understand how God as a whole has been understood to relate to time. Unfortunately, there is no consensus on this issue. To begin to assess the relationship between God and temporal reality, one must first reflect on the nature of God. Only then are we equipped to address how such a being might relate to time.

There are two ways one might go about describing God, distinguished by the method used. These two approaches can be called the "God of the philosophers" and the "God of the theologians." The philosophical approach tends to describe God as a highly abstract bearer of maximally perfect properties. God is perfectly good, God is all powerful, etc. The theological approach adds that God is a person with a historical relationship with a specific group of human beings and his own divine history. If and when there is a conflict between some philosophically formulated divine attribute (e.g., divine immutability, the idea that God does not change) and a scriptural depiction of the Christian God (e.g., that God took on human form, on Earth, and died) each discipline may prioritize one description over another. Which characteristic is more important will matter when trying to untangle the nature of the God–time relationship. Though these two need not be in opposition—and indeed it is the hope of many Christian philosophers of religion that they are *not* in opposition to theological tradition—a philosophical description of God's nature may deviate from a theological description in various ways.

When theologians and philosophers try to understand the relationship between God and time, a promising approach is to work out which are God's most important characteristics and which theory of time best preserves these. Some of these are: omniscience (all-knowing); omnipotence (all-powerful and perfectly free); omnibenevolence (perfectly good and all-loving); sovereignty (ruler of all things); simplicity (not comprised of parts and without unrealized potential); transcendence (existing over and above physical creation); immanence (being intimately related to, and present within, creation); and, finally, personhood, in the broadest sense of the word (i.e., a being with intellect and a will). Much of this can be captured by "perfect being theology," i.e., the position that if God were to exist, he would be the most perfect being possible. According to

---

4. Much of this section was first published in Qureshi-Hurst, "God and Philosophy of Time."

perfect being theology, God possesses in a maximal way all the positive attributes a person can possess, making him the greatest being metaphysically possible.

Divine Temporality

Scriptural depictions of God's relationship to time are complex and cannot easily be sorted into a single clear model. Generally, however, God is depicted as being intimately involved in the unfolding of creation, interacting within history in a way that seems to show that he is a temporal being. A temporal being is a being who has temporal properties, temporal extension, temporal location, and an experience of temporal passage. In other words: a being who exists in, and experiences, time. Psalm 102:23–28, for example, says of God:

> Long ago you laid the foundation of the earth, and the heavens are the work of your hands. They will perish, but you endure; they will all wear out like a garment. You change them like clothing, and they pass away; but you are the same, and your years have no end.

This passage weaves together two different ways one might experience time, comparing and contrasting divine temporality with the temporality of the created world. God is described as creating the cosmos "long ago," with each creative act being finite and fleeting, in contrast to God's ever-fixed eternity. An unchanging God is contrasted with a changing cosmos. Even if God might appear timeless, insofar as he does not experience the passage of time and its decaying properties, divine *action* is temporal. You may be forgiven for thinking the biblical portrayal of God and time is metaphysically muddled, showing him as being both within and outside of time.

The temporal nature of God's creative acts is never clearer than in the Genesis narratives. In Genesis 1 God creates the universe in stages, with creation coming into being over the course of six creatively active epochs. God creates worldly time (Gen 1:4–5) and this time continues to structure the creation narratives and the divine action taking place within them. Similarly, in Genesis 3, God converses with and walks alongside Adam and Eve, interacting with them in a temporal mode. Throughout the Hebrew Bible, God is shown to be active in the unfolding of human history. He commands (Exod 3–4), he punishes (Gen 7), he rewards (Job

42:10–17), and he enters into a covenant with his people (Gen 6:18; Isa 54:9; Num 25:10–13). In other words, he responds to events as they happen, engaging in a dynamic relationship with the world. Similarly, the New Testament tells of God taking on flesh, becoming human, and living as a temporal being (John 1:14). If God is triune, as Christianity claims, then the temporal status of one trinitarian person should be shared by the others. Each divine person must have the same divine nature. All of this seems to indicate that the God of the theologians is temporal.

This view has risen to prominence in recent years, led by scholars like William Lane Craig, Richard Swinburne, Nicholas Wolterstorff, and R. T. Mullins. Mullins, for example, defends what he calls the "identification view." According to this view, time is identified with God, perhaps as an essential divine attribute or mode.[5] One reason to think that God *is* time is because, according to Mullins, the existence and nature of God becomes the source of moments. God exists in the precreation moment, and the exercise of his free will gives rise to all subsequent moments of time. Both the existence and the order of moments depend upon God's decisions about how to freely exercise his power. Mullins also argues that God should be thought of as mutable (i.e., changeable), not immutable. Although God's essential attributes never change, God can undergo other kinds of changes, such as becoming the creator, redeemer, and Lord of humanity. Since God is a necessary being, and God undergoes such change, God must be *inside* time.

A more basic way of understanding divine temporality is simply that which I set out at the beginning of this section: God is temporal because God has temporal properties, temporal extension, temporal location, and an experience of temporal passage. In effect, while God is everlasting—without beginning or end—God exists within time.

Divine Atemporality

Despite the modern enthusiasm for the temporal view, the majority of the Christian tradition has not understood God as temporal.[6] In fact, it has largely understood God as eternal, meaning God exists not only without beginning or end, but also "beyond" the temporal dimension that frames creaturely existence. The work of the ancient Greek philosopher

---

5. Mullins, "Divine Timemaker."
6. There are, of course, exceptions.

Plato had a significant impact on the development of Christian thought, particularly in this regard. In *Republic* 381b–c, Plato argued that a perfect being cannot change because they are unable to improve, being already perfect, and they cannot deteriorate as this would mean they cease to be perfect. This leads to the doctrine of divine immutability—the idea that a perfect God cannot change in any way at all. Plato's student Aristotle went on to argue that time and change were inseparable, meaning that a being who cannot change must be outside of time.

Theologian Saint Augustine of Hippo (354–430) made a distinction, one that has been reached for many times since, between divine eternity and created temporality. The former is the atemporal mode that characterizes God's eternal life, while the latter is imperfect and limited by the experiential context of creatureliness. Augustine seems to have believed that the creaturely experiential context leads us to encounter time as though it is dynamic and tensed, in that it flows and is fragmented into past, present, and future. For the perfect and immutable God, however, there is no distinction between tenses, nor is there passage between different moments of time; instead, all moments are held together in eternity. Divine eternity is tenseless and unified and stands over and above created time. While our senses "flutter between the motions of things past and things still to come," God dwells in "the glory of everfixed eternity"—these states are radically different in kind.

Perhaps the most influential piece of medieval theology on the relationship between God and time was Boethius's (c. 475–c. 526) definition of divine eternity:

> Eternity, then, is the *complete possession all at once of illimitable life*. This becomes clearer by comparison with temporal things. For whatever lives in time proceeds as something present from the past into the future, and there is nothing placed in time that can embrace the whole extent of its life equally . . . , it does not yet grasp tomorrow but yesterday it has already lost; and even in the life of today you live no more fully than in a mobile, transitory moment. . . . Therefore, whatever includes and possesses the whole fullness of illimitable life at once and is such that nothing future is absent from it and nothing past has flowed away, this is rightly judged to be eternal, and of this it is necessary both that being in full possession of itself it be always present to itself and that it have the infinity of mobile time present [to it].[7]

---

7. Boethius, *Title V.*6. Emphasis added.

Saint Thomas Aquinas (1225-1274) was the medieval thinker whose writings have left the most significant impact on the development of Christian theology. Aquinas argued that God has no beginning or end and does not experience succession, passage, or change. Along with most other medieval philosophers, Aquinas endorses Boethius's definition of eternity. Echoing Boethius, Aquinas holds that all times are atemporally known by God at once. Aquinas illustrates this through the metaphor of standing at the summit of a mountain with an entire landscape before you:

> God, however, is wholly outside the order of time, stationed as it were at the summit of eternity, which is wholly simultaneous, and to Him the whole course of time is subjected in one simple intuition. For this reason, He sees in one glance everything that is affected in the evolution of time, and each thing as it is in itself, and it is not future to Him in relation to His view as it is in the order of its causes alone (although He also sees the very order of the causes).[8]

One ought not to take the metaphor too literally, however. It may be a little simplistic to claim that God perceives events in time like some eternal and external onlooker. For Aquinas, God atemporally knows all the facts about history by knowing their cause (i.e., himself). Since God predetermined all things, he knows all things before they exist. God does not need to be within time to have knowledge of what happens within the temporal, created sphere. As this brief summary indicates, for a significant portion of Christian history God was understood as existing *outside* time, i.e., as atemporal.

There are also philosophical arguments for affirming that God is atemporal. In fact, I would argue that the "God of the philosophers" is more likely to be understood as atemporal, in contrast to the "God of the theologians," who is probably better understood as temporal, given the biblical depiction of God as acting in time on a regular basis. The first philosophical argument for divine atemporality is concerned with the property "sovereignty." Theism holds that God is sovereign, meaning he is ruler of all things and is not subject to any external power or force. According to those who endorse an atemporal God, God is able to remain both sovereign and omnipotent (all powerful) by not being subject to the passing of time. A temporal God, on the other hand, has been accused of

---

8. Aquinas, *Commentary on Peri Hermeneias* I.14.20.

being trapped within time, subservient to the inexorability of its passing. Such a God can only directly access one moment of time: now. He cannot act in the past because it is gone, nor can he act in the future because it is not yet real. For this reason, this argument is also known as the "prisoner of time" objection. There is a solution, though. You can bite the bullet and argue that if God is a prisoner of time, then this is only because he has allowed himself to be so. If he *allows* it, then his power is not really restricted, and so the problem is not as significant as it first appeared.

This leads to a further problem with the temporal God that is harder to satisfyingly solve. If God can only experience *the present*, he cannot know certain facts about the future. There are two reasons for this. First, the future has not happened yet (if you endorse a temporal God, you probably also endorse a theory of time with a future that has not yet happened—more on this in the next chapter). Second, Christians will typically want to claim that human beings have free will, meaning they are able to make free choices about which actions they take and which of their possible futures they can work toward actualizing. But if the future is open and can be shaped by the free choices of human agents, then God cannot know the future. If God does know the future, then our choices stop being free. Or so the argument goes.

Why might God's foreknowledge get in the way of human freedom? The answer is best explained through the following example. If I am deciding what to have for breakfast, I might choose toast or cereal. We typically think that I am free when making this choice if I could genuinely pick between either option. Until the moment of choosing, it is possible for me to have either. But if God knows in advance that I will eat toast for breakfast, then in what sense did I freely choose? It seems, in that case, like I was only ever able to make one choice. God's knowledge is perfect and infallible, so if he knows that I will eat toast before I experience having made the choice, then I was only ever going to make that choice. I was never really free to choose cereal at all. Richard Swinburne argues on the basis of this problem that God cannot have knowledge of our future choices if those choices are to be truly free. This poses a threat to God's omniscience (perfect knowledge). The atemporal God, on the other hand, is outside of time, able to apprehend all events at once. As such, God atemporally knows everything that happens in creation. He has perfect knowledge of the present and past, as well as perfect knowledge of the events that lie in our future.

God, Time, and the Incarnation

The question is, what does all this mean for the incarnation? Many of those who believe that God is a temporal being direct us to the doctrine of the Trinity, claiming that if one trinitarian person existed in time (Jesus Christ) then all trinitarian persons must be temporal (Father, Son, and Spirit). To argue the contrary would be to deny that God is one substance, slipping into tritheism, which affirms three separate gods instead of one monotheistic God. Despite this, it is the atemporal understanding of God that dominated theological tradition. This view sees God as atemporal, with God the Son entering into space and time for only a short while before exiting again after his work was completed. Not many of these historical theologians saw a problem with a timeless God becoming incarnate in a temporal world. Whether they were right not to be worried is of course another matter entirely.

In the next chapter, we will look at some further arguments for and against divine temporality, bringing in considerations from physics about how best to understand the nature of time. For now, I leave you with the thought that understanding the relationship between God, time, and the incarnation relies on a heady mixture of science, philosophy, and theology, none of which agree in all areas. For this reason, it is a particularly thorny area of overlap between God and modern physics. My own thinking is that physics and philosophy gives us compelling reasons to think that time does not really flow and that the future and past are as real as the present, something I will discuss at length in the next chapter. This view is most compatible with God being atemporal, or outside of time. The reason for this is simple—if time does not really pass or flow, then God cannot experience temporal passage or flow. If this argument is right, and God is atemporal, then the incarnation faces some problems. It is difficult to see how God can be both atemporally transcendent and temporally incarnated. These problems are probably not insurmountable, but there is certainly more difficulty reconciling the incarnation with an atemporal God than with a temporal God.

History

One final point worth noting in relation to time and the incarnation is that of history. Paul Tillich has some particularly helpful insights on this topic. Tillich defines history methodologically and with an emphasis on subjectivity, meaning history is understood primarily as a mode of enquiry that aims to construct narratives and find meaning in past events. History is not just the neutral recording of past facts. History, and the significance of historical events, lies in the subjective interpretation of the past and not in what objectively occurred. For Tillich, events are ambiguous and transitory; their significance only really emerges through the meaning human thought forms out of them. As such, history should be understood as one of the ways that humanity explains its place and purpose in the world. Tillich argues that a spiritual life is able to produce cultural artifacts and religious experiences with almost inexhaustible meaning, all of which can reflect God and move history toward its intended purpose.

Although individual human beings are centers of meaning, they exist within wider historical narratives. For this reason, only *groups* can bear history. As individual polyps form complex coral reefs, so too do generations of individuals sharing a language and upholding cultural traditions comprise the body of history. This history is transmitted, not primarily by remembering events, but through traditions. In this way, past events reverberate down the generations through their symbolic repetition. On this understanding of history, becoming part of a history-bearing group is an essential part of what it is to be human. Therefore, if God is to become truly human, he must form part of a cultural group that has both a history and a purpose. Any proper understanding of time and the incarnation must make space for the central importance of shared history and common purpose in human identity.

Salvation and history are also fundamentally interconnected. Tillich puts the point rather well. He argues that salvation occurs in history through the concrete manifestation of the kingdom of God. The kingdom of God is realized at a point of *kairos*—a Greek term he uses to mean "fulfillment of time."[9] It must be understood in contrast to *chronos*, a moment of measured/clock time. At a point of *kairos*, history had matured to the extent that it was ready to receive the centerpoint of history: the incarnation, death, and resurrection of Jesus Christ. The word "center" does not mean the literal mid-point in the history of the cosmos in terms of time elapsed versus time to come. Rather, it is used symbolically to represent the fact that everything before this moment was preparation and everything after it is reception. Through the incarnation, the true meaning of

---

9. Tillich, *Systematic Theology III*, 369–72.

history becomes knowable: "the time is fulfilled, and the kingdom of God is at hand; repent and believe in the gospel" (Mark 1:15).

As we have seen, the doctrine of the incarnation speaks of a God who clothed himself in human flesh and entered the material world of space and time. He became embodied. He entered an earthly community whose shared history unfolds in time, bringing a new purpose toward which that history is directed. Because of all this, the incarnation cannot be disentangled from the spatial and temporal context in which it took place. The same can be said for salvation, and indeed incarnation and salvation cannot be completely separated, so we will return to these themes in the next chapter. In what remains of this chapter we will examine the spatial dimensions of the incarnation, considering both this world and worlds beyond.

SPACE

As we saw in chapter 1, the doctrine of creation *ex nihilo* describes the cosmos as utterly dependent upon God for its existence, both in terms of its inception and in each subsequent moment. This means that God created, and continues to sustain, everything that exists. This, of course, includes physical space. Yet classical theism is also committed to the idea that God is a non-corporeal being, meaning God is a non-physical person who does not occupy any spatial location or have any kind of physical body. In effect, God created space, despite being non-spatial himself.

The doctrine of the incarnation complicates things. For a few decades two thousand years ago, Christians believe God *did* enter space and take on physical form. A good place to start when trying to understand the incarnation is the Nicene Creed, the only Christian statement of faith accepted by the Roman Catholic, Eastern Orthodox, Anglican, and major Protestant churches. Formally adopted by the early church fathers in 325, it affirmed that the eternal Son of God "for us and for our salvation came down from heaven," claiming that God is actively present within the space and time of our world. Theologian Thomas F. Torrance explored this idea in *Space, Time and Incarnation*. He argued that the special and general theories of relativity have demonstrated that space and time are not mere abstractions, instead they are the ontological foundation of the contingent events inseparably and objectively rooted in them. Essentially, these form the context of God's self-revelation, meaning we cannot fully understand the content of that revelation unless we take space and time seriously. He makes an important point—in order to understand the incarnation in its entirety, space and time must receive thorough consideration. In this chapter, we take up this task.

For Torrance, time and space are created forms of rationality that exist in distinction from, but are related to, the rationality of God. He writes that the incarnation:

> Asserts the reality of space and time for God in the actuality of His relations with us, and at the same time binds us to space and time in all our relations with Him. We can no more contract out of space and time than we can contract out of the creature–Creator relationship.[10]

Essentially, Torrance argues that because the incarnation has occurred, and because it has occurred within the spatiality and temporality of our world, all other conceivable routes to God have been invalidated. Jesus' spatial existence makes space—material, embodied existence in this particular cosmos—central to the way humanity relates to God. If Torrance is right then the relationship between God and creatures in the spatiotemporal realm, including creatures' ability to receive the Christian message and be saved, is inescapably bound up with physical space.

Difficulties arise, of course, in conceiving of how a non-physical God can take on physicality without somehow diminishing his power or divinity. Christ remains united with humanity by virtue of the incarnation and at one with God outside the spatial context in which he took on flesh and died. Jesus, as *fully human*, is finite and located in a particular point in space and moment in time. The Son, however, as *fully God* must exist everywhere and nowhere; he is present throughout all of creation without being trapped in or confined to one particular location. If we deny this, we deny either his divinity or his humanity. To an extent, the Christian may have to retreat into mystery, as these puzzles may not have adequate solutions. Whatever solution is offered, what we learn is that the incarnation did not happen in a vacuum. It happened here, within space and time, showing that space and time are themselves sacred. We learn not only that our relationship with God is shaped by our embeddedness in space; we also learn that this material existence is profoundly important. For all its flaws and fallenness, our world is good and worth redeeming.

10. Torrance, *Space, Time, and Incarnation*, 67.

One further point that follows from a consideration of space and the incarnation is that of embodiment, a theme we will return to in the next chapter. The incarnation happened in physical space *and* in a physical body. After Christ took on human flesh, humanity and God are forever able to relate to each other more deeply and more completely. The material world and the embodied form are evidently of great theological importance. We are not just rational souls temporarily encased in irrelevant or disposable flesh. The body itself is essential to being human—if not, Christ would not have taken on embodied physical form. This is why fields of study like embodied cognition are becoming increasingly relevant theologically.[11]

Deep Incarnation

A related idea has been developed and defended by Niels Henrik Gregersen, namely that of *deep incarnation.* Coined in 2001, the term "deep incarnation" refers to the idea that the second trinitarian person, God the Son, is present in and with every creature, at every moment in time, at every point of space. This reading of the incarnation holds that the incarnation cannot be confined to the temporal life of the historical Jesus alone. Gregersen believes that restricting the incarnation in this way is superficial, going no further than skin deep. Instead, in the incarnation, God should be understood as taking on the material conditions of this creaturely life in ways that hold significance throughout the entire cosmos.[12] Gregersen criticizes readings of Christian doctrine that prioritize time over space, including Tillich's aforementioned *kairos.* Instead of focusing too heavily on a specific moment of historical time, Christian theologians should be emphasizing the fact that the incarnation penetrated all space and all time, the effects of which ripple outward throughout the entirety of creation.[13] God is incarnate in the material world, taking on the forms of creation from humans to grass to celestial objects. On this view the incarnation is *deep*, seeping into the very cracks between the subatomic particles of our world. The incarnation is also *broad*, sweeping throughout evolutionary history and out into the furthest reaches of the cosmos.

---

11. For example, Tanton, *Corporeal Theology.*
12. Gregersen, "Deep Incarnation," 2.
13. Gregersen, "Deep Incarnation," 3–4.

If all of the cosmos is fallen, then the incarnation must penetrate all of creation. As such, Gregersen argues that Christ must be considered a cosmic force who reaches into the depths of biological and cosmic existence, reconciling all of creation to God and opening up the possibility of salvation for the entire cosmos. Christ's human body exchanged atoms with the material world. His life shared in the earthly realities of suffering and death. He was born out of a long human lineage that was traced back to Adam, and behind this lineage lies millions of years of biological evolution. Christ did not just become incarnate in human form; he became a part of the cosmos and all of its natural processes. As Gregersen writes:

> Just as leaves of grass, Jesus was susceptible to death; just as any other animal, Jesus was susceptible to pain; and just as any other human he was exposed to social exclusion and unfair judges. In short, Jesus was a microcosm of the cosmos at large, and took upon himself all the sinful meshwork of social life. . . . The life of Jesus is the story about a God who is speaking, acting, and suffering everywhere in time and space. This story began in time and space and yet is going on forever and at every place in the cosmos. As a historical figure, Jesus is a bygone person, but the face of Christ is present in, with, and under any creature, as put by the great Franciscan theologian Bonaventure of the 13th century. As a result, Christ is still near to us today who are living even two thousand years after his death.[14]

This is the idea of deep incarnation. Christ is cosmic; he has deep and intrinsic relationships with all aspects of the world, both matter and minds. Because of the depth and breadth of the incarnation, the entire cosmos can benefit from its effects. Of course, the idea that God is present in an incarnate way in every creature and at every moment of time is a controversial one. Does this diminish the unique particularity of Jesus? What makes Jesus special, if God is everywhere and in all things? Whatever your perspective, the scope of the incarnation is an extremely important theological issue. Indeed, this issue is made even more prescient by developments in the pioneering field of astrobiology. How should we understand the incarnation if it turns out that we are not the only intelligent life in the universe?

---

14. Gregersen, "Deep Incarnation and the Cosmic Story of Christ."

Astrobiology

The Bible was written long before the invention of telescopes, and the traditional formulations of the doctrine of the incarnation were shaped before the word "science" even entered human vocabulary. It is no surprise, then, that these sources focus only on the incarnation here on Earth. The writers had no knowledge of other planets, let alone any life those planets may harbor. But what should we make of the incarnation in the context we are living in now, where the existence of life elsewhere in the universe is becoming ever more plausible?

Before it even becomes possible to suggest that alien life has emerged and evolved into something intelligent, rational, and moral (thus falling within the class of beings that may require, or at least benefit from, an incarnation), scientists need to ascertain whether there are any other habitable planets with conditions similar to Earth.[15] We have known for decades that there are more stars in our galaxy than the human mind can really comprehend. Until very recently, however, it was possible that planetary systems were vanishingly rare. As Andrew Davison writes in his pioneering book on the topic, *Astrobiology and Christian Doctrine*, there were two leading theories about how planetary systems emerge, and only one of them predicted a high number of other planets.

The first theory was that planets are formed out of the same celestial clouds of cosmic dust that make stars. On this model, gravity draws nebulae together, eventually causing them to collapse into centers of matter. The immense gravitational pressure causes the star to begin to shine, set alight by the fires of nuclear fusion. The dust that remains in orbit undergoes a similar process, causing the formation of various different types of planets, including gas giants like Jupiter and small rocky planets like Earth. If planets are formed alongside their stars, then they are extremely common. The second theory of planetary formation claimed that planets are caused by stars colliding. Given that the number of stars is minuscule compared to the space between them, stellar collision is extremely rare. It is much more likely that two bullets would hit each other during a battle,

---

15. The assumption here is that life would be similar to life on Earth, and would thus require liquid water (or similar life-sustaining liquid), stable temperatures, a breathable atmosphere, etc. Of course, alien life may be radically different to life as we know it. In which case, we would probably struggle to detect it, as we would not know what we are looking for. Theological questions about such life would be even more difficult to answer than the ones I tackle in this chapter, so I will leave them to one side.

itself a highly unlikely event. If planetary systems emerge this way, ours could be one of very few ever to exist.

We now know that the first model is correct. Our immensely powerful telescopes have allowed us to peer into the very furthest reaches of the cosmos, as well as to explore our local region in much greater detail than was previously achievable. Davison points his readers to *The Extrasolar Planets Encyclopaedia*, which, as of March 5, 2025, lists 7,417 planets, 5,089 planetary systems, and 1,035 multiple planet systems. And this only accounts for the planets we have been able to observe in our local region of the galaxy. Based on a statistical estimate from their Kepler Space Telescope, NASA suggests that there are more planets than stars in our galaxy, meaning that they are formed alongside their stars in a rather routine fashion.

The discovery of these planets is an incredible achievement, made even more impressive when you understand the methods used. Stars are immensely bright, while planets emit almost no light at all. Even with very sophisticated telescopes, it is not easy to spot a grain of dust orbiting a speck of light many billions of miles away. NASA has developed several sophisticated techniques to identify planets in other solar systems.[16] The first is to look for the gravitational effects of the planet(s) on their star, and it was this method that led to the 1995 discovery of the first exoplanet (planet outside our solar system). Astronomers at NASA noticed a wobble in a particular star that they realized was caused by a rapidly orbiting gas giant, now known as 51 Pegasi b. Since this initial breakthrough, this technique has brought about the discovery of many other gas giants.

For smaller planets, whose gravitational effects are much less noticeable, a different technique is required. To detect the presence of small rocky planets like Earth, the most likely candidates for hosting life, scientists must make long observations on specific patches of sky, paying particular attention to the light emitted by the stars in that region. This light is monitored, and any regular dips in the light emitted are evidence of a planet passing in front of the star as it orbits. What's more, NASA can now analyze the atmosphere of these planets using a technique called transit spectroscopy. Chemical elements absorb and emit particular wavelengths of light, which can be read like a barcode. You may remember holding copper salt over a Bunsen burner in a chemistry class and

---

16. NASA, "How We Find and Classify Exoplanets."

watching the distinctive blue-green flames. Each chemical element has a fingerprint, a barcode that can be read using a technique called spectroscopy. By analyzing the light emitted from these distant planets, scientists can work out the chemical composition of their atmospheres and look for telltale signs of life. As our telescopes get better and better, we are coming closer to being able to take direct, high-resolution images of distant planets as well. The questions these discoveries raise are theological and philosophical, as well as scientific. Is there life on these planets? What is that life like? Do extra-terrestrial life forms experience fallenness, sin, and alienation from God? And, if so, we must ask the most important question in this chapter: *Did the incarnation take place more than once?*

To answer, some basic reasoning needs to be done on the basis of the data that we have. In this, I follow Davison's estimate of how many habitable planets there likely are in our Milky Way galaxy.[17] First, we might reasonably conclude that solar systems with stars like ours are the best bet for life—our star is hot but not too hot, large but not too large, and, most importantly, it is stable enough to provide consistent conditions on Earth over the extremely long time span required for complex, intelligent life to evolve. Around 4 percent of the stars in our galaxy match this description, so around four billion. We now know that most stars have planets, but that many of these are not habitable. Gas giants are a no-go[18] and rocky planets too close or too far from their stars would be too hot or too cold for life to thrive. We need to identify planets in the so-called Goldilocks zone, named after the character Goldilocks, who preferred the things in the three bears' house that were *just right*. The Goldilocks zone is a region around a star where the temperature on an orbiting planet is mild enough that surface water can exist in liquid form. Life would neither be scorched nor frozen and would have access to liquid water. In other words, the conditions in the Goldilocks zone are *just right* for life. There are approximately two billion such planets in our Milky Way. The number soars to four hundred billion billion if we extrapolate these findings to the observable universe as a whole. Clearly, there are lots of chances for the spark of life to ignite and go on to evolve into something intelligent, rational, moral, and spiritual.

---

17. Davison, *Astrobiology and Christian Doctrine*, 3.

18. Although it may be possible for their moons to hold life of some kind. For example, Jupiter's moon Europa is one of the key candidate locations for finding life elsewhere in our solar system.

We do not know whether life emerges easily or not. Even if it is very difficult for life to evolve in perfect conditions like those we enjoy on Earth, it is quite a stretch to say it could not have happened at least once more given four hundred billion billion chances. The scientific field that deals with these questions is astrobiology, and the theological questions it raises are as challenging as they are awe-inspiring. Davison is a pioneer in bringing astrobiology and theology together, and he offers several options for how an incarnation may work elsewhere in the cosmos. Before delving into these, we ought to reflect a little further on a few related theological concepts, including those that relate to one of the purposes of the incarnation: our salvation. What does it mean to be a human being? In what ways are we fallen? Our answers to these questions will shape how we understand the possibility of incarnations elsewhere in the cosmos.

Fallenness and Human Nature

How theologians interpret the fall narratives in the Bible can aid us in speculating about the nature of fallenness—and any corresponding salvation—elsewhere in the cosmos. By understanding fallenness here, we will be able to make progress on understanding if and how other incarnations may have taken place. One point of contention is whether the fall was a literal historical event or whether the Genesis narratives offer a symbolic and mythical explanation of the conditions of existence. After much debate in biological and anthropological circles, most scientists now agree that although modern humans did arise from a single ancestral population in Africa, humanity cannot trace its origins back to a single couple. Even if it could, these would not be the first humans to have walked this Earth. They would have had human parents themselves and would have lived in a small tribal group with other humans, perhaps even interacting with other hominid species like neanderthals.

The implications of this are clear. We cannot claim with scientific credibility that all human beings descended from two real people named Adam and Eve who were the first humans to walk the Earth. Human beings emerged gradually, sharing continuity with all other creatures who have ever called this planet home. Like them we are born, and like them we die. This natural rhythm has always been a feature of life on Earth. As such, it becomes far less likely that sin and death were brought into the world by a single historical act committed by the first human couple, the consequences of which are passed down the generations. Far from being antagonistic to Christian theology, it instead opens up the possibility of innovative interpretations of sin and fallenness, freeing theologians to take up more creative and layered interpretations of Genesis.

Those more committed to reading Genesis as an account of historical events may wish to understand Adam and Eve as a pair of early humans in whom the *imago Dei* (the image of God, as described in Genesis 1:26–27) first reached its previously unrealized potential. These two could be understood as entering into a covenant with God and facing, for the first time in human history, the choice to obey God or to defy him. As the story explains, they chose to defy God, shaping the nature of their descendants' relationship with the divine forevermore. Others might prefer to take a less literal reading, viewing the Bible as symbolically representing something that took place gradually. As humanity matured into the kind of species that is able to make moral decisions and be held responsible for them, we strayed from God and the divine purpose set out for us. A final alternative is that the Genesis stories are allegories for the real moral choices each of us will face in our own lives. However one chooses to interpret the stories, what each interpretation shares is the central claim that human beings face moral choices that are (perhaps) uniquely human, and that human nature tends toward using our moral abilities poorly. We are created in the image of God (a doctrine that is given the Latin name *imago Dei*), and yet we often fail to live up to God's likeness.

It may be worth pausing here a moment to reflect on the doctrine of *imago Dei*, as it is an important piece of the theological puzzle and will help clarify some of the issues raised by contemporary astrobiology. As Helen De Cruz and Yves De Maeseneer write, "human uniqueness remains a central element in theological views about the imago Dei: it is by virtue of their unique status in nature that humans occupy a privileged position in creation, and derive their dignity."[19] The doctrine of *imago Dei* is highly significant—it is the source of humanity's inherent dignity and grounds our moral obligations toward each other. Humanity shares in the divine image, and because of this we have an inherent dignity and must be treated with the utmost respect.

There are several ways that the doctrine can be interpreted, but to the extent that human uniqueness is required, the possibility of alien life

---

19. De Cruz and De Maeseneer, "Imago Dei: Evolutionary and Theological Perspectives," 96.

could be seen as a threat. The first view, the *structural* view, claims that humans are uniquely made in the image of God by virtue of their characteristics. Such characteristics may include humanity's rationality, moral capacities, sophisticated levels of intelligence, or free will. It is named the structural view because it is the existence of certain structural features that ground the likeness between humanity and the divine. The second view, the *functional* view, claims that humans bear the image of God through the role or function they play in creation, perhaps by stewarding creation or perhaps by having dominion over it. Both dominion and stewardship understand humanity as being God's chosen representative on Earth, selected to aid creation in its ability to fulfill the divine purpose. By occupying such a privileged position in the natural order, we are gifted a glimmer of God's sovereignty over creation. The final option, the *relational* view, claims that the *imago Dei* is made manifest through humanity's unique relationship with God. Proponents of this view may argue that only humans enter into a covenant with God, only humans develop relationships with God that they develop over the course of their lives, and only humans can be drawn deeper into relationship with God via redemption. It is this that makes us divine image-bearers, who struggle and strive toward divine likeness.

These three approaches are not mutually exclusive, and it may well be the case that the best formulation of the doctrine of *imago Dei* includes all of them. As will be clear by now, what unites these accounts of the doctrine of *imago Dei* is their emphasis on human uniqueness. What, then, might the implications of alien life be for the doctrine of *imago Dei*? If distant alien life could bear structural similarities to God, enjoy a dominant role in their corner of creation, or enter into a deep and meaningful relationship with God, then we may have to give up on claims of absolute human uniqueness. But, as Davison asks, why should this be of concern? It is rarely the case that something becomes less special because it is not unique. As Davison writes, "even if human beings alone stand in the image of God in Genesis 1, that does not mean that the image *consists* in a difference from every other creature, and thus can only apply to one species, such that if another turned out to bear it, that would prove that we are not made in the image of God after all."[20] The image of God may belong only to humanity on Earth, but on other planets in far off reaches of the cosmos, other creatures could bear the divine image in their own

---

20. Davison, *Astrobiology and Christian Doctrine*, 158.

unique ways. The boundless perfection of God can be reflected in myriad ways in the finite creatures of the cosmos.

This picks up on a point made by Aquinas, who argued that God's creation must contain a great variety of creatures in order to adequately represent an infinitely good, loving, and intelligent God. Jamie Boulding, for example, has argued that Aquinas's commitment to diversity in creation can be fruitfully applied to the cosmos, specifically in relation to the multiverse theory.[21] As Boulding writes, "Aquinas understands diversity to be an integral characteristic of the cosmos, expressing the diversity of ways in which all parts of creation participate in God, the source of existence on which all of creation is utterly dependent."[22] Creation is both one and many; a diverse set of many creatures (and perhaps also many universes) is united within the one God on whom they all depend for their existence. Creation could not adequately reflect God if it were not extremely diverse and filled with multiplicity. Thus diversity is a good and valuable thing, without which creation would fail to reflect God's nature. In Aquinas's own words:

> Since every created substance must fall short of the perfection of divine goodness, in order that the likeness of divine goodness might be more perfectly communicated to things, it was necessary for there to be a diversity of things, so that what could not be perfectly represented by one thing might be, in more perfect fashion, represented by a variety of things in different ways.[23]

Boulding applies this idea to the multiverse, suggesting that multiple universes may be the best way for the physical cosmos to reflect the infinite God. If Aquinas's thoughts on diversity can apply to multiple universes, it is not such a stretch to suppose it applies to multiple instantiations of the *imago Dei* as well. Davison himself makes such a point, writing that all creatures by virtue of being creatures (literally "created beings") reflect some element of the divine. Perhaps human beings are uniquely bearers of the *imago Dei* on Earth, but we need not hold unwaveringly to human uniqueness in the cosmos as a whole. To use Davison's analogy, parents can have many children, with each child receiving some aspects of their parents' likeness that the other children

---

21. Boulding, *Multiverse and Participatory Metaphysics*, section 3.1.
22. Boulding, *Multiverse and Participatory Metaphysics*, 83.
23. Aquinas, *Summa Contra Gentiles* III.97.2, cited in Davison, *Astrobiology and Christian Doctrine*, 83.

do not.[24] Nor does the value of the existing children diminish if further children are born. Following this line of thinking, other, diverse, bearers of the *imago Dei* may be required throughout the cosmos if creation is to reflect properly God's infinite wisdom, love, and creativity. To suppose otherwise may be to make the idolatrous mistake of assuming God must closely resemble human beings.

If the *imago Dei* can be shared, perhaps in different ways, by other creatures in the cosmos, then it is possible (perhaps even likely) that those other creatures may also experience sin and fallenness. Only those possessing the divine image have the capacity to turn away from God and tend toward sin. Each formulation of the *imago Dei* contains a commitment to the role of morality in conferring the divine image onto humanity; it is this moral awareness, and the choice of what is morally wrong, that lies at the root of fallenness. Analyzing the various understandings of sin and fallenness here on Earth may offer insights about how these concepts work elsewhere in the cosmos. Perhaps all beings who develop reason and morality end up being pulled toward sinful expressions of these capacities and require some form of divine corrective. Perhaps each alien species must enter into its own covenant with the divine and each has its own chance to choose whether to obey God or fall into sin and disobedience. Although all this is highly speculative, we can make some educated guesses about the various ways incarnation, salvation, and astrobiology intersect. With this in mind, we are now able to turn to the incarnation—is the incarnation on Earth unique, or are there multiple incarnations across our vast and expansive cosmos?

The Incarnation(s)

The first option is that of a non-event: there are no other creatures in the cosmos who experience fallenness or who can be reconciled to God. In this case, we are living in the only place in the entire universe that contains spiritual and moral sophistication, and thus no other incarnation is needed. In my view, this is the least likely. Although we simply do not have enough information to know for sure, I believe this option to be the least likely for two reasons. First, the sheer volume of other planets gives life many billions of chances to evolve. Second, we now know that life emerged on Earth almost as soon as it could, even if it took a very

---

24. Davison, *Astrobiology and Christian Doctrine*, 164.

long time for intelligent, moral, and spiritual beings to evolve. Earth's fecundity may suggest that the universe as a whole is fertile, meaning exoplanets with the right conditions will house other highly developed species. Of course, we do not have answers yet, but it seems to me that we have good reason to take the possibility of other intelligent, rational, moral, and spiritual lifeforms seriously.

A sharp dividing line must be drawn between the remaining options, distinguishing those committed to uniqueness and those to plurality. In the case of *uniqueness*, the incarnation happened once in and through Jesus of Nazareth. Earth, on this view, sits at the soteriological center of the cosmos, its redeeming consequences reverberating outward. Perhaps other creatures on far-flung planets learn of the good news of our incarnation, or perhaps grace affects them without their knowledge. In the case of *plurality*, there are multiple incarnations that occur in and through God hypostatically uniting himself to other kinds of creaturely natures, as Christians believe he did here on Earth. A final option is that God redeems alien creatures in non-incarnational ways that are suited to their natures, which must remain, to us, shrouded in mystery.

Davison himself urges us to be creative and open to the possibility that redemption occurs in a plethora of ways. God, being supremely powerful and radically free, ought to have many routes to redemption for creatures. Moreover, different kinds of beings may well experience fallenness and sin differently. It would make sense to save each species in the way that best suits their particular needs. As Davison writes, even across the various Christian traditions,

> We have many different images of redemption because they refer to something too expansive and remarkable to be captured in one image, be it ransom, healing, sacrifice, victory, or some other way of talking about what Christ did for human beings. We do not need to choose, or even highlight, just one.[25]

He goes on to argue that we should expect the rich, even extravagant, plurality of redemption that we see on Earth to apply elsewhere in the cosmos.

Let us begin with the possibility that there are other intelligent, moral creatures, and that they are fallen in ways resembling human fallenness. Let us also suppose that there is one, unique incarnation, the one that occurred on Earth in and through Jesus of Nazareth. It is

---

25. Davison, *Astrobiology and Christian Doctrine*, 190.

possible that "rationality" or "personhood" could be universal categories, meaning that they are instantiated similarly in various different physical forms. Aliens could bear enough similarities to humans that God taking on rational personhood and dying can have repercussions for all rational persons, human or otherwise. On this view, Christ takes on materiality, embodiment, and creaturehood in a way that represents or in some way contains all forms that can instantiate these properties. Aquinas would frame this as God uniting his nature with that of a rational animal, redeeming rational animals everywhere.[26]

There is an obvious problem here. The Bible is very clear that knowledge of Christ is the only route by which humans can reach redemption, for example "Jesus said to him, 'I am the way, and the truth, and the life. No one comes to the Father except through me'" (John 14:6). How could alien life forms follow Christ's moral example, or engage in devotional worship, if they do not know of his existence? In fact, it is highly likely that even if Christ's revelatory message was given to them, alien life will differ from us in ways that render it incomprehensible.

This point is developed by theologian Tobias Tanton, who argues that religiosity and theological knowledge is fundamentally embodied. Engaging with empirical research from the cognitive sciences, his book *Corporeal Theology* develops a convincing argument in favor of the position that theological knowledge is not a disembodied affair. Instead, the means and methods by which we come to know theological truths are shaped by the particularities of human embodiment. Neither religious belief nor religious practice can be properly understood if we do not appreciate the role that our bodies play in navigating religious rituals and in forming religious beliefs. Because our understanding of theological concepts and our engagement with religious liturgies is inescapably bound up with our bodies, and the incarnation involved God taking on *human* flesh, creatures with different embodied forms may be utterly unable to engage with our earthly incarnation. In Tanton's own words:

> There may . . . be "corporeal" epistemic restrictions associated with our incarnation. Namely, if the human conceptual repertoire is shaped by human embodiment, as the cognitive science [I] have explored suggests, then creatures with significantly different bodily configurations and sensory modalities may have a very different and potentially incommensurable conceptual repertoire. . . . Hence other creatures may require a different

26. Davison, *Astrobiology and Christian Doctrine*, 217.

incarnation if our incarnation is not sufficiently accommodated to their cognitive profiles.[27]

The cognitive capabilities of alien life forms may be so utterly different to our own that they would be simply unable to comprehend an incarnation accommodated to the needs of human beings. Similarly, we would be wholly unable to understand an incarnation that took place in union with alien flesh and the corresponding alien psychology that goes along with it.

Tanton's point is persuasive. Perhaps it makes more sense to suppose that all intelligent civilizations will need their own incarnation if they are to properly understand and appreciate its significance. If you adopt universalism, namely the idea that everyone is eventually saved, then perhaps this conclusion does not follow. Nonetheless, I suggest that we ought to be wary of using humanity as a template for all other life. It risks overemphasizing our importance in the cosmic story. We can be important and loved by God without being the *only* important and beloved life forms. A parent does not love their first child any less when they have more children. As such, it should not threaten us if alien life exists in distant reaches of the cosmos and has its own species-specific incarnational interaction with God.

Another problem with the idea of only one incarnation is that the timing of the earthly incarnation may be too late in the cosmic day for other life forms. Life emerged on Earth 3.5 billion years ago, but the universe existed for around ten billion years before then. If life abounds in the universe, previous civilizations will have already been born and destroyed by the explosive death of their star (or by their own hubris, as we risk doing here). The earthly incarnation, two thousand years ago, will be too late for earlier alien civilizations to enjoy reconciliation to God.

That being said, most Christians do not believe that humans who died before Christ was born are doomed and unable to enjoy the soteriological fruits of his incarnation. These issues—whether those who have no awareness of Christ can benefit from his work—are not new to Christian theology. Astrobiology, however, throws them into sharp relief. What's more, popular solutions tend to fall back on the ontological union of divine and human natures, claiming that this union reaches out to all of humanity and redeems everyone who shares in this bodily form. It is

---

27. Tanton, *Corporeal Theology*, 258.

a greater stretch still to apply this beyond humanity and into the depths of the distant cosmos.

Perhaps multiple incarnations may be simpler, even if the idea is much more controversial among theologians today. Controversial or not, the benefits of multiple incarnations may be extensive. God is able to achieve intimacy with a range of creatures at various different times in many locations across the cosmos. This may make sense of why the universe is so vast and so old—God did not intend it to be for humans alone, but for a whole host of species, each of whom realize different facets of the divine being. As Aquinas noted, multiplicity may better represent the unbounded nature of God's power and love than unique singularity. Moreover creatures may best respond to face-to-face encounter with a God clothed in a recognizable form, rather than having the incarnation revealed to them indirectly. Tillich was one theologian who remained open to the idea, arguing that other worlds cannot be without the potential for salvation if salvation was something they required.

Most theologians who entertain the idea of multiple incarnations stress that it is possible but ultimately unknowable. Davison argues that the best way to approach the issue of multiple incarnations is *not* to use our incarnation as too specific a template. In order to remain properly Chalcedonian, we should not think that Jesus Christ, the first-century Palestinian Jew, appears on all other planets and dies for the sins of all other intelligent, rational, moral species. The idea that the human Jesus planet-hops, dying and rising again in various celestial locales, is the wrong way to think about multiple incarnations. Instead, we ought to think of other incarnations as involving the hypostatic union of God the Son to other forms of created embodiment, the consequences of which may well play out very differently across the various worlds. Each of these would be different creaturely expressions of the divine form, fulfilling distinct revelatory and soteriological functions. As Davison writes, "to pick up the language of the Council of Chalcedon, they would have their own rational soul and body, of a different kind from Jesus."[28]

There are, of course, legitimate criticisms of a pluralistic approach to the incarnation. For example, it is not clear what happens to these incarnational beings in the afterlife—are they distinct persons, and can they communicate with each other? Moreover, how can God the Son exist in so many different forms while remaining one person? As

---

28. Davison, *Astrobiology and Christian Doctrine*, 253.

Brian Hebblethwaite argues, "we do not, in the eschaton, expect to be encountered by a group of divine Incarnations, themselves in theory capable of interpersonal relation."[29] You could be forgiven for thinking this idea makes a mockery of personal identity. It is difficult to see how two incarnated beings, each radically different from the other by virtue of being different species from different planets at different times in cosmic history, can be thought of as the same person (God the Son). If two objects or persons are one and the same, then they should have all the same properties. The current King of England and the late Queen Elizabeth II's eldest son are one and the same person: Charles III. Similarly, the morning star and the evening star are identical objects: the planet Venus. Two distinct incarnations would have different properties, however, including belonging to different species and living at different times in the universe's history. They could not coherently be thought of as two names for the same thing, as in the examples of Charles III or Venus. Metaphysics would struggle to make sense of these conflicting identity claims, leading critics of multiple incarnations to dismiss the idea as incoherent.

Davison warns against making critiques like this with great confidence. We do not know what it is like to be God, nor can we understand the nature of the divine personhood. Perhaps it does make sense for God to be united with multiple created beings and for these to meet in the eschaton. Those incarnated beings would not be identical persons—in fact they could not be, without losing their distinctive creatureliness. Instead, they could be thought of as distinct instantiations of creatureliness in union with divinity. Although this is hard to imagine, that does not mean it is impossible.

Doing Christology in the context of modern physics is challenging, not least because there are so many unanswered questions. As to their answers, we can only speculate. Although excellent work has been done in this area, so much remains to be explored. Problems persist for the Christian story when we consider other worlds containing rational, moral, and spiritual beings. As our technological capabilities advance, so must our theological imaginations. This topic is not going anywhere. In fact, I expect cosmic Christology to blossom into one of science and religion's most important research areas in the decades to come.

---

29. Hebblethwaite, "Impossibility of Multiple Incarnations," 329 (cf. Davison, *Astrobiology and Christian Doctrine*, 255).

FURTHER READING

Bertka, Constance M. *Exploring the Origin, Extent, and Future of Life: Philosophical, Ethical, and Theological Perspectives*. 1st ed. Cambridge: Cambridge University Press, 2009.

Crisp, Oliver D. "Incarnation." In *The Oxford Handbook of Systematic Theology*, edited by Kathryn Tanner, John Webster, and Iain Torrance, 160–75. Oxford: Oxford University Press, 2007.

Davison, Andrew. *Astrobiology and Christian Doctrine: Exploring the Implications of Life in the Universe*. Cambridge: Cambridge University Press, 2023.

Gregersen, Niels H., ed. *Incarnation: On the Scope and Depth of Christology*. Minneapolis: Fortress, 2015.

Moser, David. "Jesus' Preexistence and Incarnation." In *St Andrews Encyclopaedia of Theology*, edited by Brendan N. Wolfe et al., 2024. Online.

Torrance, Thomas F. *Space, Time and Incarnation*. London: Oxford University Press, 1969.

5

Salvation

THE CHRISTIAN DOCTRINE OF salvation is the final piece of the theological puzzle—once in place, the entire picture emerges. Christians understand the world as being created with a purpose in mind. That purpose is, among other things, for the created order and its creaturely inhabitants to be brought into deeper relationship with God. As such, salvation is the necessary corollary of the doctrine of incarnation and the final fulfillment of the doctrine of creation. The problem is, Christianity understands humanity and the world to be fallen. Whatever details one adds to the doctrine of fallenness, at its core it represents an alienation between God and the world that is the result of creaturely freedom. In other words, creatures used their freedom to turn away from God, bringing a profound separation between creature and creator that must be overcome.[1] Redemption, atonement, and salvation are all ways of understanding the overcoming of this separation to reach a state of unity and healing. For Christians, creation is continually striving toward this redemption. Christians also hope that this process of personal salvation can begin to happen during an individual's lifetime, even if its ultimate fulfillment must come at the end of the world after time itself has come to an end.

---

1. There are various ways this can be understood that do not rely upon a real, historical fall brought by an original act of disobedience committed by Adam and Eve. Perhaps, as humanity developed moral sophistication, we began to perform acts we knew to be wrong which created an ever-increasing gulf between humanity and God. Or perhaps fallenness is a necessary dimension of created existence.

For this reason, hand in hand with the doctrine of salvation goes eschatology, the study of final things. Through these two intertwined threads of theological reflection, Christianity teaches that God, by grace and mercy, extracts each redeemable sinner out of the depths of fallen existence, offering them the chance to live again. This second life, now eternal rather than finite, will redeem all that has gone before. The sinner and the God who saves them are reconciled at last, healing deep wounds that would be fatal if left untended. Essentially, Christianity teaches that following the death and resurrection of Jesus Christ—believed to be the second person of the Trinity, Son of God, and redeemer of humanity—each human being receives the potential to be saved. Whether this salvation occurs is up to God and up to them.

The terminology "salvation" and "eschatology" have extensive histories and a multiplicity of interpretations, which I am unable to go into here. For our present purposes, I will use "salvation" to refer to the process of saving an individual from sin, redeeming them, and reconciling them to God. Such salvation involves a process of chronological transformation, a change over time, and can occur both during this earthly life and in whatever lies beyond. "Eschatology," on the other hand, refers to the end times. It is concerned almost exclusively with what happens at the end of the universe, and the promises made by God about what, if anything, comes next. Although these two terms are profoundly intertwined, I will be considering them one after the other in this chapter. We will begin with the kind of salvation available during this earthly life, and then we will examine what salvation looks like after this life—indeed, the cosmos itself—is over.

There are many ways to frame a chapter on salvation and eschatology. I have chosen to use the physics of time as a focal point, as this has been a significant research area of mine in recent years. As well as writing my master's and doctoral dissertations on the topic, I have also published two books on time and salvation, *God, Salvation, and the Problem of Spacetime* (Cambridge University Press, 2022) and *Salvation in the Block Universe: Time, Tillich, and Transformation* (Cambridge University Press, 2024). I draw heavily on this research in this chapter.

Over and above my own personal interest in this area, time is the perfect scientific companion for understanding salvation and eschatology. Christianity teaches that salvation happens in this life (i.e., within time) and also after this life, when the cosmos will come to an end (i.e., at the end of time). Thus, in this chapter, we will examine soteriological issues that arise for understanding salvation as a transformation in time, both relating to the nature of this transformation and whether sin can be eliminated. Then, we will examine whether bodily resurrection and the transformation of this cosmos into a new creation is plausible given insights from contemporary physics. Einstein's relativity theories will provide the scientific framework within which these discussions will take place, as these are the theories that concern space and time.

PERSONAL SALVATION AS A TRANSFORMATION IN TIME

Special Relativity

Toward the end of the nineteenth century, physicists had allowed themselves to slip into a false sense of security. Immense achievements in the study of motion, electromagnetism, thermodynamics, and others besides led many physicists to believe that physics was almost over. Most serious problems had been solved, and the remainder of physics would be spent ironing out the details. They could not have been more wrong. While physics had its head turned, a young patent clerk was about to publish four papers that would change the scientific landscape forever. Without any professional ties to physics, the twenty-six-year-old Einstein's "wonder year" saw him prove the existence of atoms via a phenomenon called Brownian motion, introduce the idea of the photon, which pushed Max Planck's ideas further and truly kickstarted quantum mechanics, show the equivalence of mass and energy with his famous equation $E=mc^2$, and revolutionize our understanding of space and time with his special theory of relativity. Einstein later described this period of intense creativity as one in which a storm broke loose in his mind.[2]

The crisis that pushed Einstein to develop a new theory of space and time came about following physics' most famous, and unexpected, null result. A null result occurs when an experiment does not find the result it was looking for. If I want to see who has been stealing all the raspberries from my garden, and I suspect that it is the pack of squirrels that lives in the trees behind my house, I might set up a motion-triggered camera next to my raspberry patch and leave it overnight. Looking at the footage in the morning and seeing nothing at all would be a null result—my

2. Kumar, *Quantum*, 33–34.

experiment has discovered nothing, failing to prove the hypothesis I set out to test.

The null result in question was that of the 1887 Michelson-Morley experiment, which was designed to detect the existence of a substance believed to carry light waves throughout the cosmos dubbed the luminiferous aether. Light has two properties that led physicists to predict the existence of this ethereal substance. First was its speed. Maxwell's equations concerning electromagnetism show that the speed of light in a vacuum is constant, the value of which has since been labeled c. As the speed of light is constant, physicists believed that there must be some background structure, i.e., the luminiferous aether, against which the fixity of this speed could be measured. Second was light's wave-like nature. Because of the way light behaves, it was believed to be a wave, and waves require a medium through which to propagate. Sound waves cannot travel in a vacuum because they need a substance through which to move, but light can. As such, physicists very reasonably expected to discover this substance that could carry light waves and thus explain light's ability to travel through a vacuum.

Electromagnetic radiation (of which visible light is part) was believed to be a kind of stress in the aether analogous to stresses in solid, liquid, and gaseous materials that transmit sound waves. The idea for the experiment went like this: if such an aether exists, then it would function as some kind of background structure against which things have absolute motion, and it should be possible to detect motion through it. Think of it like the ocean—to measure how fast a submarine is moving, you need to know where in the ocean it started and where in the ocean it is now. The ocean is the substance through which the motion happens, and so also provides a backdrop against which distance and speed is measured.

Albert Michelson and Edward Morley designed an experimental device that measured the speed of light in perpendicular directions. What they expected was that the light would travel at different speeds dependent upon the Earth's motion through the aether, and this would both provide empirical evidence for the aether's existence and allow them to calculate the Earth's velocity relative to the aether. Light moving against the aether would travel slower, just as you would be slowed down if you were swimming through the ocean against the current. The result stunned the world. Michelson and Morley did not detect any variation in the velocity of light, meaning that there was no detectable aether. What could explain it? Fortunately, Einstein was only a few years away from developing his revolutionary solution that would usher in an entirely new understanding of space, time, and motion.

That solution was the special theory of relativity. Special relativity contains two postulates, or two key claims, from which the rest of the theory follows. The first, the *relativity principle*, claims that the laws of physics are invariant between inertial frames. In simpler language, the relativity principle claims that the laws of physics do not change depending on whether an observer is stationary or in uniform motion. An inertial frame is a coordinate system used to represent a particular observational perspective that is either at rest or moving uniformly. Inertial frames play an important role in understanding special relativity, and we will return to them shortly. The second postulate is the *light postulate*, according to which the speed of light in a vacuum is c, irrespective of the speed of the source.

In the previous scientific paradigm ruled by Newtonian mechanics, there is a tension between these two postulates. Velocity is cumulative, meaning that the velocity of light that is emitted from a moving source should have the velocity of the speed of light c + the velocity of the source. In other words, if I flash a torch out of the front window of a train, we should expect the light to move at a speed of c + the speed of the train. If the speed of light is not always c, however, then the relativity principle is violated, because there is an observational perspective from which a law of physics (the fixity of the speed of light) is broken. Within Newtonian mechanics, the light postulate and the relativity principle cannot both be true.

Einstein managed to reconcile these postulates by throwing out the rulebook on our understanding of space and time. The price we must pay for the relativity principle and the light postulate both being true is abandoning the Newtonian commitment to absolute time, which passes at a uniform rate for all observers, and absolute space, which acts as an unmoving and unchanging receptacle. To ensure that observers always agree that the speed of light in a vacuum is c, then they cannot always agree on either *time* or *distance*. Why? Because velocity is calculated by dividing the distance traveled by the amount of time that it takes: velocity = distance ÷ time. In simple terms, special relativity reveals that your measurements of distance, duration, and simultaneity will be dependent on your observational perspective (or, more technically, your reference frame). Although this mind-bending conclusion feels very counter intuitive, many experiments have since verified that it is indeed the case.[3] The reason we do not notice that distance and duration vary between observational perspectives is because it only becomes noticeable at speeds approaching the speed of light. Humans did not evolve to experience such speeds, so we hold the intuitive belief that space and time are fixed absolutes. We are wrong.

These features of the theory are best explained using a thought experiment that Einstein himself developed. The thought experiment begins by asking the reader to imagine two observers moving relative to each other; let's call them Alice and Joe. Alice is on a train traveling from west to east at a significant fraction of the speed of light, while Joe sits on a platform at a station somewhere along Alice's route. Just as the train passes Joe, two bolts of lightning strike, one a mile to the west and one a mile to the east. An imperceptibly short time later, Joe *sees* both flashes simultaneously. Presuming that he knows how far he is from each flash of lightning, Joe concludes that the lightning strikes *happened* simultaneously. Is he correct?

Alice, however, sees the eastern lightning strike *before* she sees the western strike. Joe thinks he has a simple explanation for this discrepancy. Because Alice is in motion, the light coming from the west had to catch up with her, whereas she is approaching the light coming from the east. This explanation only works, however, if we have grounds to suppose Joe is really at rest and Alice is really in motion. But Joe is not really at rest. He is sitting on the surface of the Earth, a planet turning on its axis as it hurtles through the solar system which is itself on a vast journey through the cosmos. From Joe's perspective, he is at rest and Alice is in motion, but this is not the only way to look at things. In fact, according to special relativity, there is no objective, observer-independent, way of deciding between these divergent perspectives. Alice is just as justified in believing that the lightning flashes did not occur simultaneously as Joe is in concluding that they did. Each is describing the situation from the standpoint of their particular perspective—more technically, their frame of reference—and there is no feature of special relativity, or, as far as we know, any physical theory, that would allow us to say who is right and who is wrong. Because of this, Einstein concluded that the relation of simultaneity is relative. There is no absolute simultaneity in the universe.

---

3. Kennedy and Thorndike, "Experimental Establishment of the Relativity of Time"; Ives and Stilwell, "Experimental Study of the Rate of a Moving Atomic Clock."

From this it follows that an observer's measurement of temporal duration is frame-dependent, meaning it is shaped by their observational perspective (their location, whether they are in motion, etc.). Highly specialized experimental set-ups have since demonstrated that atomic clocks, the most finely tuned and accurate clocks we have, run at different rates when one is accelerated and the other remains stationary. This phenomenon, known as time dilation, leads to the counter-intuitive twin paradox. The twin paradox is paradoxical because of (very reasonable) assumptions we hold about twins being, and always remaining, the same age. But, in an advanced era of space travel, twins could be separated by sending one off in a spaceship traveling at a significant fraction of the speed of light and allowing one to remain on Earth. The effect this kind of motion has on time (particularly as it approaches the speed of light) leads to the paradoxical result that when the twins reunite, one will have aged much more than the other. Relativity shows that it is possible for twins to age at different rates because time does not flow at a uniform rate across the cosmos.

A subsequent development in our understanding of special relativity was introduced by Hermann Minkowski, who realized that space and time ought to be unified into a more fundamental substance: spacetime. While observers will disagree on how they measure duration and distance, i.e., time and space, the *spacetime interval* between events is fixed. There are many ways to slice the spacetime interval pie into distances and durations, but no matter how the pie is sliced its total size does not change. Time and space are not fixed, but four-dimensional spacetime is. This leads to a fascinating philosophical phenomenon known as the spacetime interpretation of special relativity, which describes the metaphysics of the cosmos in terms of a "block universe." It is this block universe that has important implications for salvation.

The Block Universe

To understand the block universe, we need to take a brief detour through the philosophy of time. Contemporary philosophy of time, at least that which sits in the analytic tradition, dwells in the long shadow cast by a 1908 article by J. M. E McTaggart entitled "On the Unreality of Time." In this seminal piece of philosophy, McTaggart argued that time must flow, by definition, but that a flowing understanding of time is plagued by an irresolvable contradiction. Therefore, according to McTaggart, time is unreal. His argument has been written on by many, myself included,[4] and it is not necessary for me to repeat this here. What is useful for this chapter is the conceptual architecture that McTaggart introduced and that has gone on to sit at the foundations of temporal metaphysics ever since.

McTaggart separated out three different ways that one could formulate a temporal series out of moments or events, calling these the A-series, B-series, and C-series. Contemporary philosophy of time has built these into more substantial theories of time, the A-theory, B-theory, and C-theory, each of which takes one temporal series to provide a fundamental description of time. Though there are several A-theories, all are committed to the following three claims:

1. Time is dynamic in that it passes or flows.
2. Events possess the objective tensed properties, past, present, and future.
3. There is an objective and universal present moment we call now.

The most popular A-theory among Christian philosophers writing on this issue is *presentism*, a view that is committed to the existence of the present only. Presentists believe in an objective, universal, present moment, and claim that only things simultaneous with this present moment (i.e., things that are happening "now") exist. The past is gone, and the future does not yet exist. Presentism has the most diminished ontology of all the A-theories because it claims fewest things exist. In other words, presentism paints the smallest picture of reality.

An alternative A-theory, the *growing block*, agrees that the future does not exist, and the present is sharp as a razor's edge. In contrast to presentism, however, it is committed to the concrete existence of the past. Growing block theorists argue that there is a "block" of past and present moments that is continuously growing as ever more present moments come into existence. A third A-theory, the *moving spotlight* view, claims that all moments of time (the past, present, and future) exist, but that some moments are privileged. As a spotlight might move across a dark street illuminating each house in turn, so too does flowing time pick out "nows" which are then objectively present, and this is what it means for time to pass. These are the three A-theories: one that is committed to the existence only of the present, one that is committed to the existence of

---

4. Qureshi-Hurst, *Salvation in the Block Universe*, chapter 1.

the present and the past, and one that is committed to the existence of the past, present, and future.

The B-theory, on the other hand, contains less variation for the simple reason that a B-theory denies that time passes and affirms the existence of the past, present, and future. It makes the following three claims:

i. Time is static in that it does not pass or flow.

ii. Events do not possess objective tensed properties (instead, time is fundamentally tenseless).

iii. All moments of time always exist.

What this means metaphysically is that all moments in time exist in a four-dimensional "block," which is sometimes referred to as the *block universe*. It is helpful to think about the block universe like an iceberg, with each frozen molecule of water representing a moment in time. All the moments exist, and their position is fixed. If you were a mammoth frozen in the ice, from your perspective there would be ice ahead of you (the future), ice around you (the present), and ice behind you (the past). Crucially, though, what counts as past, present, and future is not objective or observer-independent. Instead, it is dependent on your own position. A mammoth frozen in a different location would be equally real even if they were in your "future," and from their perspective some of your "future" would be their "past." An A-theory, on the other hand, described time like a flowing river where what counts as "past," "present," and "future" is continuously changing as the river flows.

The C-theory is also committed to the existence of a block universe. It differs from the B-theory by denying that time has any particular direction. Rather, it makes just as much sense to "read" the story of the universe as beginning at the Big Bang (as we always do) as it does to begin describing the universe with the Big Crunch or heat death and closing with the Big Bang. As long as the events aren't in the incorrect places relative to each other (e.g., if the moon landing were to be erroneously placed between the First and Second World Wars), then you have captured everything essential about the nature of time.

With this conceptual framework in hand, we are able to return to special relativity. A couple of interpretations of special relativity are available, but the one that dominates scientific circles is the so-called spacetime interpretation (or, Einstein-Minkowski interpretation). The spacetime interpretation does not commit itself to the existence of anything outside the bare bones of the theory, meaning it endorses the following claims:

a. Space and time are distinct dimensions of the more fundamental entity spacetime.

b. Absolute simultaneity relations do not exist within the special theory because they do not exist in the world.

c. One's measurement of duration and length is determined by one's frame of reference.

These claims place the spacetime interpretation of special relativity firmly with the block universe camp. The reasoning is simple: all A-theories are committed to the existence of an absolute, universal present moment that divides the real present from the not-yet-real future. But according to special relativity, there is no such thing as objective simultaneity (recall Joe and Alice observing lightning). If there is no clearly defined present moment, then it cannot be a robust boundary between the actual present and the potential future.

The take-home points from this rather technical philosophical discussion are as follows. Special relativity leads us to believe in a block universe in which all objects exist in a four-dimensional spacetime continuum. In the block universe time does not pass, because the future and past are as real as the present. The block universe raises two problems for the Christian doctrine of salvation. The first problem relates to the idea that salvation requires a transformation in time. The second problem relates to the idea that salvation requires the elimination of past sin. As we shall see, neither of these are straightforward if the block universe is true.

Personal Salvation

There are many different formulations of the doctrine of salvation, each of which characterizes the nature and scope of salvation differently. For example, the Orthodox tradition understands salvation to be a form of *theosis*, a process by which an individual becomes united with God by participating more fully in the divine being. An individual who has undergone *theosis* has fundamentally changed their very nature, with the word itself meaning "being made of God" or "becoming God." Other traditions may understand salvation to be less about the transformation of the individual into God and to be more about overcoming a separation that exists between God and fallen humanity. Salvation, on this understanding, is about reconciliation. Yet another way of conceptualizing salvation is that it involves being cleansed of sin, a corrupting substance that is brought about both by humanity's fallen state generally and by specific wrongful acts committed during one's lifetime. Regardless of the precise formulation of salvation, Christianity is committed to the idea that individuals become saved by undergoing some kind of transformation in their relationship to God, in the very core of their being, or by being cleansed of sin (most likely, it will be a combination of these). A common theme that crops up in all doctrines of salvation is that salvation is the search for authentic life.

Broadly, the doctrine of salvation assumes that both humanity and the world are distorted, self-destructive, and falling short of our true potential. For Christians, salvation or atonement depends upon a particular moment in time and space at which point Jesus of Nazareth was crucified on a cross. This event is believed to be the centerpoint in human history, dividing the fallen old creation from the eschatological promise of a new creation made possible by Jesus' resurrection. We will arrive at eschatology later. For now, let us focus on how to understand a personal transformation in the block universe.

The Problem of Personal Salvation

The first problem spacetime poses is that personal salvation requires a temporal transformation. In other words, if someone is saved then they have undergone a transformation in time from being "fallen" to being "saved." The Bible describes such a transformation as becoming a new creation: "if anyone is in Christ, he is a new creation. The old has passed away; behold, the new has come" (2 Cor 5:17). As Richard Holland writes, "These passages and others indicate a finality: a transformation achieved through the work of Christ that brings about a new standing before God."[5] For salvation to have occurred, something fundamental must have changed about that person. They are utterly new, both in their status as "saved" and in their relationship to God.

The problem is, in the block universe, it is not clear exactly how an objective change is to occur. When we say some object or person has changed, what we tend to mean is that they possess incompatible properties at different times. For example, perhaps I have blonde hair on

5. Holland, *God, Time and Incarnation*, 183–84.

Monday and choose to dye it brown on Tuesday. When the date (and thus the time) changes from Monday to Tuesday, and the event of my dying my hair takes place, my hair changes from blonde to brown. Without the passage of time, or the possibility of genuine newness entering reality, our ordinary understanding of this kind of change is harder to accommodate.

In the block universe, every moment and their corresponding events exist, somewhere out there in the four-dimensions of spacetime. The beginning of the universe is just as real as the end of the universe, and my birth is just as real as my death. The fact that I remember one and not the other is a consequence of psychology and my *position* in the block universe; it does not mean that the past is real and the future is not. What this means for the hair dying example, and of course for salvation as well, is that Monday and Tuesday are equally real. From the tenseless perspective of the block universe, I have both blonde and brown hair. There is no objective or observer-independent way to say whether my hair is *actually* blonde or brown, because each exists tenselessly at different points in the four-dimensional extension of myself.

One way to understand this is that I have temporal parts, one of which has blonde hair and exists on Monday, and one of which has brown hair and exists on Tuesday. Let's explore what this idea means for salvation. If all of my temporal parts exist, then it must be the case that if I am saved, or if a process of salvation begins to occur during my lifetime, then I have both fallen temporal parts and saved temporal parts. If both are equally real, how can we ever really say an individual has been transformed from being fallen to being saved? The fallen parts are not really gone, making the idea of personal salvation as a total transformation hard to recover.

We have reached the crux of the issue: the Christian doctrine of salvation appears to require that individuals undergo, or at least begin to undergo, an objective change in this lifetime. The problem is, in the block universe nothing new comes into being and nothing old fades away. An individual's sinful, fallen temporal parts exist for as long as the block universe does and are just as real as any subsequent, saved parts. To return to the metaphor I used earlier, the sinful parts remain frozen in the iceberg of the block universe. They cannot be thawed out and discarded, meaning the individual has not really changed. It does not seem that the block universe can support Christianity's central claim that individuals can become a "new creation," with God transforming their lives from being fallen to being saved. In other words, if you have a block universe, can you have salvation? There are a number of possible solutions to this problem, but here I want to consider two. The first is to reject the block universe, and the second is to reject the idea that salvation requires an objective change in time.

Solution 1: Reject the Block Universe

Above, I explained that the spacetime interpretation of special relativity is the interpretation that is favored in the scientific community, and is also popular with philosophers of time. Nevertheless, it is not the only option available. The block universe, also known as the B-theory or eternalism, is less popular with contemporary theists whose work focuses on the relationship between time and theology. It is fair to say that theists are divided on issues of temporal metaphysics, and that there are firm supporters of a dynamic A-theory like presentism and a static B-theory like the block universe.

One notable figure in the first camp is William Lane Craig, who argues that Christians ought to be A-theorists. The A-theory is the theory of time that is most compatible with a temporal God. We touched on some theological reasons why modern theists are moving toward a temporal understanding of God in the previous chapter. Craig names his approach the "neo-Lorentzian" interpretation because it is inspired by the work of physicist Hendrik Lorentz, who argued for the existence of an invisible aether that could act as a background structure that functions as an absolute frame of reference. As special relativity deals a heavy blow to the plausibility of the A-theory, Craig was motivated to develop an alternative interpretation that builds on the defunct aether theory by trying to find some other background structure against which some kind of "absolute time" can be recovered. Craig is a committed presentist who has devoted much of his career to defending the A-theory through his contributions to a wide variety of philosophical and theological debates. Craig's argument for his neo-Lorentzian interpretation of special relativity has three essential features.

The first is a commitment, shared with Lorentz, to the existence of some form of background structure that functions as a preferred frame of reference. If such a reference frame exists, then there is an objective, observer-independent way to say whether two events are simultaneous or not. If absolute simultaneity is recoverable, then it once again makes sense to claim that there is an objective "now" which gives rise to the future and from which the past slips out of being. Craig suggests a range of possibilities that might replace the defunct luminiferous aether, but none of these have yet been taken up with any great enthusiasm by scientists working in this area.[6]

The second component of Craig's argument invokes the Newtonian distinction between absolute, metaphysical, time on the one hand, and relative, physical, time on the other. Craig argues time dilation (that gives rise to the twin paradox and indicates that there is no absolute universal passage of time) is actually only a feature of physical, local time. There is, Craig maintains, absolute, metaphysical time, which exists in the mind of God and is perhaps also echoed in something called "cosmic time." Cosmic time is the temporal metric of the entire universe. It imagines the universe as a whole is a frame of reference and claims that there is an objective fact of the matter about exactly how much time has passed since the Big Bang from the universe's perspective. This metric can give us absolute time, according to Craig and several others who want to recover the A-theory for theological reasons. Although there are some arguments to this end, I have argued elsewhere that they are ultimately unconvincing.[7]

Craig's third point is theological. God, he argues, must be temporal for theological reasons, and a temporal God only makes sense in a universe in which time flows. In claiming that God is temporal, as we saw in the previous chapter, theists are claiming that God is *within* the flow of time. This means that God is subject to the passage of time, experiencing the unfolding of world history as it occurs. God is everlasting, existing at every moment of created time, rather than eternal, existing outside of time altogether. Supporters of such a view argue that a temporal God is more intimately connected to creation. A temporal God can act in the world because he is part of the temporal ordering of the world. It is hard to imagine a timeless God acting in the world because an act in the world happens in time, and it is precisely this being in time that the timeless God lacks. While classical theologians were aware of this issue and sought to address it, many contemporary divine temporalists are increasingly confident that this problem cannot be solved and that divine action in time is incompatible with an atemporal God.

6. Craig, *God, Time and Eternity*, 165.
7. Read and Qureshi-Hurst, "Getting Tense About Relativity."

A second reason one might want to endorse a temporal understanding of God is because this view makes more sense of the scriptural depictions of God as a person with a history that is tied up with his chosen people. God does not seem, in the Bible, to be detached and atemporal. Rather, he seems to be personal and involved in the temporal unfolding of historical events. A third reason one might want to be a temporalist is because of the incarnation. Some theologians have argued that if one trinitarian person was temporal, they all must be. It is for these reasons that Craig argues for presentism, arguing that the best option for the theist is to endorse a neo-Lorentzian interpretation of special relativity.

Problems persist with both Craig's scientific and theological claims, which make this debate far from settled. In a review of Craig's neo-Lorentzianism, Yuri Balashov and Michel Janssen offer a comprehensive assessment of the scientific viability of neo-Lorentzian special relativity, and show "how forcefully the physical evidence militates against such a return to the days before Einstein."[8] In effect, they argue that reinterpreting special relativity in a framework of Newtonian spacetime contradicts the vast amount of physical evidence, amassed over the last century, that supports the spacetime interpretation. They criticize Craig on several very technical points, which we need not detail here, but their conclusion is that there is simply not enough evidence to abandon the spacetime interpretation for Craig's neo-Lorentzian alternative. The fact that Craig's proposal has made little impact on those working in physics and the philosophy of physics also shows that it leaves many experts unconvinced. While this in and of itself is not enough of a reason to reject it—arguments from consensus are typically rather weak—it does encourage us to ask why expert opinion has not shifted in favor of Craig's proposal.

The theological problems are primarily those raised by the idea of a temporal God. While divine temporality has become rather popular in recent years, it was not the majority view throughout most of the Christian tradition. By far the more popular (though not universally accepted) view was that God was eternal and atemporal. We considered some arguments for divine timelessness/atemporality in the previous chapter. Philosopher Brian Leftow offers a further argument against the temporal God that draws upon relativity. Special relativity teaches us that space and time are actually united by the more fundamental spacetime. What this means is that anything that has a temporal location has a spatial

---

8. Balashov and Janssen, "Review: Presentism and Relativity," 330.

location. But we know that God is non-spatial; he has no physical body and transcends the physical world. The argument, then, is as follows:

(1) God is an immaterial substance.
(2) Immaterial substances are not in space. So,
(3) God is not in space. . . . But,
(4) according to relativity theory, anything that is in time is also in space.
Therefore,
(5) if relativity theory is correct (in essentials), then God is not in time.
(6) Relativity theory is correct (in essentials). So,
(7) God is not in time. So,
(8) God is timeless.[9]

According to Leftow, this gives us good reason to accept a timeless God. From the previous discussion, it is not abundantly clear that Craig's rejection of the block universe is scientifically or theologically compelling. Nevertheless, this is an extremely vibrant area of philosophical, scientific, and theological debate, and spirited arguments continue about all these matters. Some readers may find Craig's argument more compelling than I do. If you do not, there is a second solution to the problem of salvation in the block universe.

Solution 2: Salvation as Subjective

An alternative approach to solving this problem was the subject of my master's and doctoral dissertations, several peer-reviewed articles, and my second book, *Salvation in the Block Universe*. In these works, I developed an approach to understanding a salvation-transformation that is compatible with the block universe. The essence of this argument is that the best way to think about salvation in the block universe is as a *subjective* transformation, rather than an objective one. The long version of the argument is philosophically technical and requires a lot of groundwork. Space restrictions prohibit me from giving the full version here. Instead, I will sketch out the essence of the argument and leave readers to decide whether this initial form sounds plausible.

Despite the fact that the block universe does not contain temporal passage of the kind the A-theorist thinks is essential to time, we do seem

9. Leftow, *Time and Eternity*, 272.

to experience time flowing from one moment to the next. We watch our reflections age over the years, we feel the movement of rainwater as it trickles down our face, and we experience the sharp psychological shift from nervously anticipating a future event (like attending a job interview) and the relief we feel when the event is over and has gone well. There is something dynamic about our ordinary experience. Indeed, it is precisely this quality of our subjective experience that makes A-theorists so convinced that time must actually pass.

B-theorists and supporters of the block universe have developed several proposals that try to explain why our temporal experience is dynamic if time itself is not. Some proposals look at other areas of perception and argue that static images can generate dynamic perception (like magic-eye images); others argue that immediate memory plus current experience generates something in the mind that feels like temporal passage, although it is not. Philosopher Adolf Grünbaum offers one such proposal. Grünbaum, along with several philosophers since, compares temporal properties like nowness with sensory properties like color. These properties are mind-dependent. Color does not objectively exist; it is a consequence of particular wavelengths of light being reflected off objects and processed first by our retina and then by our brains. The wavelengths of light are objectively real, as are the objects that reflect them, but the color they appear to us is constructed in the mind. Philosophers call these kinds of properties secondary qualities and point out that we could all experience them slightly differently. What I see as red you might see as pink, orange, or even blue. There is no way to know for sure, because we cannot get inside each other's heads. Secondary qualities have an inescapably subjective element, because they depend on conscious experience. Similarly, Grünbaum argues that the mind constructs temporal passage out of the static events of the block universe.

Grünbaum also denies that presentness exists mind-independently, as there is no flow of time to make it mind-independently real. Instead, presentness or nowness are no more than mental representations. It is when we go from experiencing one moment as *now* to another that the mind generates the illusion that time is passing. I argue that we can take the essence of this proposal, namely that we *experience* change from one state, moment, or event, to another, even if there is no objective change out in the world, and then apply it to salvation. Just as the mind constructs passage phenomenology (i.e., the experience of the passage of time) out of ordered events in the block universe, so too can the mind construct a salvation-transformation.

Does this mean that salvation is an illusion? Not necessarily. The events in the block universe are real, even if the flowing time that connects them is an illusion. Similarly, saved individuals go through a subjective, psychological, qualitative change, which for them both constitutes and provides evidence for personal salvation. On this view, conscious awareness plays a highly important role in creating the type of change required to transform an individual's life from a state of fallenness to a state of salvation. My proposal for how salvation might work in the block universe is as follows: individuals freely choose to perform certain actions which lead to an authentic, soteriologically directed, life.[10] God can be understood as saving them in response, or at least beginning the process by which they will become a new creation. The saved state they then enter into *feels* new, even if their earlier, fallen, temporal parts still exist.

The philosopher Robin Le Poidevin also examines a similar kind of problem, which he puts as follows:

> With no passage of time, there is no scope for any change in what is real. For "real" is not similarly perspectival. On this theory, then, the Atonement, if real at any time, is real with respect to all time: its reality does not change over time. It seems that we are left with a choice between two uncongenial possibilities: (i) since the Atonement is at all times part of reality, and since the Atonement is sufficient for restoring our relationship with God for all time, then at no time is God unreconciled to humanity; (ii) since the sin that broke our relationship with God is at all times part of reality, and since that sin separates us from God, then at no time are we reconciled to God.... Either way, there is no change from fallen to redeemed state for man.[11]

If a state exists in the block universe, it does not come into or go out of existence. It always exists. But salvation requires an objective change that leaves sin objectively in the past, perhaps even eliminating that sin altogether, bringing about a *new* relationship with the divine. Le Poidevin's solution is to appeal to the directionality of time, specifically asymmetrical relations of cause and effect. What matters is that my fallen parts exist *before* my saved ones, and that there is some causal relation between Christ's atoning act and the existence of my subsequently saved

---

10. This kind of freedom would have to be compatibilist in nature (i.e., compatible with determinism).

11 Le Poidevin, "'Once for All': The Tense of the Atonement," 189-90.

parts. For Le Poidevin, because my sinful temporal parts are causally prior to my saved parts, it makes sense to say that I have undergone a progressive soteriological transformation *from* fallen *to* saved. While this does not solve the problem of the elimination of past sin, it does appeal to the temporal structure of the block universe to make sense of my later, saved parts taking priority over my earlier, fallen parts.

In my own view, an individual in the block universe can undergo a qualitative, experiential change from fallen to saved by possessing the properties associated with each state at different times. As they experience these properties successively, they experience this as robust change. This is analogous to the experience of time as robustly passing, despite neither robust change nor robust passage being mind-independently or objectively real. Nevertheless, on this view it remains the case that your past sinful parts are not gone. They may *seem* gone from your later temporal parts' perspective, but from a God's eye perspective those sinful parts remain. For some theists, this is not good enough. Salvation must require the elimination of past evil. This brings us to the second problem for personal salvation in the block universe: the problem of persisting sin.

The Problem of Persisting Sin

Scripture identifies the root of sin as Adam and Eve's first disobedience, the consequences of which are passed down throughout human history (Gen 2–3). Christian doctrine that has been constructed upon these scriptural foundations teaches that sin infected human nature, like rot from a single apple quickly causing the whole box to fester. In the very broadest terms, sin is that from which individuals are saved. Sins (plural) are the morally objectionable acts an individual performs; these may indicate that the individual is affected by sin (singular).

If a block universe is the right way to understand the ontology of spacetime, then it follows that all your temporal parts eternally exist. You are best thought of as a four-dimensional "worm" that is extended across all the events in your spatiotemporal lifetime. If you have fallen temporal parts in the block universe (which Christianity claims is the case for everyone), then you always have fallen parts, even if those parts are in your distant past. These cannot be truly left behind, even if you do possess subsequent saved temporal parts. While they may *seem* left behind from the perspective of your later parts, as per the argument I discussed in the previous section, this is only subjectively the case. Your four-dimensional ontology cannot change, and so your fallen parts remain as much a part of you as any other parts. This seems to lead to the striking conclusion that sinners cannot really change, and past sin or evil can never be eliminated. Even if sin is, from the perspective of the saved individual, in their past, it is still real and visible from God's perspective. For God, sin is an everlasting part of creation.

R. T. Mullins raises this problem for four-dimensional models of time, arguing that in the block universe, God is *at best* an "evil balancer" and not an "evil defeater." He rightly points out that a core claim of Christian theology is that evil will cease to exist, and that the suffering of those who are redeemed will come to an end.[12] On the block universe, however, neither creation nor an individual's past temporal parts can be purged of evil, because the past always exists. If this is the case, then God is no longer an "evil defeater." His best hope is balancing or outweighing evil and suffering in the eschatological future; he cannot eliminate it completely. In fact, the view also raises a rather terrifying form of the problem of evil. If all your temporal parts exist, then the parts of you that suffered the worst events of your life are stuck in that moment, forever suffering. Such a prospect must make even the most confident block theorist shiver.

Andrew Hollingsworth develops this problem, arguing neither salvation nor eschatology are possible without the total elimination of sin and evil. Therefore, if you want evil to be eliminated, you have to be an A-theorist about time. In fact, Hollingsworth argues that you cannot be just any A-theorist. You must be a presentist, because any temporal ontology that is committed to the concrete existence of the past is incompatible with the elimination of sin and evil.[13] Hollingsworth returns us to Craig's position—you cannot affirm both the doctrine of salvation and the block universe. They are simply not compatible. The only solution, for theologians of this persuasion is rejecting the block universe outright and saving salvation itself.

The block-universe-supporting theist does have the option of biting the bullet here and agreeing that evil is not eliminated during this phase of creation. It is theologically plausible to claim that neither the sinner nor the world can be purged of sin until everything we know ends and is utterly transformed into a new creation. At this point, the block universe may be no more, and creation may instead resemble something currently

---

12. Mullins, "Four-Dimensionalism, Evil, and Christian Belief," 130.

13. Hollingsworth, "Eschatology, the Elimination of Evil, and the Ontology of Time."

unimaginable. Redemption may overthrow even time itself, leading to the release of all our suffering temporal parts from their unfortunate fate and purging creation of evil once and for all. Indeed, perhaps it is precisely because sin cannot be totally eliminated from this creation that it is appropriate to call it fallen. Only in the fully redeemed kingdom of heaven is sin no more.

It is safe to say that whether you adopt an A-theory or a B-theory of time, i.e., whether you are a presentist or a supporter of the block universe, you will face theological problems. The A-theory makes more sense of the elimination of past evils, but, as we explored in the chapter on the incarnation, it struggles with divine sovereignty and divine omniscience. Presentism is also more compatible with divine providence and the incarnation, as it is hard to imagine how a timeless God can remain timeless and also live a temporal life. Nevertheless, the block universe fits better with the Christian theological tradition's claims about God as eternal, viewing all events in time from an outside perspective, and being impervious to change of any kind. Perhaps the best route down which to travel is the one with the problems that seem to you less damning. But before you make such a decision, we must consider one last problem. This problem arises as a direct result of presentism in combination with cosmology's prediction that the physical universe will come to an end.

ESCHATOLOGY AND THE END OF THE UNIVERSE

Eschatology

Both theology and physics have fields of study devoted to studying the end of the universe, although they unsurprisingly focus on rather different facets of the issue. Theology has the subdiscipline of eschatology, the study of final things. Namely, death, judgment, heaven, hell, and the end of this iteration of creation. Christianity teaches of a creator God who brought the universe into being for a divinely intended purpose. That purpose is believed to be, in part, for the universe and its inhabitants (maybe a select few or maybe all of them) to enter into a loving, covenantal, relationship with God. For this purpose to be realized, God decrees that humanity must live first in this created physical universe, which is fallen and sinful. During their earthly lifetime, humans exist in a state of estrangement from God. Indeed, this estrangement is the very mark of fallenness and sin. Without some kind of intervention, sin and fallenness would stand in the way of humanity ever developing a close relationship with God. As we saw in the previous chapter, Christianity's solution to this existential estrangement was provided by the soteriological work of Jesus Christ and the ongoing presence of the Spirit. Because of these, humanity is able to freely come to God and begin to undergo a process of personal salvation. Then, we die.

At some time in the future, Christians expect that God will bring the physical universe—this iteration of creation—to an end. At these endtimes, people (maybe a select few or maybe all of them) are raised from the dead and redeemed, reaching the eschatological goal of creation by being transformed into a "new creation" characterized by eternal life and unity with God. Essentially, those who are saved will experience something that was foreshadowed by Christ's resurrection; they will "be raised imperishable, and . . . shall be changed" (1 Cor 15:52). While the raised body will be new—and will therefore differ from the body you currently inhabit in various ways—it must nonetheless be continuous with that body in certain important respects. If not, then it is not *your* body, and *you* have not been raised. After being resurrected, humanity will live for eternity in the new creation in a state of reconciliation with God.

For the above to be true, the rest of the cosmos must also be redeemed, renewed, and resurrected. Romans 8:18–30, for example, speaks of the groaning of creation and the promise of eschatological redemption for the entire physical universe. Scriptural verses that discuss this draw parallels between the eschatological promise of bodily resurrection and the redemption of creation as a whole. In the words of John Polkinghorne, "the resurrection of Jesus is the seminal event from which the whole of God's new creation has already begun to grow."[14]

In summary, eschatology concerns the kind of salvation, redemption, and transformation that occurs at the end of time, after this earthly life is over. As Susanna Ticciati writes, "resurrection life is not continuation in time, but the consummation of a time that has been brought to an end. Its newness is not temporal newness. Its futurity is not temporal futurity."[15] It stands, therefore, in sharp contrast to the kind of salvation discussed in the previous section that happens within the temporality of this world. In what remains, I want to explore we might learn about Christian eschatology from the world of physics.

---

14. Polkinghorne, *God of Hope and the End of the World*, 113.
15. Ticciati, "Resurrection of the Dead," online.

General Relativity

I mentioned above that both theology and physics have branches of study devoted to the end of the universe. Theology has eschatology and physics has cosmology. Cosmology is the study of the entire cosmos, including its origin, structure, history, and future development. The intellectual backbone of modern cosmology is Einstein's general theory of relativity. Like the special theory before it, general relativity revolutionized how humanity understood one of physics' core concepts. In this case, gravity. In contrast to the Newtonian idea that gravity is a force between bodies, general relativity understands gravity as the warping of spacetime itself.

Grasping how the mass of celestial bodies curves spacetime can be achieved by visualizing a sheet that is held taut at the four corners. Imagine placing a bowling ball at the center. The mass of the bowling ball would stretch and warp the sheet around the curvature of its surface, and the heavier the ball the greater this distortion will be. If a smaller ball, say, a tennis ball, were rolled past it, the tennis ball's trajectory would be affected by the curvature of the sheet, perhaps even to the point that it would begin traveling around the bowling ball as though it is in orbit. The effect of the bowling ball's mass on the two-dimensional surface of the sheet resembles the warping of four-dimensional spacetime by massive celestial bodies like stars and planets.

Given that it concerns the warping of time itself, the strength of gravity affects observers' measurements of temporal duration. The reason for this is as follows. Light always takes the shortest path between two points. In flat spacetime, this is a straight line. In curved spacetime, however, light must travel a greater distance between the same two points. A helpful way of visualizing this is using the Earth. The distance you must travel between the north and south poles depends on whether you drill straight through the Earth in a straight line or if you travel along its curved surface. The straight line through the Earth's core is far shorter, so if there was such a hole between the north and south pole, that would be the quickest route between them. Instead, we must travel along the Earth's curved surface, a much longer route, which adds significantly to the time taken to travel between the two poles.

The shortest line between two points in curved space-time is known as a geodesic. In general relativity, light follows space-time geodesics, meaning that the greater the curvature of space-time the greater the distance light must travel. As we learned earlier in our discussion of special relativity, it is a law of nature that the speed of light is always *c*. Because speed = distance ÷ time, the fixity of the speed of light means that two observers will disagree on their measurements of distance and duration if they are at different places in a gravitational field. Essentially, time passes faster in flatter spacetime. The closer you are to a massive body, the greater the spacetime curvature and the slower time passes. This means that an astronaut visiting a massive planet would experience a much stronger gravitational force than her companions back on the spaceship. If the astronaut spent an hour on the planet and then returned to the spaceship much further out in the gravitational field, she could find that many years had passed for her colleagues who remained on the ship. This science-fiction-like idea, memorably explored in the Christopher Nolan 2014 film *Interstellar*, is actually founded upon robust relativistic physics. General relativity's equations have been used to study the universe as a whole and make predictions about its future, and these predictions raise questions about eschatology.

Freeze or Fry?

Astronomers have long gazed up to the heavens and recorded the behavior of the celestial bodies they find there. Our ability to map the night sky, to peer into its depths and discover some of the cosmos's many secrets, is utterly dependent upon our technological capabilities. Galileo Galilei was the first to use a rather rudimentary telescope to look up at the night sky. He was able to discover Jupiter's four largest moons and Saturn's rings, although he could not see the latter clearly and so described them amusingly as "ears." Since then, our scientific apparatus has greatly improved, and we now have the James Webb Space Telescope that allows us to capture images of the most distant reaches of our observable universe. We are staggeringly lucky to live in a time period with so many scientific discoveries at our fingertips.

The first discovery relevant to eschatology and the ultimate fate of the universe was Edwin Hubble's observations of universal expansion. These observations, in combination with the equations of general relativity, allowed physicists to predict how the universe will evolve over time. Currently, our best predictions reveal that at some point, many billions of years in the future, the cosmos will come to an end. The two primary contenders for how this will occur have been nicknamed *freeze* and *fry*.

Freeze refers to a phenomenon called heat-death, i.e., the idea that the universe will continue to expand and cool for the rest of time. Over many billions of years, galaxies will vanish over the horizon, stars will burn out, atoms will decay, and the universe will reach maximum entropy in a soup of black holes and radiation whose temperature tends toward absolute zero. This universe would be totally dark and extremely cold, and no life of any kind could hope to survive. *Fry*, also known as the Big Crunch, is essentially the opposite of the Big Bang. If *fry* occurs, the universe will eventually stop expanding and will begin collapsing back in on itself like a rubber band that is stretched and then released. Eventually, everything will be crushed in an almost infinitely hot, infinitely dense singularity.

Whether *freeze* or *fry* will come to pass is dependent on the value of the cosmological constant (Λ), namely the energy density of the vacuum of space. Insofar as it acts as a counterbalance to gravity, the cosmological constant will determine the ultimate fate of the cosmos. If Λ is weaker than some critical value, the universe's expansion will be halted by gravity, and all matter in the universe will be drawn back together. Inhabitants of planets will see their skies ablaze with the brightness of a thousand suns as galaxies rush toward each other at increasingly astronomical speeds. Eventually, everything that ever has or ever will exist will implode into a singularity. If Λ turns out to be stronger than a certain critical value, however, then gravity will be unable to overcome the expansion caused by the Big Bang. Instead, the universe will spend eternity expanding and cooling. The cosmos will decay into a radioactive soup of formless nothingness, and darkness will once again roll over the face of the deep.

Bodily Resurrection

The way contemporary science and religion scholars have approached eschatology has been shaped by what physics reveals about the future of the cosmos. Christian tradition affirms bodily resurrection, namely the idea that the chosen dead will be raised to live in the new creation. Although there is widespread agreement over this core principle, who is saved, how this happens, and what the new creation looks like have been hotly contested since the beginning of theology itself. One question is whether the new creation restores the world to the Edenic state enjoyed before the fall or whether it brings a kind of newness never experienced by creation until the eschaton. Will the raised body and the new creation be a continuation of the old, or something completely fresh and utterly different to what went before?

Answering such questions requires careful interpretation of scripture. Revelation 21:1 speaks of "a new heaven and a new earth, for the first heaven and the first earth had passed away," emphasizing radical newness and discontinuity with this world. Whereas in 1 Corinthians 15:52, Paul writes that "the dead will be raised imperishable, and we shall be changed," depicting continuity as well as transformation. If the scriptural promises are to be fulfilled, what comes next cannot be so different from this world that it no longer makes sense to say that *this* creation and *this* body have been saved. If there was radical discontinuity, the new creation and its inhabitants would be a second attempt at creating a world, rendering this creation obsolete.

Although physicists cannot be certain about whether the universe will decay or burn, recent findings indicate that the universe's expansion is accelerating, perhaps due to a higher value of Λ than previously expected. If correct, this swings the balance of probability in favor of *freeze*. Regardless of which scenario plays out, physics tells us that the universe *will* come to an end. Everything that has ever existed will die, decay, or be destroyed. Scholars of science and religion have rightly noticed that this raises problems for eschatology. Robert John Russell puts the problem this way:

> For those who defend the bodily resurrection . . . the challenge is obvious and severe: if the predictions of contemporary scientific cosmology come to pass ("freeze" or "fry") then it would seem that the universe will never be transformed into a new creation, that there will never be a general resurrection, and this, in turn, means that Christ has not been raised from the dead, and our hope for resurrection and eternal life is in vain.[16]

There are two distinct problems here. First, the end of the universe raises concerns about bodily resurrection because the end of the world brings the destruction of all human remains. Second, the end of the universe seems incompatible with the idea that the cosmos will be transformed into a new creation because there will be nothing left to transform. In my view, these catastrophic conclusions must be caveated: the problem only persists *if presentism is true*. The block universe,

---

16. Russell, "Eschatology and Physical Cosmology," 267.

and A-theories committed to the concrete existence of the past, allow all previous states of the universe to remain intact. The block universe resembles a novel, with the ending no more than the final page of the narrative. A novel does not vanish out of existence once the final sentence has been read; the characters remain imprinted on its pages ready for new readers to delve into their story. Similarly, each moment of time still exists in the block universe, meaning their inhabitants are preserved and able to be resurrected or redeemed. According to presentism, however, creation vanishes in its entirety when the universe ends, destroyed as it fades into the non-existent past. Every moment vanishes out of existence into nothingness as soon as it has happened, leaving nothing to be resurrected once decomposition is complete.

Both bodily resurrection and the possibility of a new creation are utterly integral to the Bible and the tradition, and therefore to Christianity as a whole. Are they still scientifically credible options? A range of positions are available, varying in accordance with the extent to which continuity is prioritized over discontinuity. If you emphasize discontinuity over continuity, you may favor the idea that the body is destroyed and only the soul is resurrected or lives on. New creation, on this view, is occupied by a sea of souls floating free of any physical form. If you do want some kind of body, but think the new creation and the resurrection should be discontinuous with this earthly existence, you may argue that the soul is preserved and placed into an entirely new body. Perhaps this will be a spiritual body, or perhaps it will be a physical body made of entirely new matter. If you favor continuity over discontinuity, you may endorse the idea that this earthly body, and the matter out of which it is made, is the exact body that is resurrected. Even if it undergoes a significant transformation, the matter matters. Let us explore these views in more detail.

The first option is that God saves only immaterial souls and leaves the physical bodies of this world to decay. The new creation would then be populated by disembodied souls. Would this be consistent with scriptural depictions of the resurrection and the kingdom of heaven? On the one hand, human beings are more than machines made of meat. We exist in a network of relationships, structure our lives in accordance with narratives that give us meaning and purpose, and we cannot truly understand ourselves without appreciating the social, familial, and interpersonal contexts that define us. What makes me *me* is more than my physical embodiment; it is my memories, my personality, my relationships, my regrets from the past, and my hopes and dreams for the future. It is possible that the kingdom of heaven could preserve all these important features without the need for a physical body.

On the other hand, our sense of self, even in the above respects, is inescapably physical. In other words, we are not just minds. We are *bodies*. And these bodies are important markers of our individual identities. They do not just house our minds; they also shape the way we interact with the world and the way we conceptualize ourselves. This applies in the relatively superficial contexts of self-expression like clothing choice, hair-dye, and makeup. It also applies in deeper and more authentic contexts of ethnic, religious, and cultural expressions of selfhood that form the basis of communities, both in terms of natural characteristics like skin color and culturally significant body modification like religious tattooing. Our bodies draw us together as markers of community and belonging (e.g., solidarity between those in oppressed racial groups), and our bodies can become sources of conflict (e.g., racist violence). In numerous ways that vary in how deeply they relate to our core sense of self, physical embodiment is a very important part of our identity.[17] This point is becoming increasingly recognized in the fields of psychology and science and religion.[18]

David Wilkinson considers these issues at some length and argues that the solution must be found in the biblical narratives. First Corinthians 15 discusses resurrection through the metaphor of a seed. In the words of Paul, the author of 1 Corinthians, "the body that is sown is perishable, it is raised imperishable; it is sown in dishonor, it is raised in glory; it is sown in weakness, it is raised in power; it is sown a natural body, it is raised a spiritual body" (1 Cor 15:42–44). It is clear that although Paul understood resurrection as a change in the raised person, the body that is raised must be the body that died. A tension plays out in the text between continuity and discontinuity, and when biblical scholars and theologians debate the meaning of this passage they often focus on this tension. It is a matter for debate whether Paul wishes to emphasize continuity between the "sown" sinful body and the raised glorious body, or whether he understands the raised body to be so different that it is utterly discontinuous with the original sinful body. The Gospels paint a diverse picture of resurrection, but each of them emphasizes the empty

---

17. Developments in science and religion are also indicating that the body is integral to religious life and religious knowledge. Tanton, *Corporeal Theology*.

18. Tanton, *Corporeal Theology*.

tomb. The same body that died is raised, even if it undergoes a significant transformation.

Biblical scholar N. T. Wright argues that the resurrection must be thought of as transformed re-embodiment.[19] Wilkinson, too, argues that the dualistic idea of a soul that can be separated from the body after death is both unbiblical and unscientific.[20] The Gospels emphasize the bodily continuity of the risen Jesus—he is recognized (John 20:19–20), he can be touched (Matt 28:9), and he remains scarred by his crucifixion (Luke 24:39). In these passages, it is clear that it was Jesus' slain, earthly body that rose again. The original body must not be abandoned if the resurrection of believers is to echo the resurrection of Christ. Despite this, there are also important discontinuities—Jesus appears to have new physical properties that allow him to appear in locked rooms without explanation (John 20:19–20) and that cause some to doubt whether it is really him (Luke 24:37). Whatever changes resurrected people undergo, losing a physical body cannot be one of them. Christianity must find a way to explain how our current physical bodies will be resurrected, and to what extent they will be transformed.

As such, the body must be part of the eschatological story. That still leaves open exactly what bodily resurrection entails. One way of understanding the resurrection of the body that side-steps the problematic demise of the physical cosmos is to hold that God simply re-creates each saved person in the kingdom of heaven, doing away with the need to use the earthly body in the formation of the heavenly body. The soul lives again, providing continuity between the dead and resurrected person, while the raised body is utterly new, providing discontinuity. Polkinghorne argues along these lines, defining the soul as a pattern of information: "amid its evolving change, each individual soul carries specific elements of its patterning which are the signature of its own abiding and unique personal identity."[21] This echoes the hylomorphism of Aristotle and Saint Thomas Aquinas, each of whom understand the human person to be a fundamental unity of matter (body) and form (soul). Matter is pure formless substrate; it is given its particular nature and characteristics by a formal organizing principle that is best understood as a soul. As Rebekah Wallace explains, "hylomorphic dualism is holistic in that it does not separate the human person into parts but presumes the whole

---

19. Wright, *Resurrection of the Son of God*.
20. Wilkinson, *Christian Eschatology and the Physical Universe*, 142–44.
21. Polkinghorne, *God of Hope and the End of the World*, 107.

functioning human in light of which the soul exercises capacities through the material cause of the body."[22]

Polkinghorne affirms that death is real death—the soul is encoded in the body and so dies with bodily decay—but the self can be preserved in divine memory (like a shadow) until it is given a new body in the new creation. Opting for an information-based approach may involve arguing that what is essential to the identity of human beings and the cosmos is the information we bear, not the physical stuff out of which we are made. One is able to overcome the threats posed by *freeze* or *fry* if information is what will be preserved because the destruction of the physical cosmos would not necessarily destroy the information-bearing patterns recalled in the mind of God. My soul, the information pattern that makes up my psychological existence, could be placed into a new and transformed body, like old software being uploaded to new hardware. Resurrection would resemble downloading all the photos, apps, and contact information from an old phone (backed up on the cloud) onto a new phone. Similarly, the physical cosmos could have its information-based essence preserved and imposed onto new, imperishable, materiality. The form remains the same, even if the matter does not.

While this may seem appealing, this reading of Polkinghorne comes at a high price. All the physical "stuff" that you, I, and our cosmos is made from is never redeemed, saved, or transformed. God *could* create new matter to bear the old information, but in so doing he would sever the interconnectedness of information and matter that underlies this creation. Not only would this do a disservice to Genesis's claims that our physical universe is good and beloved by God, it would also imply that our present bodies are unimportant and disposable. This is simply not the picture of resurrection painted in the Gospels. If my body decays, and this world passes out of existence, it is not clear in what sense have *I* been saved or *this* world has been redeemed. A potential route out of this problem is hoping that this transformation will take place before *freeze* or *fry* become reality. Only if the new "hardware" is made out of matter from this universe will claims about being raised (albeit in a body and world that is transformed) be possible.

The benefits of this are twofold. First, it would be well within the capabilities of an all-powerful God to transform the matter of this world into something utterly new and yet continuous with our present reality.

22. Wallace, "Does Embodied Cognition Support a Hylomorphic View of the Soul?," 2.1.

Second, it acknowledges that our physical bodies are forever in flux and do not contain a fixed set of particles for the duration of our lifetimes anyway. Minute by minute we gain and lose atoms, hour by hour matter from our bodies is expelled and replaced, and over the course of around seven years our bodies undergo total regeneration. It is almost certain that not a single particle that I was born with remains in my body today. For some people, it would not pose a problem if the resurrected body replaced every cell in one fell swoop. Others might take issue on the grounds that the regeneration we undergo during our earthly life is so gradual that we never notice it happening. While some cells in our bodies regenerate rapidly, others stay with us for many years. If God allows such a stark divide between the dead body and the raised body that nothing in the original body is preserved after resurrection, this should properly be called a *recreation* not a *resurrection*. The Bible is clear: humanity's eschatological fate will mirror the resurrection and ascension of Jesus, and Jesus' raised body bore the scars of his crucifixion. God raised the same body that suffered and died.

Perhaps, instead, one might follow Anthony Thiselton, who likens resurrection to a reversal of decay that results in purposeful flourishing, like the curing of a wasting disease.[23] On this type of view, the destruction of the physical universe does little to disrupt the eschatological process, because any decay that has taken place is able to be reversed or regenerated. What is resurrected may not be the exact same physical *stuff*, but the identity is restored via a process of regeneration. Whether this contains enough continuity, or is even possible if absolutely nothing of the original body remains to be regenerated, is a matter for debate.

Wilkinson himself turns, in the end, to the transformative power of God: "the key to resurrection and new creation is not the importance of the material but the action of the creator God."[24] Physical creation contains various kinds of matter, substance, and form, all of which, on the Christian worldview, are wholly dependent on God the creator. Wilkinson argues that the new body must similarly be thought of as totally dependent on God who has transformed it from a state of decay to a state of purposeful flourishing. Resurrection must be understood as a physical, embodied, resurrection that mirrors the resurrection of Jesus. If it is not physical, then the materiality of this world is relegated

---

23. Wilkinson, *Christian Eschatology and the Physical Universe*, 97–98.
24. Wilkinson, *Christian Eschatology and the Physical Universe*, 100.

to an inferior position, something that is not consistent with scripture. As such, Wilkinson rejects Polkinghorne's argument that we ought to focus our eschatological attention on the soul. The materiality of this world, along with human embodiment, are subjects of eschatological transformation. Nevertheless, the resurrection is not only about materiality and embodiment. It is also about the context, purpose, and mode of existence. For Wilkinson, we must not oversimplify a highly complex doctrinal commitment; we must recognize that resurrection will bring about stark discontinuity as well as continuity. What is preserved—matter, context, and relationships—must also be transformed. As will now be clear, when discussing bodily resurrection, the dialogue is incomplete without consideration of the context within which the body exists. That is, the cosmos itself.

New Creation

Eschatology is not only concerned with bodily resurrection; it is also concerned with what happens to the cosmos at the end of time. The Bible speaks of a new creation formed out of the old, mirroring what is promised to happen to our physical bodies. As with the discourse on bodily resurrection, tensions arise with regard to continuity and discontinuity. On the one hand, the new creation must possess new soteriological and eschatological properties that transform it. As Wilkinson writes, "the new creation is not simply the present order with a renewed humanity. There is something essentially 'new' both for the human community and the physical universe."[25] On the other hand, as John Polkinghorne reminds his readers, this second creation must not be viewed as "a second attempt by God to do what he had tried first to do in the old creation"; it must be "a divine redemption of the old."[26] In other words, whatever transformations it will undergo, it must still be *this* creation in some sense.

Wilkinson argues that the physical matter and its spacetime context of which our cosmos is made must be present in the new creation, even if they obey different physical laws or are somehow rearranged. If nothing of this world is present in the new creation, then it would not be a transformation of *this* creation. It is, instead, an alternative creation in which fallenness is absent from the beginning. Such an option is theologically

---

25. Wilkinson, *Christian Eschatology and the Physical Universe*, 86.
26. Polkinghorne, *Science and Christian Belief*, 167.

inconsistent. If God wanted to make such a world, he would have done so the first time around and would not have bothered making this one. The point of the new creation is to bring renewal and reconciliation to this world that God is professed to love, so continuity with this world must be preserved. Yet an overemphasis on continuity with this world is difficult to reconcile with scientific predictions about the ultimate fate of the universe.

Polkinghorne's solution is that the new creation will be *creatio ex vetere*—creation of something new out of old materials. While this cosmos was created *ex nihilo*, out of nothing, the new creation must reform the substance of this world into something glorious and reconciled completely to God. Such *creatio ex vetere* is dependent upon a delicate balance of continuity and discontinuity. If the new creation is also made out of matter, energy, forces, and spacetime, then continuity will be preserved. If new creation is made out of something entirely new, however, then it will exhibit discontinuity. One of the ways that the new creation could preserve continuity while being formed entirely of new matter is if the information of this cosmos were imposed onto new, spiritual, matter, as discussed in the previous section. This may still count as *creatio ex vetere*, as the information counts as the old material that is carried over. Polkinghorne favors discontinuity over continuity, however, writing that "the matter-energy of the world to come will certainly have to be radically different in its physical properties to the matter-energy of this creation."[27] Our world is constituted by change, bringing with it the benefits of the evolutionary process and the corresponding costs of death and decay. These processes allow creation to create itself, and so they are valuable to us in this aeon. Nevertheless, if the new creation is to be permanent rather than impermanent, then matter and energy will have to have an entirely different kind of organization. Moreover, in Polkinghorne's view, the new creation will be panentheistic. In other words, God will remain greater than new creation, but new creation will become part of God, almost like becoming God's body. Thus, the new creation will be constituted by a deep relationship between God, creation, and creatures.

Russell endorses Polkinghorne's argument that a total eschatological transformation will occur in the mode of *creatio ex vetere*, suggesting that this may well include "the radical transformation of the background conditions of space, time, matter, and causality, and with this, a permanent

---

27. Polkinghorne, "Eschatology," 39.

change in at least most of the present laws of nature."[28] Despite giving space for discontinuity between this creation and the next, however, Russell endorses a certain level of realized eschatology, namely the idea that the new creation is in some sense already manifesting in present creation. If the future can manifest concretely in the present, helping to imbue the present with spiritual significance, perhaps this might secure enough continuity between our world and the new creation.

Russell does not leave it there, however. He also wants to draw a distinction between what a scientific theory predicts will happen, and the metaphysical claim that this will in fact come to pass. Science can only make predictions in contexts where the laws of nature are not broken and where the cosmos proceeds into the future in step with how it has behaved in the past. Russell argues we do not have sufficient justification for believing that physics will correctly predict the end times. Nancey Murphy agrees, writing of the eschatological transformation of the cosmos, "we can say nothing of what this transformation will be like in scientific terms because all science is based on the way things are in this aeon."[29] Not only do we not know for certain that the laws of nature will continue to hold many billions of years into the future, but eschatology itself claims that God will end this current iteration of the cosmos himself anyway. Christians expect God to act in radically new ways that cannot be predicted by science. *Freeze* or *fry* might have been inevitable had God not acted at Easter to raise Jesus from the dead and bring the promise of a new eschatological future into the finite realm of creaturely existence. As God did act, however, these predictions can no longer be accepted with certainty.

It is fair to criticize this kind of response on the basis that it illegitimately disengages from the problem by denying that *freeze* or *fry* will occur. The entire enterprise of science and religion depends upon trust that the scientific disciplines provide valuable, accurate insights into the functioning of the natural world that can inform theological reflection. By pursuing this route, Russell risks cherry picking the parts of science that conform to his worldview and eschewing or denying those that do not. My own view is that this type of approach is best avoided. Physics ought to be taken seriously, unless there is overwhelming evidence

---

28. Russell, "Eschatology and Physical Cosmology," 296.
29. Murphy, "Immortality Versus Resurrection in the Christian Tradition," 81.

against doing so. Of course, the Christian may respond that the eschatological promise of a new creation is precisely such evidence.

Indeed, Wilkinson takes such a view, reassuring his readers that we should not be concerned with the distant annihilation of the universe. Recall the resurrection of Christ. First he was killed, then he rose again. What we learn from this is that one cannot rise if one does not die. Death and destruction are as integral to this process as the resurrection itself, and so physics is not in conflict with the hope of Christian eschatology.[30] Keith Ward echoes this, writing that "the Christian faith is wholly consistent with the idea that this space-time will have a temporal end. Christians do not hope for a continuation of this space-time, just as it is, forever."[31] Instead of being concerned with the end of the universe, they should welcome it as an opportunity for bringing the new creation into being. This echoes the Pauline proclamation in 1 Corinthians 15:35–36: "But someone will ask, 'How are the dead raised? With what kind of body do they come?' You foolish person! What you sow does not come to life unless it dies."

Has the Problem Been Solved?

As the previous discussion shows, the problems raised for eschatology by physics have been taken seriously by scholars of science and religion, and various solutions have been offered. The Christian reader may find the various responses to *freeze* or *fry* scenarios promising, grounded as they all are in the resurrection of Jesus. In my view, the solutions that focus on the cosmos itself are more encouraging than those that focus on bodily resurrection. As long as God does not wait so long to transform the cosmos into a new creation that everything has decayed and disappeared, enough materials will remain to secure the promised continuity between this world and the next. Particularly if this cosmos contains an element of realized eschatology, a foreshadowing of the new creation in this present world.

The arguments surrounding bodily resurrection leave much more to be desired. If presentism is true, then as soon as your body decays completely *nothing physical is left to be resurrected*. Because the past does not exist if presentism is true, the deceased body is doomed to fade out of

---

30. Wilkinson, *Christian Eschatology and the Physical Universe*, 187.
31. Ward, "Cosmology and Religious Ideas About the End of the World," 246.

existence with it. Astute readers will be aware, however, that presentism is a mixed blessing. It may significantly problematize bodily resurrection, but it does do an excellent job of solving the problem of annihilating past sin. If the past versions of you are gone, and you have been saved, then your past sin has vanished out of existence forever. The problem is, presentism quite literally throws the baby out with the bathwater. The sinner is annihilated along with the sin. Even if God acts before *freeze* or *fry* takes place, the bodies of most human beings will have decayed and disappeared into the non-existence of the past.

Despite the illuminating work of Russell, Polkinghorne, Wilkinson, and Ward, it remains the case that the inevitable end of the spatiotemporal universe raises problems for Christian eschatology that have not been wholly addressed. Perhaps, if the Christian wishes to retain the continuity between old and new creation that is essential to scripture, the predicted end of the physical universe should encourage them to reject presentism and favor a block universe view. While this raises the aforementioned problem of eliminating past sin, maybe that cannot take place until the end times anyway. At that point, and perhaps *only* at that point, fallenness will be overcome and sin will be defeated. Only if matter and spacetime continue to exist when the final events of the universe have unfolded can they be available to fulfill God's eschatological purposes.

FURTHER READING

Baron, Sam, and Kristie Miller. *An Introduction to the Philosophy of Time*. Cambridge: Polity, 2019.

Craig, William Lane. *Time and Eternity: Exploring God's Relationship to Time*. Wheaton, IL: Crossway, 2001.

Deng, Natalja. *God and Time*. Cambridge Elements in the Philosophy of Religion. Cambridge: Cambridge University Press, 2019.

Qureshi-Hurst, Emily. *God, Salvation, and the Problem of Spacetime*. Cambridge Elements in Problems of God. Cambridge: Cambridge University Press, 2022.

Russell, Robert J. "Bodily Resurrection, Eschatology and Scientific Cosmology." In *Resurrection: Theological and Scientific Assessments*, edited by Ted Peters, Robert J. Russell, and Michael Welker, 3–30. Grand Rapids: Eerdmans, 2002.

Ward, Keith. "Cosmology and Religious Ideas About the End of the World." In *The Far-Future Universe: Eschatology from a Cosmic Perspective*, edited by G. F. R. Ellis, 235–48. Philadelphia: Templeton Foundation, 2002.

Wilkinson, David. *Christian Eschatology and the Physical Universe*. London: T&T Clark, 2010.

Conclusion

WE HAVE NOW ARRIVED at the end. Throughout the previous pages, we have traversed the complex and variegated landscape of theology and physics. We have seen how the Christian story is structured in a narrative arc, beginning with creation and directed purposefully toward salvation. Theology also describes a universe designed for life to flourish and a God who acts within that universe in terms of providence and through the incarnation. Both humanity and the wider cosmos are believed to be fallen, and so both require redemption.

How should we understand all this in the modern world? These are ideas that have been crafted, honed, and reimagined over the two thousand years since Jesus' lifetime. Modern physics, with its insights about space, time, matter, and energy, provides yet more impetus to revisit and revise certain areas. As long as core Christian claims are not threatened, this can be a fruitful and mutually beneficial relationship. Without prompting from science, we would still believe that the sun revolved around the Earth and the universe itself was less than ten thousand years old. Keeping the two books metaphor in mind, Christians can be confident that science can provide an alternate route to understanding God. Surely, if there is a creator, then his handprint must be embedded in his creation.

That being said, modern physics and Christian theology do not fit together perfectly. We have covered some examples in the preceding pages. Many areas of tension remain, and more theological work is required to address these if the Christian is to be confident that their worldview is wholly scientifically credible. We must remain open to the possibility that this may not end up being possible.

At the outset, I was clear that I am not in the business of defending religion from scientific critique, nor am I interested in dismantling religion using scientific tools. The purpose of this book was to provide readers with the knowledge to make those sorts of decisions for themselves. We have seen that there are areas of deep synergy between Christian theology and modern physics, and we have seen undeniable tensions. No sound bite can be given about the compatibility of theology and modern physics. I hope you will close this book with an appreciation of how complex this relationship is, and has always been. I also hope that you are now armed with the tools to continue to interrogate how knowledge of the physical cosmos should shape the spiritual lives of human beings, and vice versa.

We are meaning-making creatures—each of us is searching for greater understanding. Religion and science are humanity's greatest efforts in this search. Each of these intellectual giants has provided a framework within which humanity has understood itself and its place within the vast and majestic cosmos we call home. For this reason, we ought to continue to bring these meaning-making modes of thought together. There are no better companions to accompany us on our never-ending search for deeper explanation.

Bibliography

Adams, Marilyn McCord, and Stewart Sutherland. "Horrendous Evils and the Goodness of God." *Proceedings of the Aristotelian Society, Supplementary Volumes* 63 (1989) 297–323.
American Museum of Natural History. "James Hutton: The Founder of Modern Geology." Accessed March 19, 2025. https://www.amnh.org/learn-teach/curriculum-collections/earth-inside-and-out/james-hutton.
Aquinas, Thomas. *Commentary on Aristotle's Peri Hermeneias*. Finished by Cardinal Cajetan; translated by Jean T. Oesterle. Milwaukee: Marquette University Press, 1962. https://isidore.co/aquinas/english/PeriHermeneias.htm#14.
Augustine. *City of God, Volume VII: Books 21–22*. Translated by William M. Green. Loeb Classical Library 417. Cambridge: Harvard University Press, 1972.
Balashov, Yuri, and Michel Janssen. "Review: Presentism and Relativity." *The British Society for the Philosophy of Science* 54 (2003) 327–46.
Barbour, Ian G. *Religion and Science: Historical and Contemporary Issues*. London: SCM, 1998.
Baron, Sam, and Kristie Miller. *An Introduction to the Philosophy of Time*. Cambridge: Polity, 2019.
Barrow, John D., and Frank J. Tipler. *The Anthropic Cosmological Principle*. Oxford: Oxford University Press, 2009.
Bertka, Constance M. *Exploring the Origin, Extent, and Future of Life: Philosophical, Ethical, and Theological Perspectives*. 1st ed. Cambridge: Cambridge University Press, 2009.
Bishop, Robert. "Chaos." In *The Stanford Encyclopedia of Philosophy*, edited by Edward N. Zalta. Spring 2017 edition. https://plato.stanford.edu/entries/chaos/.
Boethius. *The Consolation of Philosophy*. Translated by David R. Slavitt. Cambridge, MA: Harvard University Press, 2008.
Bonhoeffer, Deitrich. *Letters and Papers from Prison*. Edited by John W. De Gruchy. Minneapolis: Fortress, 2009.
Boulding, Jamie. *The Multiverse and Participatory Metaphysics: A Theological Exploration*. 1st ed. London: Routledge, 2022.

Brooke, John Hedley. *Science and Religion: Some Historical Perspectives*. Cambridge: Cambridge University Press, 2014.

Brown, William P. "Creation in the Old Testament." In *St Andrews Encyclopaedia of Theology*, edited by Brendan N. Wolfe et al. 2022. https://www.saet.ac.uk.

Burns, Robert. M. "Richard Swinburne on Simplicity in Natural Science." *Heythrop Journal* 40 (1999) 184–206.

Craig, William Lane. *God, Time and Eternity*. Dordrecht: Kluwer Academic, 2001.

———. *The Kalām Cosmological Argument*. 1979. Reprint, Eugene, OR: Wipf & Stock, 2000.

———. *Time and Eternity: Exploring God's Relationship to Time*. Wheaton, IL: Crossway, 2001.

Crisp, Oliver D. "Incarnation." In *The Oxford Handbook of Systematic Theology*, edited by Kathryn Tanner, John Webster, and Iain Torrance, 160–75. Oxford: Oxford University Press, 2007.

Dalrymple, G. Brent. "The Age of the Earth in the Twentieth Century: A Problem (Mostly) Solved." *Geological Society Special Publication* 190.1 (2001) 205–21.

Davison, Andrew. *Astrobiology and Christian Doctrine: Exploring the Implications of Life in the Universe*. Cambridge: Cambridge University Press, 2023.

Dawkins, Richard. *The Blind Watchmaker*. London: Penguin, 2006.

———. *The God Delusion*. London: Black Swan, 2007.

———. *The Root of All Evil?* Episode 1. Channel 4 (UK), 2006.

De Cruz, Helen, and Yves De Maeseneer. "The Imago Dei: Evolutionary and Theological Perspectives." *Zygon* 49.1 (2014) 95–100.

Dembski, William A. "In Defence of Intelligent Design." In *The Oxford Handbook of Religion and Science*, edited by Philip Clayton, 715–31. Oxford: Oxford University Press, 2008.

Deng, Natalja. *God and Time*. Cambridge Elements in the Philosophy of Religion. Cambridge: Cambridge University Press, 2019.

Fergusson, David. "Creation." In *The Oxford Handbook of Systematic Theology*, edited by Kathryn Tanner, John Webster, and Iain Torrance, 72–90. Oxford: Oxford University Press, 2009.

———. *Creation*. Guides to Theology. Grand Rapids: Eerdmans, 2014.

———. "Providence." In *St Andrews Encyclopaedia of Theology*, edited by Brendan N. Wolfe et al., 2022. https://www.saet.ac.uk/.

Gregersen, Niels H. "Deep Incarnation and the Cosmic Story of Christ." Biologos, January 9, 2024. https://biologos.org/articles/deep-incarnation-and-the-cosmic-story-of-christ.

———. "Deep Incarnation: From Deep History to Post-Axial Religion." *Hervormde Teologiese Studies* 72.4 (2016) 1–12.

———, ed. *Incarnation: On the Scope and Depth of Christology*. Minneapolis: Fortress, 2015.

Harrison, Peter. *Some New World: Myths of Supernatural Belief in a Secular Age*. Cambridge: Cambridge University Press, 2024.

———. *The Territories of Science and Religion*. Chicago: The University of Chicago Press, 2017.
Hazen, Robert M. "How Old Is Earth, and How Do We Know?" *Evolution Education Outreach* 3 (2010) 198–205.
Hebblethwaite, Brian. "The Impossibility of Multiple Incarnations." *Theology* 104.821 (2001) 323–34.
Heilbron, John L. *The Sun in the Church: Cathedrals as Solar Observatories*. Cambridge: Harvard University Press, 1999.
Hick, John. *Evil and the God of Love*. Basingstoke, UK: Palgrave Macmillan, 2010.
Holland, Richard A. *God, Time and the Incarnation*. Eugene, OR: Wipf & Stock, 2012.
Hollingsworth, Andrew. "Eschatology, the Elimination of Evil, and the Ontology of Time." *Theologica (Louvain-La-Neuve)* 8.1 (2024).
Hume, David. *An Enquiry Concerning Human Understanding*. Edited by Tom L. Beauchamp. Oxford: Oxford University Press, 2000.
Hunsinger, George, and Keith Johnson, eds. *The Wiley Blackwell Companion to Karl Barth*. Hoboken, NJ: Wiley Blackwell, 2020.
Huxley Thomas H. *Lay Sermons, Addresses and Reviews*. Cambridge: Cambridge University Press, 2009.
Ives, H. E., and G. R. Stilwell. "An Experimental Study of the Rate of a Moving Atomic Clock." *Journal of the Optical Society of America* 28.7 (1938) 215–26.
Johnson, Keith. "Barth on Natural Theology." In *The Wiley Blackwell Companion to Karl Barth: Barth in Dialogue*, edited by George Hunsinger and Keith L. Johnson, 95–107. Hoboken, NJ: Wiley-Blackwell, 2020.
Kennedy, R. J., and Edward M. Thorndike. "Experimental Establishment of the Relativity of Time." *Physical Review* 42.3 (1932) 400–418.
Koperski, Jeffrey. "God, Chaos, and the Quantum Dice." *Zygon* 35.3 (2000) 545–59.
Kragh, Helge, and Malcolm S. Longair, eds. *The Oxford Handbook of the History of Modern Cosmology*. Oxford: Oxford University Press, 2019.
Kuhn, Thomas S. *The Structure of Scientific Revolutions*. 1962. Reprint, London: Folio Society, 2020.
Kumar, Manjit. *Quantum: Einstein, Bohr and the Great Debate About the Nature of Reality*. Thriplow, UK: Icon, 2008.
Leftow, Brian. *Time and Eternity*. Ithaca, NY: Cornell University Press, 1991.
Lemaître, Abbé G. "A Homogeneous Universe of Constant Mass and Increasing Radius Accounting for the Radial Velocity of Extra-Galactic Nebulæ." *Monthly Notices of the Royal Astronomical Society* 91.5 (1931) 483–90.
Le Poidevin, Robin. "'Once for All': The Tense of the Atonement." *European Journal for Philosophy of Religion* 8.4 (2016) 179–94.
Lorenz, Edward N. "Deterministic Nonperiodic Flow." *Journal of the Atmospheric Sciences* 20 (1963) 130–41.
Mackie, John L. *The Miracle of Theism: Arguments For and Against the Existence of God*. Oxford: Clarendon, 1982.

McGrath, Alister. "Natural Theology." In *St Andrews Encyclopaedia of Theology*, edited by Brendan N. Wolfe et al., 2022. https://www.saet.ac.uk/.

———. *Science and Religion: A New Introduction*. Maldon, MA: Wiley-Blackwell, 2010.

———. *The Territories of Human Reason: Science and Theology in an Age of Multiple Rationalities*. Oxford: Oxford University Press, 2019.

McGrew, Timothy, and Robert Larmer. "Miracles." In *The Stanford Encyclopedia of Philosophy*, edited by Edward N. Zalta and Uri Nodelman, 2024. https://plato.stanford.edu/entries/miracles/.

Mortenson, Terry. "Systematic Theology Texts and the Age of the Earth." *Answers Research Journal* 2 (2009) 175–200.

Moser, David. "Jesus' Preexistence and Incarnation." In *St Andrews Encyclopaedia of Theology*, edited by Brendan N. Wolfe et al., 2024. https://www.saet.ac.uk/.

Mullins, R. T. "The Divine Timemaker." *Philosophia Christi* 22.2 (2020) 211–37.

———. "Four-Dimensionalism, Evil, and Christian Belief." *Philosophia Christi* 16.1 (2014) 117–37.

Murphy, Nancey. "Immortality Versus Resurrection in the Christian Tradition." *Annals of the New York Academy of Sciences* 1234.1 (2011) 76–82.

NASA. "How We Find and Classify Exoplanets." Accessed March 5, 2025. https://science.nasa.gov/exoplanets/how-we-find-and-characterize/.

Navarro, Jaume. "Electron Diffraction chez Thomson: Early Responses to Quantum Physics in Britain." *The British Journal for the History of Science* 43.2 (2010) 245–75.

Paley, William. *Natural Theology*. Edited by Matthew D. Eddy and David Knight. Oxford: Oxford University Press, 2008.

Patterson, C. C., G. Tilton, and M. Inghram. "Age of the Earth." *Science (American Association for the Advancement of Science)* 121.3134 (1955) 69–75.

Peebles, P. J. E. *Cosmology's Century: An Inside History of Our Modern Understanding of the Universe*. Princeton, NJ: Princeton University Press, 2020.

Plantinga, Alvin. *God, Freedom, and Evil*. 1974. Reprint, Grand Rapids: Eerdmans, 1989.

Polkinghorne, John. "Chaos Theory and Divine Action." In *Religion and Science: History, Method, Dialogue*, edited by W. M. Richardson and W. J. Wildman, 253–54. London: Routledge, 1996.

———. "Eschatology: Some Questions and Some Insights from Science." In *The End of the World and the Ends of God: Science and Theology on Eschatology*, edited by J. Polkinghorne and M. Welker, 29–41. Harrisburg, PA: Trinity, 2000.

———. *The God of Hope and the End of the World*. London: SPCK, 2002.

———. "Physical Process, Quantum Events, and Divine Agency." In *Quantum Mechanics: Scientific Perspectives on Divine Action*, edited by Robert J. Russell et al., 181–90. Notre Dame, IN: Center for Theology and the Natural Sciences Vatican Observatory, 2001.

———. *Science and Christian Belief: Theological Reflections of a Bottom-Up Thinker*. London: SPCK, 1994.

———. *Science and Theology: An Introduction*. London: SPCK, 1998.
Qureshi-Hurst, Emily. "Does God Act in the Quantum World? A Critical Engagement with Robert John Russell." *Theology and Science* 21.1 (2023) 106–21.
———. "God and Philosophy of Time." In *St Andrews Encyclopaedia of Theology*, edited by Brendan N. Wolfe et al., 2024. https://www.saet.ac.uk/.
———. *God, Salvation, and the Problem of Spacetime*. Cambridge Elements in Problems of God. Cambridge: Cambridge University Press, 2022.
———. "Is Simplicity That Simple? An Assessment of Richard Swinburne's Argument from Cosmic Fine-Tuning." *Theology and Science* 19.4 (2021) 379–89.
———. "Many Worlds and Moral Responsibility." *Theology and Science* 22.3 (2024) 456–73.
———. "Many Worlds and Narratives of Personal Identity." *Scientia et Fiddes*, forthcoming 2025.
———. "The Many Worries of Many Worlds." *Zygon* 58.1 (2023) 225–45.
———. *Salvation in the Block Universe: Time, Tillich, and Transformation*. Cambridge: Cambridge University Press, 2024.
Qureshi-Hurst, Emily, and Christopher T. Bennett. "Outstanding Issues with Robert Russell's NIODA Concerning Quantum Biology and Theistic Evolution." *Zygon* 56.1 (2021) 75–95.
Read, James, and Emily Qureshi-Hurst. "Getting Tense About Relativity." *Synthese* 198 (2020) 8103–25.
Rees, Martin. *Just Six Numbers: The Deep Forces That Shape the Universe*. London: Phoenix, 2000.
Reichenbach, Bruce. "Cosmological Argument." In *The Stanford Encyclopedia of Philosophy*, edited by Edward N. Zalta and Uri Nodelman, 2024. https://plato.stanford.edu/entries/cosmological-argument/.
Rubenstein, Mary-Jane. *Worlds Without End: The Many Lives of The Multiverse*. New York: Columbia University Press, 2014.
Russell, Robert John. "Bodily Resurrection, Eschatology and Scientific Cosmology." In *Resurrection: Theological and Scientific Assessments*, edited by Ted Peters, Robert J. Russell, and Michael Welker, 3–30. Grand Rapids: Eerdmans, 2000.
———. "Cosmology and Eschatology." In *The Oxford Handbook of Eschatology*, edited by Jerry L. Walls, 563–80. Oxford: Oxford University Press, 2009.
———. "Eschatology and Physical Cosmology: A Preliminary Reflection." In *The Far Future Universe: Eschatology from a Cosmic Perspective*, edited by G. F. R. Ellis, 266–315. Radnor, PA: Templeton Foundation Press, 2002.
———. "Quantum Physics and the Theology of Non-Interventionist Objective Divine Action." In *The Oxford Handbook of Science and Religion*, edited by Philip Clayton, 579–95. Oxford: Oxford University Press, 2006.
———. "Special Providence and Genetic Mutation: A New Defense of Theistic Evolution." In *Evolution and Molecular Biology: Scientific Perspectives on Divine Action*, edited by Robert John Russell, William R. Stoeger SJ, and

Francisco J. Ayala, 191–224. Note Dame, IN: Center for Theology and the Natural Sciences Vatican Observatory, 1998.

Saunders, Nicholas. *Divine Action and Modern Science*. Cambridge: Cambridge University Press, 2002.

———. "Does God Cheat at Dice? Divine Action and Quantum Possibilities." *Zygon* 35 (2000) 517–44.

Schlosshauer, Maximillian, Johannes Kofler, and Anton Zeilinger. "A Snapshot of Foundational Attitudes Toward Quantum Mechanics." *Studies in the History and Philosophy of Modern Physics* 44 (2013) 220–30.

Sollereder, Bethany N. "Compassionate Theodicy: A Suggested Truce Between Intellectual and Practical Theodicy." *Modern Theology* 37.2 (2021) 382–95.

Spencer, Nick. *Magisteria: The Entangled Histories of Science and Religion*. London: Oneworld, 2023.

Stanford, Kyle. "Underdetermination of Scientific Theory." In *The Stanford Encyclopedia of Philosophy*, edited by Edward N. Zalta and Uri Nodelman, 2023. https://plato.stanford.edu/entries/scientific-underdetermination/.

Stevenson, Austin. "Christian Vaccine Hesitancy: The Church Between Science and State." *Zygon*, forthcoming.

Stump, Eleonore. *Aquinas*. London: Routledge, 2003.

Swinburne, Richard. *The Existence of God*. 2nd ed. Oxford: Clarendon, 2004.

———. *Simplicity as Evidence for Truth*. Milwaukee: Marquette University Press, 1997.

———. "The Universe Makes It Probable That There Is a God." In *Science and Religion in Dialogue*, edited by Melville Y. Stewart, 1:203–34. Chichester, UK: Wiley-Blackwell, 2009.

Tanton, Tobias. *Corporeal Theology: The Nature of Theological Understanding in Light of Embodied Cognition*. Oxford: Oxford University Press, 2023.

Ticciati, Susannah. "Resurrection of the Dead." *St Andrews Encyclopaedia of Theology*, edited by Brendan N. Wolfe et al., 2023. https://www.saet.ac.uk/.

Tillich, Paul. *Systematic Theology II*. London: Nisbet, 1957.

———. *Systematic Theology III*. London: Nisbet, 1964.

Torrance, Thomas. *Space, Time and Incarnation*. London: Oxford University Press, 1969.

Wallace, Rebekah. "Does Embodied Cognition Support a Hylomorphic View of the Soul?" *Theological Puzzles* 9, June 19, 2022. https://www.theo-puzzles.ac.uk/2022/06/19/wallace/.

Ward, Keith. "Cosmology and Religious Ideas About the End of the World." In *The Far-Future Universe: Eschatology from a Cosmic Perspective*, edited by G. R. F. Ellis, 235–48. Philadelphia: Templeton Foundation Press, 2002.

Whitehead, A. N. *The Concept of Nature: The Tarner Lectures Delivered in Trinity College, November 1919*. Cambridge: Cambridge University Press, 1964.

Wilkinson, David. *Christian Eschatology and the Physical Universe*. London: T&T Clark, 2010.

Wright, N. T. *The Resurrection of the Son of God*. London: SPCK, 2012.

www.ingramcontent.com/pod-product-compliance
Lightning Source LLC
Chambersburg PA
CBHW031428150426
43191CB00006B/447